THE OFFICIAL® PRICE GUIDE TO MICKEY MOUSE COLLECTIBLES

1st Edition

ILLUSTRATED CATALOGUE & EVALUATION GUIDE

by

TED HAKE

GEMSTONE PUBLISHING

J.C. Vaughn, Executive Editor & Associate Publisher
Brenda Busick, Creative Director • **Lindsay Dunn**, Editor
Tom Gordon III, Managing Editor • **Mark Huesman**, Production Coordinator
Diana Hundt, Advertising Assistant • **Courtney Jenkins**, Marketing Manager
Amanda Sheriff, Editorial Coordinator • **Heather Winter**, Office Manager

House of Collectibles
New York

Gemstone Publishing

THE OFFICIAL® PRICE GUIDE TO MICKEY MOUSE COLLECTIBLES. Copyright ©2008 by Theodore L. Hake and Gemstone Publishing, Inc. All rights reserved. No part of this book may be used or reproduced in any manner whatsoever without written permission except in the case of brief quotations embodied in critical articles and reviews. For information, write to:
Gemstone Publishing, P.O. Box 12001, York, PA 17402.

Mickey Mouse, Minnie Mouse and related characters ©2008 Disney Enterprises.
All rights reserved.

THE OFFICIAL® PRICE GUIDE TO MICKEY MOUSE COLLECTIBLES (1st Edition) is an original publication of Gemstone Publishing, Inc. and House of Collectibles. Distributed by Random House Information Group, a division of Random House, Inc., New York and simultaneously in Canada by Random House of Canada Limited, Toronto. This edition has never before appeared in book form.

House of Collectibles
Random House Information Group
1745 Broadway
New York, New York 10019

www.houseofcollectibles.com

 House of Collectibles is a registered trademark and the colophon is a trademark of Random House, Inc.

Published by arrangement with Gemstone Publishing.

ISBN: 978-0-375-72307-0

Printed in the United States of America

10 9 8 7 6 5 4 3 2 1

First Edition: October 2008

Table of Contents

Advertiser Index

About the Author

Ted Hake is recognized as the founding father of America's collectibles industry. A collector from age seven beginning with coins and fossils, Hake's first presidential campaign item sales lists were issued from New York City while he was employed by General Electric at the 1964-65 New York World's Fair. In the Fall of 1965, he entered New York University's graduate film program and then in January, 1967 transferred to the Annenberg School for Communication at University of Pennsylvania, receiving his master's degree in 1968. While in Philadelphia, he founded Hake's Americana & Collectibles in 1967, the first auction house to specialize in 20th century American popular culture. Disney collectibles have been his primary specialty for forty years. His early initiatives in hundreds of collecting areas contributed significantly to establishing collectibles as a major pastime for millions of Americans. Over the years, Hake has shared his expertise by writing eighteen reference/price guides covering such subjects as presidential campaign artifacts, pinback buttons and vintage collectibles in the areas of advertising, comic characters, cowboy characters and television. His lifelong interest in Disneyana culminated in the publication of the *Official Price Guide to Disney Collectibles*, a comprehensive companion (10,000 color photos) to this book published 2007 in its second edition. He is a frequent guest on radio, was an appraiser on the first two seasons of the PBS series *The Antiques Roadshow* and was a featured expert on the History Channel's 2003 program *History of Toys*. In March, 2004, Hake sold his business which is now a division of Geppi's Entertainment Publications & Auctions and he continues as Chief Operating Officer. Hake's four annual catalogue and internet (www.hakes.com) auctions, internet sales lists and books are produced at the company's home office in York, Pennsylvania.

Acknowledgements

Many contributors joined forces to make our guide possible. I'm indebted to Maurice Sendak who gave me access to his collection of vintage Mickey items. Doug and Pat Wengel, noted Disneyana collectors and dealers, kindly provided photos of many rare 1930s Disney tin wind-up toys and consulted with me on the values. Thanks also to David Smith, Walt Disney Archives Director, for information on Disney copyright markings used on merchandise since 1930.

There are numerous items pictured in this guide provided by their actual creators. From the 1930s into the 1970s, Gordon Gold and his father Sam Gold, known as the "premium king," created thousands of toys used as sales incentive premiums. Over the past decade, Hake's Americana & Collectibles offered at auction many of these toys from the Golds' archive where usually one example of each was preserved. Items in the guide of this origin are noted "Gordon Gold Archives." Our guide also includes the original art for numerous toy concept designs by Disney character merchandising executive Al Konetzni. As the "idea man" in Disney's New York office from 1953 to 1981, Konetzni proposed toy concepts to Disney's many licensees. His most famous creation is the Disney school bus design lunch box which became the best selling lunch box ever. In 1999, Disney honored Konetzni with the title "Disney Legend."

Two collectors made major contributions to this comprehensive guide. John K. Snyder, Jr., President of Geppi's Entertainment Publishing & Auctions, of which Hake's Americana is a division, made many pieces from his personal collection available. Steve Geppi, the CEO of Geppi's Entertainment Publishing & Auctions and Diamond Comic Distributors, made the creation and continuation of this guide possible, as well as offering access to his personal Disneyana collection.

For additional photos and information, my thanks to Dan Morphy, Tom Sage Jr., and Shanelle Weaver of Morphy Auctions, Gary Selmonsky for items from his collection, Harrison Judd for photos of the Sendak collection, Carl Lobel, Phil Hecht, Jamie Hillstead, and Paul Merolle.

The scope and detail of this guide requires contributions from many people on the production staffs of three Geppi's Entertainment companies. At Hake's Americana, a special thanks to my assistant Joan Carbaugh, General Manager Alex Winter and Mike Bollinger, Jack Dixey, Mark Herr, Terence Kean, Kelly McClain, Linda Snyder, Sarah Snyder, Mark Squirek, Deak Stagemyer, and Sally Weaver.

At Geppi's Entertainment Publishing & Auctions, headed by John K. Snyder, Jr., for production and marketing assistance, my thanks to Joe McGuckin, Mike Wilbur, and Heather Winter. All our efforts came together under the auspices of Gemstone Publishing. A special thanks to Robert M. Overstreet for use of information from his authoritative reference *The Official Overstreet Comic Book Price Guide*. Shouldering much of the responsibility for this guide's integration and look are Lindsay Dunn, Editor; Mark Huesman, Production Coordinator; and Brenda Busick, Creative Director. My thanks to each and a special acknowledgement to Tom Gordon III for his recommendations. Also at Gemstone, thanks to Courtney Jenkins, Marketing Manager; Diana Hundt, Advertising Assistant; David Gerstein, Archival Editor; and J.C. Vaughn, Executive Editor and Associate Publisher.

Rounding out our numerous contributors on various fronts, my appreciation is extended to Ken Chapman, John Hone, Steve Ison, Ken Sequin, Jim Halperin, Ed Jaster, Bill Hughes, Harry Matetsky, Dave Anderson, David Callahan, Bruce Hamilton, Joe and Nadia Mannarino, Robert Rogovin, Jay Parrino and Tom Tumbusch. Special credit goes to my wife, Jonell, both for her support and insightful ideas.

From myself and everyone in the Geppi's Entertainment family of companies, we thank our advertisers for their support. We also appreciate the support of our audience and urge our readers to mention this guide when responding to advertisements.

ORGANIZATION

This book pictures and prices 1476 items. Following the item title is the year of issue if known exactly or stated as c. for circa if the date is approximate. Following the date, most items are detailed by the item's maker, publisher or sponsor name along with relevant details of size, number of pages, identifying marks, number in a set, and so on.

The description ends with three current market values for the item in Good, Fine and Near Mint condition.

TYPES OF ITEMS

Mickey Mouse collectibles come in all shapes and sizes, made from a diversity of materials. This guide includes examples of everything from the earliest years to the most recent. Sizes range from 13/16" pin-back buttons to a 9-foot long outdoor banner promoting the French publication "Le Journal de Mickey."

While the majority of items are of United States origin, Disney, for decades, has been a worldwide marketer. Accordingly, our listings include select items intended for distribution in Australia, Canada, Germany, Great Britain and other areas.

Aside from product advertising collectibles, original art and other Disney Studio-related collectibles, most items we list are "toys." Webster's New World Dictionary defines a toy as "any article to play with, especially playthings for children." This definition includes both store-bought toys as well as those distributed as a premium by a sponsor. Premium toys may be free or sometimes require a small payment and/or proof of purchase of the sponsor's product.

While guide listings are comprehensive, they are selective and by no means all inclusive. Items included are not necessarily more common or rarer than items not included.

DATES OF ISSUE

Items are listed chronologically by decade starting with the earliest specific year, followed by the earliest approximate year followed by those items of an unknown year but approximated to the earliest decade. The sequence then repeats for each successive decade. When a specific year or decade is open to question, the date is listed with the abbreviation c. for circa.

To determine issue dates, most often the copyright date is used when this is obviously consistent with the date of issue. Other primary sources for dating include Disney merchandise catalogues, wholesale or retail toy catalogues, and newspaper or other advertisements. When an item was available over several years, the earliest known date is specified. Most original art used to create cartoons or animated features is undated and obviously pre-dates the movie's release date, but the release date is typically used since the creation date is unknown.

Other dating clues may come from the character's design. For example, most five-fingered Mickeys are circa 1930 and of European origin. Similarly, most Mickeys prior to 1938 are referred to as having "pie-eyes" due to the white notch accents on the eyes. Mickeys with solid black pupils generally began in 1938. Of course, there are exceptions. Most notably, all the Mickeys from his revival era of the mid-1960s until today which are created with pie-eyes to capture his vintage appearance.

One of the following copyright notices usually appears on an item issued during these specific years. However, there are exceptions and overlaps as licensees sometimes used an older copyright notice if an item was in production when the rule changed and Disney adopted a new copyright specification. Along with the copyright notices are a few dates that relate to information sometimes found on the items, tags or packaging. Disney's first character merchandise contract dates to February 3, 1930 with the New York City novelty firm Geo. Borgfeldt & Co.

1930-32: © Walter Disney, © W.E. Disney, © Walter E. Disney

1932-9/30/38: © Walt Disney Enterprises, © W.D.E., © Walt Disney Ent.

9/30/38 – 2/6/86: © Walt Disney Productions, ©WDP

2/6/86 – current: © The Walt Disney Company, © Walt Disney Co., © Disney

May 1, 1943 – June 30, 1963: Postal zone numbers in use by large and some medium-sized cities.

July 1, 1963 – current: ZIP codes in use.

1975: Universal Product Codes (UPC) begin on packaging.

1970s: Two letter state name abbreviations become standard.

GUIDE VALUES

Values in this guide are estimations of retail prices for each item in Good, Fine and Near Mint condition. The prices stated are based on the author's 40 years of experience in auctioning and selling all types of popular culture collectibles, with a concentration on Disneyana since 1967. Most prices are based on actual sales at auction during the past decade, adjusted for any lapse of time and with the extreme results of an occasional "bidder war" eliminated.

Also considered were sales lists, show prices, transactions between individuals and advice from collectors and dealers with expertise in certain specialties.

Few vintage items are still truly Mint, so the highest grade listed for each item is Near Mint. However, there are those rare exceptions. Strictly Mint items with no traces of wear might command 25% or even more than the listed Near Mint value. Those items falling between the specified grades are termed Very Good or Very Fine. A reasonable approximation of value for these items would be the midpoint value between Good and Fine or Fine and Near Mint.

Original packaging, particularly if illustrated and appealing in design, is highly valued by many collectors. This applies usually to toys of a three-dimensional nature. Thus, a wind-up toy illustrated original box may add 50%-100% to the value of the basic toy. In many cases, the price guide evaluations take these options into account and specify separate values for toy and box.

DEFINITIONS: GOOD, FINE, NEAR MINT

Value has three primary determining factors: rarity, demand, and condition. Of these, condition is paramount. If a very rare, very desirable item has a significant condition problem, a large part of the potential buyer universe ceases to exist.

Accurately assessing an item's condition is a crucial step in using the Good, Fine and Near Mint prices specified in this guide. For any given item, issued before the advent of collector targeted items intended to be preserved, the percentage of items still surviving in Near Mint condition is likely to be very small. This low supply, coupled with collector demand for outstanding condition, accounts for the disproportionately high values assigned to Near Mint examples versus those in Fine or Good. Furthermore, the survivability of an item depends on its material construction. The chances of a bisque figure remaining Near Mint over seventy years far exceeds those for a coloring book. Thus, the value increase between Fine and Near Mint for a bisque is typically proportional whereas for a book the increase is a geometric progression. To correctly compare prices encountered in the marketplace with the values specified in this guide, the following condition definitions must be understood and applied. Condition factors vary according to an item's basic materials and those materials generally fall into the following four categories.

PAPER/CARDBOARD

Near Mint: Fresh, bright original crisply-inked appearance with only the slightest perceptible evidence of wear, soil, fade or creases. The item should lay flat, corners must be close to perfectly square and any staples must be rust-free.

Fine: An above average example with attractive appearance but moderately noticeable aging or wear including: small creases and a few small edge tears; lightly worn corners; minimal browning, yellowing, dust or soiling; light staple rust but no stain on surrounding areas; no more than a few tiny paper flakes missing. Small tears repaired on blank reverse side are generally acceptable if the front image is not badly affected.

Good: A complete item with no more than a few small pieces missing. Although showing obvious aging, accumulated flaws such as creases, tears, dust and other soiling, repairs, insect damage, mildew and brittleness must not combine to render the item unsound and too unattractive for display.

METAL

Near Mint: Painted or lithographed tin objects, such as toys, must retain at least 97% original color with only a few non-obtrusive random small scratches or rub marks. An object with un-painted metallic finish, such as a ring, must retain 90% or more of its original bright finish metallic luster as well as any accent coloring on the lettering or design. Badges must have the original pin intact and rings must have near perfect circular bands. Any small areas missing original luster must be free of rust, corrosion, dark tarnish or any other defect that stands out enough to render the naked eye appearance of the piece less than almost perfect.

Fine: An above average item with moderate wear. Painted items must retain 80% of original color. Metallic luster items should retain at least 50%. There may be small, isolated areas with pinpoint corrosion spotting, tarnish or similar evidences of aging. Badges must have the original pin, although perhaps slightly bent, and rings must have bands with no worse than minor bends. Although general wear does show, the item retains an overall attractive appearance with strong, bright color or luster.

Good: An average well-used or aged item missing about 35% paint or nearly all metallic luster. Badges may have a replaced pin and ring bands may be distorted or obviously reshaped. There may be moderate but not totally defacing evidence of bends, dents, scratches, corrosion, etc. Aside from a replaced pin, completeness is still essential.

CELLULOID OR LITHOGRAPHED TIN PIN-BACK BUTTONS

Near Mint: Both celluloid and lithographed tin pin-backs retain the original, bright appearance without visual defects. For celluloid, this means the total absence of staining (known as foxing to button collectors). There can be no apparent surface scratches when the button is viewed directly; although when viewed at an angle in reflected light, there may be a few very shallow and small hairline marks on the celluloid surface. The celluloid covering must be totally intact with no splits, even on the reverse where the celluloid covering is folded under the collet, a metal ring that holds the parts together. Lithographed tin buttons may have no more than two or three missing pinpoint-size dots of color and no visible scratches. Even in Near Mint condition, a button image noticeably off-center, as made, reduces desirability and therefore value to some price below Near Mint depending on the severity of the off-centering.

Fine: Both styles of buttons may have a few apparent scattered small scratches. Some minor flattening or a tiny dent noticeable to the touch, but not visually, is also acceptable. Celluloids may have a very minimal amount of age spotting or moisture stain, largely confined to the rim area, not distracting from the graphics and not dark in color. There may be a small celluloid split on the reverse by the collet, but the celluloid covering must still lay flat enough not to cause a noticeable bump on the side edge. Lithographed tin buttons may have only the slightest traces of paint roughness, or actual rust, visible on the front.

Good: Celluloid pin-backs may have moderate dark spotting or moisture stain not exceeding 25% of the surface area. There can be some slight evidence of color fade, a small nick on the front celluloid, or a small celluloid split by the reverse collet causing a small edge bump. Dark extensive stain, deep or numerous scratches and extensive crazing of the celluloid covering each render the button to a condition status of less than Good and essentially unsalable. Lithographed tin buttons must retain strong color and be at least 75% free of noticeable surface wear or they too fall into the likely unsalable range.

OTHER MATERIALS

(Ceramic, Glass, Wood, Fabric, Composition, Rubber, Plastic, Vinyl, etc.)

Near Mint: Regardless of the substance, the item retains its fresh, original appearance and condition without defect. Only the slightest traces of visually non-distracting wear are acceptable.

Fine: Each material has its own inherent weaknesses in withstanding time, typical use or actual abuse as follows:

Ceramic, porcelain, china, bisque and other similar clay-based objects are susceptible to edge chips. These are acceptable if minimal. Glazed items very typically develop hairline crazing not considered a flaw unless hairlines have also darkened.

Glass is fragile and obviously susceptible to missing chips, flakes or hairline fractures but acceptable in modest quantity.

Wood items, as well as the faithful likeness composition wood, generally withstand aging and use well. Small stress fractures or a few small missing flakes are acceptable if the overall integrity of the item is not affected.

Fabric easily suffers from weave splits or snags plus stain spots are frequently indelible. Weaving breaks are generally acceptable in limited numbers but fabric holes are not. Stains may not exceed a small area and only a blush of color change.

Composition items, typically dolls or figurines, tend to acquire hairline cracks of the thin surface coating. This is commonly expected and normally acceptable to the point of obvious severity. Color loss should not exceed 20% and not involve critical facial details.

Rubber items, either of solid or hollow variety, tend to lose original pliability and evolve into a rigid hardness that frequently results in a warped or deformed appearance. Some degree of original flexibility is preferred or at least minimal distortion.

Plastic and vinyl items have a tendency to split at areas of high stress or frequent use. This is frequently expected and excused by collectors up to the point of distracting from overall appearance or function.

Good: Items of any material are expected to be complete and/or functional. Obvious wear is noticeable, but the item retains its structural soundness. Wear or damage must not exceed the lower limits of being reasonably attractive for display purposes.

COLLECT FOR PERSONAL ENJOYMENT

Amazingly, there are few Americans alive today who were not the childhood owner of some type of Disney character toy. Disney characters, and especially Mickey Mouse, are imbedded in our deepest psyche and, indeed, the phenomenon is worldwide. Our memories of childhood, both the trials and triumphs, stay with us until our demise. Some say, in a negative way, the collectors of Disneyana or toys in general are out to recapture their youth. The reality is that collectors of these objects never lost their youth. They are collected as a way to keep us in touch with our youth. Disneyana collections bring our past experiences to life in a physical form to be sensed visually and tactically and thus enhancing precious memories. Developing all the nuances of astute collecting and the evolution of a collector's focus takes time. The journey is rewarding in many ways. In contrast to our daily obligations and concerns, collecting is an adventure to be savored, a way to express and enjoy our passions. Collecting Disneyana is about having fun. It's a positive experience and it makes sense.

MARKET REPORT

by
John K. Snyder, Jr. &
J.C. Vaughn

What an exciting time to be collecting! The general public's awareness of the impact of popular culture has never been higher and they have never been more receptive to understanding vintage pop culture artifacts.

One merely has to turn on a television or radio, pick-up a newspaper or magazine, or log on to the internet to find some story that shows just how entwined general history and pop culture history are in America. While that's also true in many other nations, nowhere else have these two sides of history been so parallel for the majority of a country's existence. When even our establishment media gets it, that's a sign that things have changed.

INFORMATION IS KING

It was not too long ago that it seemed that only record prices made the headlines and then only as a novelty. As we have detailed in *The Official Price Guide To Pop Culture Memorabilia* (a sister publication to this one, which we urge you to reference), in trying to understand why this market has performed so well, it is important to first clearly define what we mean by the term "Vintage Pop Culture Artifacts." A vintage pop culture artifact is an item, now characterized by excellence, maturity, enduring appeal, and scarcity, which was contemporary to and reflective of the lifestyle in the period during which it was produced. As a general rule, this area of study includes pieces that were not specifically created to be collectible but were instead intended to be used. While there are notable exceptions to this, this definition excludes what one might call mass-produced manufactured objects that attempt to meet an assumed demand among the col-

These giant-sized display dolls of Mickey Mouse and Minnie Mouse by Charlotte Clark sold for $151,534.35 (including the Buyer's Premium) at Hake's Americana & Collectibles in September, 2007. Mickey is 44" tall and Minnie in 48" tall.

lecting population.

As Steve Geppi, the Chief Executive Officer and Owner of Geppi's Entertainment Museum said in an interview, "There's never been a better time for pop culture enthusiasts because society as a whole has finally started to realize that history of popular culture is inexorably tied to mainstream history in this country. It seems like I say this all the time now, but take a look at the History Channel, A&E, The Learning Channel, your local PBS affiliate. Collectibles, these magnificent artifacts of days gone by, are everywhere. Whether it's a comic-themed movie sitting atop the box office charts or a top-selling video game or an actual comic book successfully utilizing well-known characters, this serves to reinforce the public's awareness of and comfort with this social acceptance."

He went on to point out that now it's possible to research in a few hours what took previous generations a lifetime to experience. While the reader must be careful in evaluating the information he or she is presented with, there is more information than ever available with just a few strokes of the keyboard.

In keeping aware of the realities of collecting, it's also keenly important to remember the *reasons* for collecting. This is a pursuit we must keep in a positive light. Rather than let it exclude family members and friends, collecting is a perfect way to bring generations together as we work toward common goals. Family members should be encouraged to participate, whether in your own particular niche or another. Since we have recognized that vintage pop culture collectibles are a major key to understanding general history, shouldn't we take a generational approach to opening its mysteries? Many of us in the collecting field are competitive, and that's not always a bad thing. However, it's very easy to let the blind spirit of acquisition accidentally replace the fun-loving life-force that brought us into the game. A family's involvement is one check against that.

As human beings, we're on this Earth for a limited time. That makes us at best custodians of these artifacts from another time. How we act on that knowledge and the insights we gain from our collections will say more about us in the end than the quantity or monetary value of our acquisitions.

For Mickey Mouse collectors specifically and Disneyana enthusiasts in general, we have a running start at keep our collecting endeavors on an optimistic track. We are collecting not only the most recognized character in the world, but a positive, upbeat and energetic character that embodies plucky can-do spirit that characterizes the successful everyman. (It's difficult to even conjure up negative reasons for collecting Mickey!)

SUPPLY AND DEMAND

Of course, when one talks to any group of experienced collectors, sooner or later the subject of record prices is bound to come up. This book lists prices and in this very market report you'll find many of the recently set benchmarks for values of Mickey Mouse collectibles. Don't let this throw you! Collecting is still about the characters.

When you get down to it, though, most of us still collect for love, not for the promise of return on investment. That said, a true understanding of our treasures includes the responsibility of being apprised of their value. Since prices are generally the product of scarcity (or supply and demand), the rarity of the item and its value most often go hand-in-hand.

This simple understanding sets the stage for what has been a fascinating market for years now. Ever since the release of the first edition of another sister publication, *The Official Price Guide To Disney Collectibles*, just a few years ago, the market seems to have responded to the information it provided in a very positive way. The trend had started long before that, though, and has sustained itself over a protracted period and through a variety of economic conditions.

RESULTS

There have definitely been some great Mickey Mouse results in the past few years:

On the top of any list would be the pair of rare, giant-sized display dolls of Walt Disney's Mickey Mouse and Minnie Mouse which shattered records and sold for $151,534.35 (including the Buyer's Premium) in the Hake's Americana & Collectibles auction that concluded Thursday, September 27, 2007. The 44" tall Mickey and 48" tall Minnie were promotional items for the highly acclaimed Charlotte Clark line of dolls from the early 1930s and were purchased by a private collector and longtime Hake's customer.

Following Mickey's successful introduction as a Clark doll in 1930, Minnie arrived in toy shops the following year. Together the popular toys were produced for the retail market in three sizes: 8.5", 13.5" and 18" – and only a significantly limited number of the giant-sized ones were made for display purposes for prominent movie theaters, retail stores and the occasional photo shoot with Walt himself.

Made of stuffed velveteen, Clark's trademark material, Mickey is detailed with four 2" diameter natural pearl buttons, and Minnie wears a silk-like skirt with pantaloons that have lace accents. Each doll has a long, 32" tail.

"The overall strength of the character collectibles market is typified by the $151,534 price realized for these dolls," Ted Hake said at the time of the sale. "They are so rare I thought I'd never lay eyes on a set, let alone get a chance to auction this remarkable, near mint pair as the capstone to Hake's 40th anniversary year. These dolls stand at the pinnacle of iconic objects symbolizing the breadth and depth of American popular culture."

Other top sales that we at Geppi's Entertainment personally witnessed included a *Mickey Mouse* and *Silly Symphony* matched pair Sunday page original comic strip artwork ($51,750), the very rare, early Mickey Mouse Scooter, by Nifty with its even rarer box ($37,041.73), Mickey Mouse Doll by Knickerbocker ($19,096), Mickey Mouse Doll in Easter Parade outfit by Knickerbocker ($11,180.40), Mickey Mouse Musical Doll as Band Leader by Knickerbocker ($10,841.60), the rare Mickey and Pluto boxed Celluloid Wind-Up Toy ($6,325.00), the rare Mickey Mouse Circus Pull Toy ($6,142.21), the standard edition Mickey and Minnie Mouse Dolls by Charlotte Clark ($5,962.88), the rarely seen, boxed wind-up toy Mickey and Minnie Mouse Playland ($4,600.00), a first edition of the first *Mickey Mouse* Book ($4,136.55), *Two-Gun Mickey* publicity artwork ($4,025.00), a celluloid figure/rattle Mickey Mouse in Bathing Suit with Life Preserver ($3,348.80), Mickey Mouse Ingersoll 1937 De Luxe Watch [with charms and chromium band] ($3,275.38), Hobo Mickey [seated on a "London XII Miles" marker] glazed ceramic figure by Wadeheath ($2,981.61), the first issue of *Mickey Mouse Magazine* ($2,794.13), the Spanish edition of the famed *Mickey Mouse Waddle* Book ($2,788.93), Dean's Mickey Mouse Jazzer Doll, boxed ($2,710.40), and the large Mickey Mouse Doll by Knickerbocker ($2,710.40).

Keep in mind that these were only a handful of the top items we actually saw being auctioned or sold. Heritage Auction Galleries, Just Kids, R&R Auctions, and many other auction houses also noted significant sales.

Those sales are, of course, augmented by transactions from dealers and private collectors, and they continue to show strength for virtually every type of collectible. Character watches, store displays, song sheets, club kits, statues, original comic book and comic strip art, dolls, rings, vinyl records, theatrical one-sheets, concept art, promotional pieces, dolls, books, pull toys, and many other specialties all attract broad interest.

As with any such undertaking, this book would not have been possible without superb direction and a dedicated group of people. Steve Geppi, Ted Hake and the Gemstone Publishing and Hake's Americana & Collectibles staffs, and numerous contributors have cataloged, described, written, edited, designed, proofed, and re-proofed this edition because we love what we do. That's how it should be, just like in collecting.

We hope you enjoy the results.

John K. Snyder, Jr. is the President of Geppi's Entertainment Publications & Auctions. J.C. Vaughn is the Executive Editor & Associate Publisher of Gemstone Publishing.

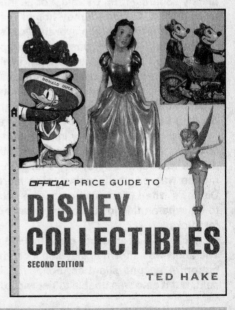

Thousands of additional Disney items can be found in *The Official Price Guide To Disney Collectibles*, second edition, also by Ted Hake and published by Random House. It is now available at your local bookstore or online at www.hakes.com.

Mickey Mouse, Minnie & Nephews

Legend has it that Mickey Mouse was born over eighty years ago during a train trip from New York to Los Angeles. Among the many passengers on that train was Walt Disney. The trip out to New York had been a very hopeful journey for young Walt. However, the return trip was the exact opposite. When he began to scribble the beginnings of Mickey Mouse on a notepad, Walt was on his way home to California after receiving some very disturbing business news.

For the preceding year, Disney had been producing cartoons for film distributor Charles Mintz. Every one of them had starred a Disney creation, Oswald the Lucky Rabbit. The cartoons were released through Universal and Mintz was operating as a middle-man. The visit to Mintz in New York was two-fold. Walt wanted to negotiate higher pay for a second season. He also intended to use the increase to improve the quality of the cartoons.

When Disney finally met with Mintz, Walt's vision for the future was dashed. He was told that there would be no increase. In fact, he had to instead accept a cut in pay or lose his control over the rabbit. It was revealed that Universal, not Disney, was the actual owner of Oswald. In addition to that shocking news, Mintz had been given the authority to produce the shorts on his own if the need arose. In preparation for that very real possibility, Mintz had already been going behind Disney's back. He had already contracted with many of Disney's current animation staff so they could continue to produce the Oswald shorts without Walt.

After being given that incredible news, Disney made the decision to completely separate from Oswald. For all intents and purposes, he left Mintz's office unemployed. On the journey home, Disney came up with the beginnings of a character that would take over the licensing world.

The original Mickey was a series of ovals that somewhat resembled Oswald, but included a good amount of originality. What was new for the mouse, and what Walt gave to him, was an enthusiastic, adventurous, determined personality. The character would drive the action as opposed to reacting to it. The then recent solo flight of Charles Lindbergh across the Atlantic in his plane *The Spirit of St. Louis* was an obvious inspiration.

There was one last, very important characteristic that Walt provided, a voice. Mickey's vocals were supplied by Walt himself through 1946. Mickey's visual design was refined by Disney's longtime associate Ub Iwerks. The name of the mouse was originally going to be Mortimer, but, again according to legend, Disney's wife Lillian considered the name "too pompous." Walt knew to listen to his wife on this idea. Mortimer was out and the mouse's name was swapped for Mickey.

Mickey's screen debut came in 1928 with a silent cartoon titled *Plane Crazy*. The short was shown in May at a local theatre, but it did not achieve wide distribution. A second silent cartoon, *The Gallopin' Gaucho* (1928), was produced next, but it also was unable to get wide distribution.

Major film distributors were preparing to move into sound production, and another silent cartoon series simply did not interest them. Disney was aware of their objections and, with those objections in mind, prepared the next cartoon for sound.

When *Steamboat Willie* (1928) premiered at New York's Colony Theatre on November 18, audiences ran wild. There had been sound cartoons before *Steamboat Willie*, but none had ever come close to the quality of Disney's new cartoon. Ironically, Mickey did not actually speak in *Willie*; a parrot is the only speaking character. Mickey and others merely grunt. It took another year for Mickey to actually speak in English. That occurred in *The Karnival Kid* (1929). That year also saw the debut of the first merchandise item to bear Mickey's likeness: a children's school tablet.

By 1930, Mickey was so well-known that Disney developed a comic strip featuring the character. Initially drawn by Iwerks, the strip was soon taken over by Floyd Gottfredson, who plotted it for fifteen years and drew it for forty-five. Gottfredson's plots were swashbuckling epics with a colorful interpretation of Mickey. His work made the strip an instant favorite. The vast majority of the Mickey children's books created during the thirties drew on the Gottfredson strip for plots, clip art, or both.

Four years after the fateful 1928 train ride, Walt Disney received a special Academy Award for the creation of Mickey Mouse. Within a few years, Mickey became the Disney company spokesman, and over time he increasingly came to be treated with the requisite respect. As a result, his screen personality lost some of its original edge. The smart-alecky, adventurous Mickey Mouse of the early days gradually became a squeaky-clean do-gooder. Over time, Disney creations such as Snow White and Donald Duck stole much of his thunder.

Nevertheless, Mickey remained a central figure at the core of Disney. Perhaps that's why, for recent TV cartoons, the studio has seen fit to restore some of Mickey's original funnier and more mischievous impulses. While he has undergone some minor physical changes over the years, the Mickey of today is essentially the same figure who rose to success in his early years; a scrappy little guy with a great big sense of adventure.

Mickey Mouse is the single most merchandised character in history.

Mickey's Nephews

Morty and Ferdie (the latter is sometimes spelled Ferdy) made their first appearance in the Mickey Mouse Sunday newspaper strip dated September 18, 1932. Their only animated cartoon appearance came in a 1934 Mickey Mouse short titled *Mickey's Steamroller*. Since then, they have mainly been active in the comics. The boys are patiently waiting for other opportunities to knock.

Merchandise exclusively depicting the two is limited, but they more frequently appear on items featuring multiple characters.

Minnie Mouse

She was with Mickey from the beginning. Minnie appeared in *Steamboat Willie* (1928), Mickey's first cartoon with sound and the first to receive national distribution. Together with Mickey, Minnie appeared in 74 classic-era theatrical cartoons over the years. When visitors arrive at a Disney theme park, Minnie is always there to greet them and have her picture taken. Many of those visitors make a special effort to seek her out. For some, she is the best-loved character in the park.

Merchandise for Minnie isn't as extensive as it is for Mickey, but she does have her fair share. There have been dolls, books, records and many other items. In many European countries, Minnie is the star of her own long-running comic book title.

MKY-1

MKY-2

❑ **MKY-1. Minnie Mouse Carrying Felix In Cages Lithographed Tin Wind-Up,** 1929. Made by Rogelio Sanchez, Spain with castle logo on left cage. 6-7/8" tall with electrical cord tail. Minnie has small points on ears and wears hobnail style shoes. Only a few known. Rare. - **$8500 $12500 $36500**

❑ **MKY-2. "Exhibitors Herald World" Featuring Mickey Mouse,** 1929. 9.25x12.25" Volume 96, No. 9 dated August 31,1929 issue. 82 pages with great 2-page ad for Mickey Mouse. - **$110 $215 $325**

MKY-3

MKY-4

❏ **MKY-3. "Mickey Mouse" Pencil Tablet,**
1929. Tablet is 8x9.75" and .5" thick. From a series of several believed to be the first Disney items licensed, possibly as early as 1929. - **$120 $240 $500**

❏ **MKY-4. "Mickey Mouse Club" Earliest Design Member's Celluloid Button,**
1930. The first movie club began January 11, 1930 at Fox Dome Theater in Ocean Park, California. The club idea came from theater manager Harry W. Woodin who in September 1929 received Disney's endorsement of his idea. Button is pictured on the membership application blank. 7/8" with small copyright symbol on the front. - **$80 $135 $265**

MKY-5

❏ **MKY-5. "The Cactus Kid" Pencil Drawing,**
1930. 9.5x12" sheet with 3.75x7" art, likely by Ub Iwerks, of Mickey with angry expression and Pegleg Pedro (Pete). - **$575 $1150 $1950**

MKY-6

MKY-8

☐ **MKY-6. "Fox Mickey Mouse Club" Button,**
1930. 7/8". The first movie club began January 11, 1930 at Fox Dome Theater in Ocean Park, California. The club idea came from theater manager Harry W. Woodin who in September 1929 received Disney's endorsement of his idea. - **$90 $165 $325**

☐ **MKY-8. Earliest Design Mickey Mouse Movie Club Officer Button,**
1930. From the earliest days of the west coast Mickey Mouse Clubs which began in 1930. Clubs elected officers from "Chief Mickey Mouse" on down and this button denotes the rank of "Courier." 2-3/16" button. - **$550 $1600 $3600**

MKY-9

MKY-7

☐ **MKY-7. "Mickey Mouse Club" Washington State Earliest Design Club Button,**
1930. 7/8" button. No maker's name and no backpaper possibly as issued. - **$90 $165 $325**

☐ **MKY-9. "Mickey Mouse Movie Club" Campaign Folio,**
1930. 9x11.5" card stock cover holds a complete multi-page set of 8.5x11" single-sided sheets. Bound on left with brass clips so that pages can be easily removed. Folio filled with information and images detailing in every way, shape and form all aspects of the club.
- **$550 $1250 $2150**

MKY-10

MKY-11

☐ **MKY-10. "Mickey Mouse Club" Second Design Member's Celluloid Button,**
1930. The first design was quickly replaced by Mickey image approved by Disney Studios. Copyright text was also added. 7/8" with Philadelphia Badge backpaper. Used briefly and replaced by designs 1.25" in size. - **$90 $145 $290**

☐ **MKY-11. "Mickey Mouse Club" Rare Imprint Celluloid Button,**
1930. Includes sponsor names of "Harris Family Theatre" and "Sears, Roebuck And Co." 7/8". - **$175 $350 $675**

MKY-12

☐ **MKY-12. Mickey And Minnie On Motorcycle Tin Wind-Up,**
1930. Tipp & Co., Germany. 10" long. Immensely popular and very few known examples. - **$15500 $36000 $82500**

MKY-13

MKY-15

□ **MKY-15. "Mickey Mouse" Celluloid Figure,**
1930. Walter E. Disney. 2.25x2.75x5" tall with movable head and arms. String tail. - **$145 $290 $500**

MKY-14

MKY-16

□ **MKY-13. "Mickey Mouse" With French Horn Large Bisque,**
1930. Figure is 2.5x3x5-1/8" tall with string tail and paper label under feet. Has incised number on back "S36." - **$275 $550 $800**

□ **MKY-14. "Minnie Mouse" With Violin Large Bisque,**
1930. Figure is 5.75" tall and has incised "S38" on back. - **$275 $550 $800**

□ **MKY-16. "Minnie Mouse" Celluloid Figure,**
1930. Walter E. Disney. 2.25x2.75x5" tall with movable head and arms. String tail. - **$135 $275 $450**

MKY-17

❑ **MKY-17. "Mickey Mouse" Celluloid Novelty,**
1930. Base is 1x1.5" and has pair of attached 7/8" Mickey figures. Underside has label "Mickey Mouse." - **$75** **$135** **$275**

MKY-18

❑ **MKY-18. "Mickey Mouse" First American-Made Toy,**
1930. Wood with rope arms, leatherette ears and a stiff cord tail. When tail is pushed down, Mickey's head rises slightly. Designed by Disney artist Burton "Bert" Gillett for distribution by George Borgfeldt Corp. Label includes "c. 1928-1930 by Walter E. Disney Des. Pat. Apd For." 2.5x3x6.25" tall. - **$1050** **$2200** **$4250**

MKY-19

❑ **MKY-19. "Mickey Mouse" Wood Jointed Figure,**
1930. "Mickey Mouse/Walt E. Disney." 2x3x4.75" tall with flat disk hands to allow balancing in various positions. - **$240** **$575** **$1150**

MKY-20

❑ **MKY-20. "The Mickey Mouse Quoit Game,"**
1930. Spears Games. Box is 7.5x11x1" deep with paper label playing surface in bottom along with wood block with slot to hold 5.5x9" cardboard Mickey figure. Also has three paper-covered cardboard rings. Object was to toss rings onto Mickey figure to land on various point value squares of insert. - **$135** **$275** **$500**

MKY-21

❑ **MKY-21. "Mickey Mouse" Glazed China Ashtray,**
1930. Measures 3.25x5x2-7/8" tall. Underside has sticker "Mickey Mouse Copr 1928-1930 By Walter E. Disney." At least four different. Each- **$135 $265 $525**

MKY-22

❑ **MKY-22. Mickey Mouse And Felix Litho Tin Sparkler,**
1930. Rogelio Sanchez, Spain marked "La Isla R.S." on front. 5" wide by 7" tall with action of them each bending over to light cigars on candle flame created by sparks that show through cellophane at flame center. No tail on Mickey as designed. Reproduced in the 1990s, Spain as a noisemaker but without any animation. - **$5250 $8500 $16000**

MKY-23

❑ **MKY-23. "Mickey Mouse" Hurdy Gurdy Tin Wind-up,**
1930. Probably Distler, Marked "Made In Germany." Dancing Minnie figure on
the top is frequently replaced. Mickey has a spring tail. Toy is 6" long by 8" tall.
- **$2650 $5250 $21500**

MKY-24

❑ **MKY-24. "Mickey The Musical Mouse" Lithographed Tin Toy,**
1930. Germany, for British import. 5.5" tall by 9.75" long with crank that moves
the heads and operates music box on reverse. Front text "Regd. No. 508041 -
All Rights Reserved, Germany, By Exclusive Arrangement With Ideal Films."
Three versions with this considered the best.
Minnie With Pram Version - **$12500 $21000 $32500**
Blue Background Dancing Mickey Version - **$10500 $18500 $24000**
Yellow Background Dancing Mickey Version - **$11500 $21000 $26500**

MKY-25

❏ **MKY-25. Minnie Mouse Pushing Baby Felix In Pram Tin Lithographed Wind-Up,**
c. 1930. Rogelio Sanchez, Spain. Minnie is 6.5" tall with metal tail. Castle logo on her apron. 5.5" long stroller. Only several known. - **$12500 $21000 $36500**

MKY-26

❏ **MKY-26. Mickey Mouse With Moving Eyes And Mouth Lithographed Tin Wind-Up,**
1930. Germany for British import. 8-7/8" tall with rubber tail. Text on back "By Exclusive Arrangement With Ideal Films Ltd. Registered No. 508041." Among the rarest wind-ups. There is also a version without facial movement.
Moving Face - **$10500 $21000 $37000**
Non-Moving Face - **$5500 $10500 $18500**

MKY-27

MKY-28

❑ **MKY-27. "Mickey Mouse Slate Dancer" Litho Tin Toy,**
1930. German with only mark a registration number 508041. Two versions, each 3.5" wide by 6.5" tall, one with hand crank only and one with crank and fly wheel for use with a steam generator. Mickey's arms and legs move rapidly when activated. Also, a third version without the text and Mickey head image on back panel.
Fly Wheel Version - **$8250 $14750 $21000**
Crank Only Version - **$6350 $12500 $19000**
No Text Version - **$4250 $8500 $13000**

❑ **MKY-28. "Mickey Mouse" Drumming Tin Litho Mechanical Toy,**
1930. Germany. There are four varieties. All are 6.5" tall with reverse plunger to activate. All show five-fingered gloves and all depict face positioned over his left shoulder. All drum heads are plain. Two versions show teeth, the example shown plus one with wide smile and teeth. Two versions without teeth showing are one with mouth open and one with mouth closed. All four came in plain generic box.
Version With Teeth - **$1050 $1900 $3150**
Version Without Teeth - **$625 $1050 $1600**

MKY-29

❑ **MKY-29. "Official Mickey Mouse
Song" English Sheet Music,**
1930. Lawrence Wright Music Co.
9.5x12.25" folder of words and music
"Inspired By The Popular Mickey Mouse
Sound Cartoons By Walter Disney For
Ideal Films Ltd." Lyrics include "Dressed In
Charlie Chaplin's Bags/One Night He'd A
Glass Of Wine/Smiling Like The Prince Of
Wales/Some Rat-Killing Stuff He Found." -
$60 $125 $285

MKY-30

❑ **MKY-30. The First "Mickey Mouse
Book,"**
1930. Bibo and Lang. 9x12" with 16 pages.
Includes pages 9-10, board game and
playing pieces to cut out. Some issues
have the Win Smith Mickey Mouse daily
strips on page 8 and back cover.
Complete - **$1250 $5500 $11500**
Missing Pages - **$225 $850 $1600**

MKY-31

❑ **MKY-31. Mickey Mouse With
Saxophone And Cymbals Tin
Mechanical Figure,**
1930. Made In Germany. 5.75" tall with
reverse wire that activates arm and leg
motion. Reverse has transparent decal
with gray printing noting copyright by Ideal
Films. - **$850 $1900 $3900**

MKY-32

❑ **MKY-32. English Photo Postcard,**
1930. "Fleetway Press Ltd." 3.5x5.5" postal
with glossy front photo titled "Toy Soldier
Display. Mickey Mouse Wipes Out The
Toy Army." Photo is two adults wearing full
Mickey Mouse costumes at a cannon while
behind them are numerous men dressed
as toy soldiers, all knocked to the ground. -
$18 $35 $70

MKY-33

MKY-35

❏ **MKY-35. "Aladdin-Tabor Mickey Mouse Club" Celluloid Button,**
c. 1930. 1.25". Scarce imprint. - **$165 $375 $800**

MKY-34

MKY-36

❏ **MKY-33. "Mickey Mouse" Pencil Tablet,**
c. 1930. Tablet is 5.5x9". This is one of several cover styles and these tablets were the first pieces of Disney character merchandise ever produced. This example precedes those produced by Powers Paper Company under a license granted in 1931. - **$115 $230 $450**

❏ **MKY-36. "Mickey Mouse Club" Celluloid Button,**
c. 1930. Western Badge & Button Co. 1.25". - **$55 $110 $175**

MKY-37

❏ **MKY-34. "Mickey Mouse Club" Member's Celluloid Button,**
c. 1930. Fox Hollywood Theatre. 1". - **$115 $175 $335**

❏ **MKY-37. "Mickey Mouse Club" Celluloid Button,**
c. 1930. Philadelphia Badge Co. 1.25". - **$55 $110 $175**

MKY-38

❑ **MKY-38. "Fox Park Plaza Theater Mickey Mouse Club" Celluloid Button,** c.1930. Philadelphia Badge Co. 1.25" shown with back paper. - **$60 $120 $180**

MKY-39

❑ **MKY-39. "Uptown Mickey Mouse Club" Celluloid Button,** c. 1930. Philadelphia Badge Co. 1.25". Unusual for being serially number with rare sponsor imprint. - **$65 $135 $225**

MKY-40

❑ **MKY-40. "Hawaii Theatre Mickey Mouse Club" Button,** 1930. 1.25". Presumably issued by the theater built in Honolulu in 1922, known as "Pride Of The Pacific." - **$65 $135 $225**

MKY-41

❑ **MKY-41. Mickey Mouse Movie Club "Sergt.-At-Arms" Celluloid Button,** c. 1930. 2.25". Earliest movie clubs elected an officer slate headed by "Chief Mickey Mouse" and "Chief Minnie Mouse." Buttons were produced for those and other club officers plus "Master of Ceremonies," "Color Bearer," Song Leader" and "Chorus."
"Chief" Rank - **$1100 $3250 $6500**
Other Ranks - **$800 $2150 $4500**

MKY-42

❑ **MKY-42. "Courier" 2-1/8" Cello. Button,** c. 1930. Cello button with back paper from set of club official buttons issued from the Mickey Mouse Club. Rare.
"Chief" Rank - **$1100 $3250 $6500**
Other Ranks - **$800 $2150 $4500**

MKY-43   MKY-44

□ **MKY-43. Mickey Mouse Early Litho Button,**
c. 1930. Made by Western Theater Premium Co., LA. 13/16". - **$70** **$135** **$250**

□ **MKY-44. Mickey Mouse Early Litho Button,**
c. 1930. Made by W&S Theater Premium Co., Pittsburgh, PA. 13/16". - **$70** **$135** **$250**

MKY-45

□ **MKY-45. "Mickey Mouse Undies" Black And White Advertising Button,**
c. 1930. Philadelphia Badge Co. 7/8". Version has image of Mickey as used on the second design Mickey Mouse Club movie theater buttons. - **$115** **$225** **$450**

MKY-46

□ **MKY-46. "Mickey Mouse Undies" Celluloid Button,**
c. 1930. Backpaper by maker Whitehead & Hoag, Newark. .5". - **$55** **$110** **$165**

MKY-47

□ **MKY-47. "Mickey Mouse/Pluto The Pup" Bisque,**
c. 1930. Japan. 2.5x2.25x5.5" tall designed with movable arm holding fabric "leash." Incised number "S178." - **$225** **$500** **$900**

MKY-48

□ **MKY-48. Minnie Mouse With Tambourine Bisque Figure,**
c. 1930. Unmarked. Likely German. 1-1/8" tall. - **$45** **$85** **$150**

MKY-49

❑ **MKY-49. "Mickey Mouse" Boxed Celluloid Novelty,**
c. 1930. Box is 1x4x1.75" tall and holds 3 figures each about 7/8" tall crossing a bridge. Box is marked "Made In Japan."
Box - **$125 $250 $385**
Figure - **$115 $225 $350**

MKY-50

❑ **MKY-50. Celluloid Figure On Base,**
c. 1930. "Made In Japan" 1.25" tall. - **$115 $165 $240**

MKY-51

❑ **MKY-51. Four Marching Mickeys Celluloid Novelty,**
c. 1930. Japan. 1-7/8" tall Mickey followed by three smaller Mickeys. Mounted on .75x4" base. - **$125 $225 $450**

MKY-52

❑ **MKY-52. Mickey Mouse Early Metal Figure,**
c. 1930. Figure is 1x1x2-3/8" tall and made of cast lead. Marked "Walter E. Disney" underneath. Some figures also say "Design. Pat. Apld. For." A scarce figure and perhaps the earliest Mickey metal figural. - **$125 $275 $600**

MKY-53   MKY-54

❑ **MKY-53. "Mickey Mouse" Bulbous Head Bisque Toothbrush Holder,**
c. 1930. Holder is 2.75x3.25x5" tall designed with one movable arm and string tail. - **$125 $250 $385**

❑ **MKY-54. Minnie Bulbous Head Toothbrush Holder,**
c. 1930. "Japan" 2.5x3x5" tall painted bisque figure with string tail. No incised number. - **$115 $225 $350**

MKY-55

❏ **MKY-55. Mickey Mouse "Pull On His Ear" Lithographed Tin Bank,**
c. 1930. Saalheimer & Strauss, Germany. Text on back explains ear should be pulled to make tongue appear for coin placement and deposit. Side text "By Exclusive Arrangement With Ideal Films Ltd. Registered 508041." 2.25x3.5x7" tall. Four reverse design versions: Mickey with clasped hands, hands apart, pointing (version pictured), and playing accordion. Each - **$10500 $15750 $26250**

MKY-56

MKY-57

❏ **MKY-56. Mickey Mouse China Figural Vase,**
c. 1930. Crown Devon, England. 6" tall. Underside has incised number "578" and text "Reproduced With The Consent Of Walter E. Disney & Ideal Films Ltd." Also issued with match striker area.
Either version - **$1100 $2150 $3750**

❏ **MKY-57. Mickey Mouse Charlotte Clark Large And Rare Doll,**
c. 1930. Velveteen-covered stuffed 8x19x21.5" doll with felt ears, oilcloth eyes, separate string whiskers and four plastic buttons on pants. Has a long 14" tail. Underside of one foot has bold marking "Walt Disney Mickey Mouse" plus design patent number. - **$1750 $3750 $7500**

MKY-58

MKY-60

❑ **MKY-58. "Mickey Mouse" Five-Fingered Celluloid Wind-Up,**
c. 1930. Germany by Rheinische Gummi Und Celluloid Fabrik Co. Figure is celluloid 6" tall with spring tail and flat tin ears that wiggle. Sticker under foot "Reproduced With The Consent Of Walter E. Disney And Ideal Films Ltd." Box is 3.5x6.5x2.5" deep.
Box - **$550 $1100 $2200**
Toy - **$1100 $2750 $5500**

❑ **MKY-60. Mickey Mouse With Felix In Basket Tin Lithographed Mechanical Toy,**
c. 1930. Made by Rogelio Sanchez, Spain, marked "Ilsa." Photo example missing Mickey's cloth tail. 4.75" long with spring action that raises basket lid to allow Felix to pop up. - **$3250 $8000 $16500**

MKY-61

MKY-59

❑ **MKY-59. Mickey Five-Fingered Walking Lithographed Tin Wind-Up,**
c. 1930. Commonly credited to Johann Distler, Germany. 2.25" wide by 9" tall with rubber tail. - **$3750 $8500 $16500**

❑ **MKY-61. "Mickey The Mouse" Early Australian Movie Theater Hand-Out,**
c. 1930. 5.75x8.75" four page folder features numerous images of Mickey and related text along with "Mickey's Theme Song, Minnie's Yoo Hoo." Art by British artist Wilfred Haughton who drew the Mickey comics for the Mickey Mouse annual. - **$115 $225 $350**

MKY-62

MKY-65

MKY-63

☐ **MKY-62. "Mickey Mouse" Flip Book,**
c. 1930. English by Flicker Productions
Ltd. 2.25x3". Front cover reads "Mickey
Mouse/Flicker No. 36/The Cheese Trap
And Fatty Boy." Pages feature actual film
scenes. - **$75 $150 $325**

☐ **MKY-63. "Mickey Mouse Coloring
Book,"**
1931. Saalfield Publishing. 10.75x15.25".
Book #871 with 28 pages. - **$125 $325
$850**

MKY-64

☐ **MKY-64. "Mickey Mouse Pictures To
Paint" Book,**
1931. Saalfield. 9x10.5" softcover "No.
210" with 48 pages of illustrations by staff
of Walt Disney Studios. Format is full color
example pages and black/white identical
pages to be colored. - **$140 $350 $900**

☐ **MKY-65. Walt Disney Studio
Christmas Card,**
1931. Card is 5x7.5" closed with tipped-in
paper sheet. - **$675 $1750 $3500**

MKY-66

☐ **MKY-66. Wood Jointed Figure With
Lollipop Hands,**
1931. Figure is 3x6x7.25" tall complete
with fabric-covered wire tail, pair of rubber-
over-fabric ears, name decal on chest.
Note: Yellow color is rare.
Red Figure - **$450 $875 $1650**
Yellow Figure - **$800 $1650 $2750**
Box - **$550 $1100 $2000**

MKY-67

❑ **MKY-67. Mickey/Minnie Fabric Pillow Cover,**
1931.Vogue Needlecraft Co. Inc. Un-cut fabric sheet to be cut in half and then sewn together to form a pillow measures 16.5x34.5". Margin includes text "Mickey Mouse Series" and "98." Unused or neatly stitched - **$55 $110 $165**

MKY-68

❑ **MKY-68. Mickey/Minnie Fabric Pillow Cover,**
1931. Vogue Needlecraft Co.Inc.Un-cut fabric sheet containing two halves that were to be sewn together to form a pillow and measures 16.5x34.5." Margin says "Mickey Mouse Series" and "97." Unused or neatly stitched - **$55 $110 $165**

MKY-69

❑ **MKY-69. "Mickey Mouse Handkerchiefs" Book,**
1931. Great Britain with Ideal Films and Disney copyright. 10x10.5" with six pages which likely held six hankies. Hanky art from Adventures of Mickey Mouse book. Versions exist with page and hanky counts of eight each or fewer.
Book - **$115 $225 $450**
Each Hanky - **$20 $35 $70**

MKY-70

❑ **MKY-70. "Mickey Mouse Jazz Drummer" Mechanical Toy,**
1931. Nifty Co. 3x6.75" lithographed tin figure of Mickey with attached 1.5" diameter drum. German made. When lever on back is pushed down, this causes a pair of knobs inside the drum to spin rapidly and beat against the drum head which also moves up and down. Mickey's arms which are attached by rivets move up and down as if he is drumming with sticks. Specified as Nifty Toy #173 on top end of box.
Toy - **$850 $1850 $3250**
Box - **$550 $1350 $3800**

MKY-71

❑ **MKY-71. "The Wedding Party Of Mickey Mouse" Sheet Music,**
1931. Stasny Music Corp. 9x12" eight pages. - **$55 $110 $175**

MKY-72

❑ **MKY-72. "Mickey Mouse" First Newspaper Premium Picture Card,**
1931. Stiff paper card 3-3/8x5-3/8". Issued by various newspapers in May, 1931. Scene includes "Butch" in suit of armor. Historic and rare premium. - **$300 $600 $1250**

MKY-73

❑ **MKY-73. "Mickey Mouse Illustrated Movie Stories" Hardcover,**
1931. David McKay Co. 6.25x8.75" with 200 pages. Includes art taken from eleven of Mickey's earliest cartoons.
Jacket - **$425 $850 $1750**
Book Only - **$265 $425 $900**
2" Red Slip-band With Instructions - **$110 $225 $335**

MKY-74

❏ **MKY-74. "Mickey Mouse Storybook" Hardcover Version,**
1931. David McKay Co. 6x8.75" with 64 pages including black and white photos from early films. - **$135 $265 $550**

MKY-75

❏ **MKY-75. "Mickey Mouse Series No. 1" Reprint Book,**
1931. David McKay Co. 9.75x10" cardboard cover version with 48 pages of reprinted Floyd Gottfredson daily strips from 1930-1931 including the famous two-week sequence in which Mickey tries to commit suicide. - **$250 $700 $1650**

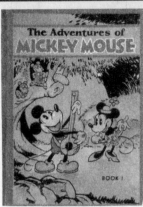

MKY-76

❏ **MKY-76. "The Adventures Of Mickey Mouse Book 1,"**
1931. David McKay Co. 6.25x8.25" softcover with 32 pages. - **$115 $235 $500**

MKY-77

❏ **MKY-77. "The Adventures Of Mickey Mouse Book 1" Hardcover,**
1931. David McKay Co. 5.5x7.75" with 32 pages. Text refers to Clarabelle Cow as "Caroline" and to Horace Horsecollar as "Henry." The name "Donald Duck" designates a non-costumed generic duck. - **$140 $275 $600**

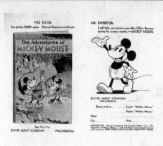

MKY-78

MKY-78. "The Adventures Of Mickey Mouse" Book Promotional Movie Theater Folder,

1931. 6x9" glossy 4-page folder with images and various merchandise also includes an order form for classic Mickey book "The Adventures of Mickey Mouse." - **$225 $450 $900**

MKY-79

MKY-79. "Mickey Mouse" Sparkler,

1931. By Nifty, distributed by Geo. Borgfeldt. 1.5x4x5.5" tall die-cut tin litho with spring plunger mechanism. Nifty Toy #174 on box. Beware of repro. boxes.
Box - **$275 $550 $1200**
Sparkler - **$225 $500 $800**

MKY-80

MKY-80. Mickey Mouse Iridescent Luster China Mug,

c. 1931. Japan. 2.25" tall. Image near identical to front cover image of 1931 book "The Adventures of Mickey Mouse." - **$115 $225 $350**

MKY-81

MKY-81. Mickey In Santa Outfit Cello. Button,

1931. Several imprints: this one "Meet Me At Hank's Toyland." - **$600 $850 $1850**

MKY-82

❏ **MKY-82. Mickey Mouse Theater Promo Cello Button,**
1931. Cello pinback with back paper. Rare. - **$300 $500 $1250**

MKY-84

❏ **MKY-84. Mickey Mouse Glazed Ceramic Napkin Holder,**
c. 1931. "Germany" on underside and "6567" on reverse. 4" tall. - **$225 $450 $850**

MKY-83

❏ **MKY-83. Mickey Mouse Glazed Ceramic Napkin Ring,**
c. 1931. Comes in two sizes. 2-5/8" tall or 3-3/8" tall. Small - **$135 $275 $450** Large - **$200 $400 $725**

MKY-85

❏ **MKY-85. Mickey Mouse Figural China Condiment Jar,**
c 1931. German. 4" tall. Incised #2820. Depicts a five-fingered Mickey. - **$125 $235 $475**

MKY-86

MKY-88

❏ **MKY-86. "Fishin' Around Mickey Mouse Game,"**
c. 1931. English By Chad Valley Co. As noted on one side of game board "The Illustrations And Text Matter In This Game Were Taken From Mickey Mouse Movie Stories And Are Produced By Permission Of Dean & Son Ltd." - **$450 $875 $1500**

❏ **MKY-88. Mickey Mouse Pencil Drawing From The Klondike Kid,**
1932. Sheet of animation paper is 9.5x12" with 2.5x4" image. #71 from a numbered sequence. - **$110 $225 $325**

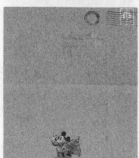

MKY-89

MKY-87

❏ **MKY-87. Mickey Classic Pose Silvered Brass Pin,**
c. 1931. 1" tall pin with silver finish and black and yellow enamel paint. - **$45 $90 $150**

❏ **MKY-89. Walt Disney Studio Christmas Card,**
1932. Mailer card about 8x9" open. This example was sent to a theater in Allentown, PA. - **$550 $1100 $2250**

MKY-90

❑ **MKY-90. "Mickey Mouse Club" Rare Sweater Emblem,**
1932. Fisch & Co. 4.5" diameter felt. From an unknown theater in the Los Angeles area. - **$525 $1050 $2000**

MKY-91

❑ **MKY-91. Fox Movie Theater Owner's Promo Booklet,**
1932. 4.5x6" with 16 pages. - **$35 $75 $135**

MKY-92

❑ **MKY-92. Movie Exhibitor Magazine With Mickey And Silly Symphonies,**
1932. "Motion Picture Herald." 9.25x12.25" December 17 weekly for movie theater owners, 76 pages. Content includes two-page ad for "Silly Symphony 'Santa's Workshop' And Mickey Mouse In 'Mickey's Good Deed'." Ad features Santa surrounded by four Mickeys reading mail sent to him. Another two-page ad introduces Boris Karloff as "The Mummy." - **$85 $175 $300**

MKY-93

MKY-94

❑ **MKY-94. Mickey Mouse Pull Toy By Steiff,**
1932. 4.5x7.25x8.5" tall toy consists of jointed Mickey figure attached to a four-wheel Irish mail which has heavy wire frame, wood seat and wheels. Metal button in ear, string whiskers, oil cloth eyes, fabric tail. Bellows in seat to squeak. - **$2650 $4800 $8000**

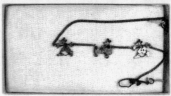

MKY-95

❑ **MKY-95. Mickey Mouse Boxed Necklace,**
1932. Cohn & Rosenberger Inc. 2.75x5.25x.75" deep box contains nice quality necklace still attached to fabric-covered insert. Metal link necklace has three .5" tall silvered brass pendants with enameled paint.
Box - **$65 $150 $250**
Necklace - **$55 $115 $175**

❑ **MKY-93. Australian Movie Exhibitor Magazine Featuring Mickey Mouse And Silly Symphonies,**
1932. 10x12" Volume 13, No. 668 dated December 14, 1932 issue. Features 4-page full color insert for United Artists Mickey Mouse and Silly Symphonies shorts with artwork by Win Smith. - **$125 $225 $475**

MKY-96

☐ **MKY-96. "Mickey Mouse And Silly Symphonies" Exceptional Film Exhibitor's Catalogue,**
1932. Book is 9x12" with 48 pages printed in limited run of around 15000 copies. Considered the first merchandise catalogue. Contents are black and white with great illustrations and photos. Attached to first page is reply postcard for theater owner stating their desire to run these features. - **$1500 $3500 $5500**

MKY-97

❑ **MKY-97. Mickey Mouse Early Glazed Ceramic Figure By Rosenthal,**
1932. Germany. About 4" tall. Likely the first figure produced. Incised #493. - **$1000 $2000 $3650**

MKY-99

❑ **MKY-99. Mickey Mouse Crossed Legs Glazed Ceramic Figure By Rosenthal,**
1932. Germany. 3.5" tall. Incised #652. - **$500 $1250 $2500**

MKY-98

❑ **MKY-98. Mickey Mouse With Revolver Glazed Ceramic Figure By Rosenthal,**
1932. Germany. 3" tall. Incised #552. Rosenthal figures usually have a green and gold foil sticker under the base in German that translates to "Mickey Mouse Brings Luck To Your House." Rosenthal never distributed Disney items in the U.S.A. - **$750 $1500 $3000**

MKY-100

❑ **MKY-100. Mickey Mouse Kicking Ball Glazed Ceramic Figure By Rosenthal,**
1932. Germany. 3.5" tall. Incised #567. - **$650 $1350 $2750**

MKY-101

❑ **MKY-101. Mickey Mouse Playing Mandolin Glazed Ceramic Figure By Rosenthal,**
1932. Germany. 3.25" tall. Incised #554. - **$750 $1500 $3000**

MKY-103

❑ **MKY-103. Mickey Mouse Grinning Glazed Ceramic Figure By Rosenthal,**
1932. Germany. 3.25" tall. Incised #551. - **$650 $1350 $2750**

MKY-102

❑ **MKY-102. Mickey Mouse Throwing Discus Glazed Ceramic Figure By Rosenthal,**
1932. Germany. 3.25" tall. Incised #651. - **$650 $1350 $2750**

MKY-104

❑ **MKY-104. Mickey Mouse With Saxophone Glazed Ceramic Figure By Rosenthal,**
1932. Germany. About 3.5" tall. Incised #553. - **$750 $1500 $3000**

MKY-105

❏ **MKY-105. Mickey Mouse Ball Toss Glazed Ceramic Figure By Rosenthal,** 1932. Germany. About 3.5" tall. Incised number. - **$750 $1500 $3000**

MKY-107

❏ **MKY-107. Minnie Mouse Bashful Pose Glazed Ceramic Figure By Rosenthal,** 1932. Germany. About 3.5" tall. Incised #556. - **$600 $1200 $1800**

MKY-106

❏ **MKY-106. Minnie Mouse With Compact Glazed Ceramic Figure By Rosenthal,** 1932. Germany. About 3.5" tall. Incised #655. - **$750 $1500 $3000**

MKY-108

❏ **MKY-108. Mickey Mouse On Ashtray Glazed Ceramic By Rosenthal,** 1932. Germany. About 3.5" diameter. Uncertain if with or without incised number. - **$600 $1200 $1800**

MKY-109

❑ **MKY-109. Mickey Mouse With Saxophone Glazed Ceramic Ashtray By Rosenthal,**
1932. Germany. 3.75x5.75" oval with 3" figure. No number. - **$800** **$1600** **$3250**

MKY-110

❑ **MKY-110. Minnie Mouse With Tennis Racquet Glazed Ceramic Figure By Rosenthal,**
1932. Germany. About 3.5" tall. Incised number. - **$750** **$1500** **$3000**

MKY-111

❑ **MKY-111. Mickey Mouse Hands On Hips Glazed Ceramic Figure By Rosenthal,**
1932. Germany. About 3.5" tall. Incised #550. - **$600** **$1200** **$1800**

MKY-112

❑ **MKY-112. Mickey Mouse China Plate,**
1932. Rosenthal. 8.25" diameter depicts a happy Mickey Mouse image at center of plate. - **$115** **$275** **$525**

MKY-113

MKY-116

❏ **MKY-113. Mickey Mouse China Plate,**
1932. Rosenthal. 8.25" diameter depicts a puzzled Mickey Mouse image at center of plate. - **$115 $275 $525**

❏ **MKY-116. Pencil Drawing,**
1932. Animation paper is 9.5x12" centered by 4.5x5.5" image for 'Wayward Canary' film short. Depicted is Mickey poking his head through what appears to be a greenhouse framework with broken windows. No. "64" from a numbered sequence. - **$150 $250 $450**

MKY-114

❏ **MKY-114. Mickey Mouse With Field Hockey Stick And Ball Glazed Ceramic Figure,**
1932. No markings. 1.25" tall. - **$75 $140 $250**

MKY-117

MKY-115

❏ **MKY-115. Mickey And Minnie Glazed Ceramic Salt & Pepper Set,**
1932. Marked "Germany." Mickey with incised number "6895." 2.5" tall. Pair - **$150 $300 $500**

❏ **MKY-117. "Mickey Mouse" Pillow Pair,**
1932. Vogue Needlecraft. First is 16.5x18", #494, second is 15.5x16." Each Unused - **$55 $110 $165**
Each Used, Nicely Formed - **$30 $60 $90**

MKY-118

❏ **MKY-118. "Mickey Mouse" Pillow Cover,**
1932. Vogue Needlecraft Co. #492 in series. 16x17.5". Unused - **$55 $110 $165**
Neatly Stitched And Formed - **$30 $60 $90**

MKY-119

❏ **MKY-119. "Mickey/Minnie Mouse" Bangle Bracelet,**
1932. Cohn & Rosenberger. Silvered brass with enameled paint .5" wide and about 2.25" diameter. - **$135 $250 $450**

MKY-120

❏ **MKY-120. "Mickey Mouse" Bracelet,**
1932. Cohn & Rosenberger. Silvered brass with 1.75" enamel Mickey figure. - **$50 $100 $225**

MKY-121

❏ **MKY-121. "Minnie" Mouse Child's Glass And Silver Beaded Necklace,**
1932. Likely By Cohn & Rosenberger. 6.75" long with 5/8" diameter glass pendant. - **$90 $175 $300**

MKY-122

❏ **MKY-122. Minnie Mouse Bracelet With Charm,**
1932. 7/8" tall enamel paint on brass figure Minnie held on a child size 2.5" diameter brass link with green segments bracelet. - **$50 $90 $150**

MKY-125

MKY-123

☐ **MKY-123. Mickey Mouse Ring and Box,**
1932. Cohn & Rosenberger Inc. 1.25x1.25x1" deep cardboard box for enameled silver/brass Mickey Mouse ring pictured above.
Ring - **$300 $450 $900**
Box Only - **$110 $225 $350**

☐ **MKY-125. Mickey Mouse ABC Bowl,**
1932. Bavaria. 7.75" diameter by 1.5" deep. - **$140 $275 $500**

MKY-126

MKY-127

MKY-124

☐ **MKY-124. Mickey Running Sterling And Enamel Pin,**
1932. 13/16" from jewelry series by Cohn & Rosenberger, New York City. - **$40 $85 $160**

☐ **MKY-126. "Mickey Mouse" China Alphabet Bowl,**
1932. Bavaria. 8" diameter by 1.75" deep 1930s marked on underside "Walter E. Disney/Made In Bavaria" plus small full figure black, white and red Mickey image. Alphabet order error of "JI." - **$125 $250 $450**

☐ **MKY-127. "Mickey Mouse/Pluto The Pup" China Soup Bowl,**
1932. Bavarian. 7.5" diameter by 1.25" deep. - **$100 $200 $400**

MKY-128

☐ **MKY-128. Mickey And Minnie Mouse Ceramic Bowl,**
1932. Krueger. 7" diameter by 1.75" deep. Reverse includes early copyright of "Walt E. Disney" as well as name "Mickey Mouse." - **$85 $165 $275**

MKY-129

☐ **MKY-129. Mickey/Minnie Mouse Ceramic Mug,**
1932. Mug is 3.5" tall. Marked on underside "Mickey Mouse/Copyright Walt E. Disney." Originally came as a set with bowl (previous item) and dish (following item.) - **$50 $100 $200**

MKY-130

☐ **MKY-130. Child's Partitioned Dish,**
1932. Dish is 7.5" diameter by 1" deep glazed ceramic segmented into three food sections. Reverse has copyright and name "Mickey Mouse." - **$90 $175 $300**

MKY-131

☐ **MKY-131. "Mickey Mouse China" Creamer,**
1932. Bavaria. 3.5" tall. Incised #992. - **$110 $225 $335**

MKY-132

☐ **MKY-132. "Mickey Mouse" China Cup And Saucer,**
1932. Bavaria. 2.5" tall cup and 4.75" diameter saucer. Both pieces have same company mark on underside that includes small Mickey image. Cup - **$55 $80 $135** Saucer - **$30 $55 $85**

MKY-133

❑ **MKY-133. "Mickey Mouse" China Sugar Bowl,**
1932. Bavaria. 4.5x6x3.25" tall. Underside has company markings plus small full figure image of Mickey and incised "590/3." Photo example missing lid. Complete. - **$150 $275 $450**

MKY-135

❑ **MKY-135. Mickey Mouse Mug,**
1932. Bavarian China. 3" tall. - **$60 $125 $250**

MKY-134

❑ **MKY-134. Minnie Mouse China Cup And Mickey Saucer,**
1932. Bavaria. 2.5" tall cup and 4.75" diameter saucer. Both pieces have company mark on underside that includes small Mickey image. Cup - **$45 $70 $115** Saucer - **$30 $55 $85**

MKY-136

❑ **MKY-136. "Mickey Mouse" German Large Plate,**
1932. China is 7.5" diameter with underside marking "Walter E. Disney/Made In Bavaria" plus small Mickey image. - **$110 $215 $340**

MKY-137

❏ **MKY-137. "Mickey Mouse" German Large Plate,**
1932. China is 7.5" diameter with under-side marking "Walter E. Disney/Made In Bavaria" plus small Mickey walking image. - **$110 $215 $340**

MKY-138

❏ **MKY-138. "Mickey Mouse" Plate,**
1932. "Bavaria Schumann." 6.25" diameter issue from chinaware series marked on underside by Mickey image and authoriza-tions. - **$85 $185 $325**

MKY-139

❏ **MKY-139. "Mickey Mouse" Plate,**
1932. "Bavaria Schumann." 6.25" diameter issue from series marked on underside by Mickey image and authorizations. - **$85 $185 $325**

MKY-140

MKY-141

❏ **MKY-140. "Mickey Mouse" Bavarian China Plate,**
1932. Plate is 6.25" in diameter and marked on reverse "Walter E. Disney/ Made In Bavaria" with small Mickey image. - **$85 $185 $325**

❏ **MKY-141. "Mickey Mouse" Bavarian China Plate,**
1932. Plate is 6.25" in diameter and marked on reverse "Walter E. Disney/Made In Bavaria." - **$110 $215 $340**

MKY-142

MKY-143

❏ **MKY-143. Mesh Purse,**
1932. Mesh metal is 2.5x3.5" with enameled metal frame bar for the clasp closure.
Attached to front by a pair of wire loops is
a 1" tall metal diecut Mickey figure with
painted accents. - **$225 $375 $600**

MKY-144

❏ **MKY-142. Mickey Mouse Glazed
Ceramic Child's Tea Set By Rosenthal,**
1932. Set consists of six 1.25x7/8" deep
cups and six 2-5/8" saucers, 3" tall teapot
with lid, 1-5/8" tall sugar bowl with lid, 1-
3/8" tall creamer and a ceramic serving
tray. Set - **$3250 $8000 $16000**

❏ **MKY-144. "Mickey Mouse Movie
Stories" Book,**
1932. Musson Book Co. Ltd. "Second
Canadian Edition" 6x8.75" clothbound
hardcover, 190 pages. - **$110 $215 $400**

MKY-146

❏ **MKY-146. "More Adventures Of Mickey Mouse" English Book,** 1932. Dean & Son Ltd. 5.5x7.75" hardcover, 32 pages. Inside front and back covers feature full color map of town where Mickey lives. - **$120 $250 $575**

MKY-145

❏ **MKY-145. "1932-33 Art Needlework Specialty Shop" Catalogue With Mickey,** 1932. Issued by Frederick Herrschner Inc., Chicago. 8x11" with 68 pages. Shows many rare fabric items. - **$65 $150 $250**

MKY-147

❏ **MKY-147. Mickey And Minnie Book,** 1932. French by Hachette. 4.5x7" with 256 pages. - **$115 $240 $375**

MKY-148

❑ **MKY-148. "Mickey Mouse Book No. 2" Of Comic Strip Reprints,**
1932. David McKay Co. 9.75x10" cardboard cover book with 48 pages of reprinted 1931 daily strips by Floyd Gottfredson. - **$225 $625 $1200**

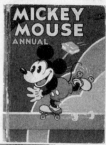

MKY-149

❑ **MKY-149. "Mickey Mouse Annual" Hardcover,**
1932. English by Dean & Son Ltd. 6.5x8.75x2" thick with 124 pages. - **$115 $275 $550**

MKY-150

❑ **MKY-150. Steiff Mickey Mouse Hand Puppet,**
1932. Velvet puppet 10" tall has sateen-covered hands, felt ears, oilcloth eyes and string whiskers. Came with ear button and cloth tag. There were two versions, this one shown with all black body and one with lower few inches in dark red with two sewn-on buttons to simulate pants. See MKY-193. With Tag And Button - **$425 $850 $1750**
With Tag Or Button - **$225 $550 $1100**
Without Tag And Button - **$125 $450 $900**

MKY-151

❑ **MKY-151. "Mickey Mouse" German Ashtray,**
1932. Bavarian China. 3x3x.5" deep. - **$60 $115 $175**

MKY-152

❏ **MKY-152. "Mickey Mouse" German Ashtray,**
1932. Bavarian China. 3x3x.5" deep. - **$60** **$115** **$175**

MKY-153

❏ **MKY-153. "Mickey Mouse" China Boxed Ashtray Set,**
1932. Bavaria. 7x7x.75" deep cardboard box with hinged lid contains set of four 3x3x.75" deep ashtrays. Underside of each ashtray has same markings which include small image of Mickey plus text "Mickey Mouse Authorized By Walter E. Disney/ Made In Bavaria."
Near Mint Boxed Set - **$900**

MKY-154

❏ **MKY-154. "Mickey Mouse" Bavarian China Ashtray,**
1932. White china 3x3x.5". - **$60** **$115** **$175**

MKY-155

❏ **MKY-155. Minnie Mouse Ashtray,**
1932. White china 3x3x.5". - **$60** **$115** **$175**

MKY-156

❏ **MKY-156. Minnie Mouse Ashtray,**
1932. White china 3x3x.5". - **$60** **$115** **$175**

MKY-157

MKY-157. Minnie Mouse Bavarian China Ashtray,
1932. China ashtray 3x3.5". - **$60 $115 $175**

MKY-158

MKY-158. Mickey Mouse Calendar,
1932. 6x11.75" die-cut stiff cardboard with attached complete 12-month calendar pad. - **$125 $250 $350**

MKY-159

MKY-159. "Mickey Mouse Home Movies" Promotion Material,
1932. Lot of four pieces issued by "Hollywood Film Enterprises Inc," to store owners. Original envelope with Mickey/Minnie images is 4x9.5", a 12x18.5" sheet of paper designed like the front page of a newspaper titled "Cine Art Amateur Home Movies Vol. 1 No. 1," 8.5x11" letter typed on "Hollywood Film Enterprises" letterhead and a 3x8.5" sheet of pink paper with "Heading Correction" for the large "newspaper" sheet.
As Issued - **$135 $265 $375**

MKY-160

MKY-160. Mickey Mouse Get Well Card,
1932. Hall Brothers. 4x5" paper card with scalloped edge. - **$30 $60 $90**

MKY-161

MKY-161. Mickey Mouse In Bullet-Nose Car Bisque,
c. 1932. 1.5" long. - **$150 $300 $600**

MKY-162

MKY-163

MKY-164

☐ **MKY-164. Mickey Mouse German Band China Figures,**
c. 1932. Set of six, each 2.25" tall. Incised numbers 4281 to 4286 consecutively. Each is a five fingered Mickey. Each - **$55 $110 $175**

MKY-165

☐ **MKY-162. Mickey Mouse German Figure,**
c. 1932. Unmarked 2.75" tall with compressed paper body, heads, hands and feet plus pipe cleaner arms, legs and tail. - **$55 $110 $165**

☐ **MKY-163. Minnie German Figurine,**
c. 1932. "Deutschland" 1.75" tall china miniature. - **$50 $90 $165**

☐ **MKY-165. Mickey Mouse In Chair German Metal Figure,**
c. 1932. Figure is 3-7/8" wide and 3.75" tall. - **$1150 $3250 $6500**

MKY-166

MKY-168

❑ **MKY-166. Mickey Mouse German Metal Figure,**
c. 1932. "Mickey Mouse" in lower relief text on one side, "Walt Disney" in lower relief text on other side. 4" wide, 3.25" tall. - **$700 $1400 $2350**

❑ **MKY-168. Mickey Mouse Metal Figure With Playing Card Suit Indicator,**
c. 1932. Germany. 'Book' pages flip to show card suits. A second version has Mickey with one arm bent down and one arm bent up. 3.25" tall by 4.25" wide. Either - **$1050 $2250 $3300**

MKY-167

MKY-169

❑ **MKY-167. Mickey Mouse With Umbrella German Metal Figure,**
c. 1932. Figure is 3.75" wide, 5" tall to top of umbrella. - **$825 $1600 $2650**

❑ **MKY-169. Mickey Mouse With Book Metal Figure,**
c. 1932. Germany. 3.5" tall. - **$825 $1600 $2650**

MKY-170

❑ **MKY-170. Mickey Mouse Metal Figure With Cigarette And Match Holders,**
c. 1932. Germany. 3.5" tall by 6" long. - **$1050 $2250 $3300**

MKY-172

❑ **MKY-172. Minnie Mouse Metal Figure With Bell,**
c. 1932. Germany. 3.25" diameter by 5.75" tall. - **$1050 $2250 $3300**

MKY-171

❑ **MKY-171. Minnie Mouse Metal Figure Ashtray,**
c. 1932. Germany. 4.5" diameter by 5.25" tall. - **$825 $1600 $2650**

MKY-173

❑ **MKY-173. Mickey Mouse Metal Figure Ashtray,**
c. 1932. Germany. 4.5" diameter by 5" tall. - **$875 $1650 $2850**

MKY-174

MKY-176

MKY-177

❏ **MKY-174. Mickey Mouse Metal German Astray With Floor Lamp,** c. 1932. Metal Mickey is 3.5" tall on 3-1/8x4.75x5/8" metal base with 6" wire lamp at rear. Germany in black ink on underside. - **$1050 $2250 $3300**

MKY-175

❏ **MKY-175. Mickey Mouse Metal German Figure With Calendar On Lamppost,** c. 1932. About 5.5" tall with paper calendar date sheets in holder. - **$1050 $2250 $3300**

❏ **MKY-176. Mickey Mouse Ceramic Bottle Stopper,** c. 1932. Germany. 3-1/8" tall. Depicts Mickey with five fingers. - **$80 $160 $250**

❏ **MKY-177. Large Mickey Mouse Candy Container,** c. 1932. German. 6.25" tall painted composition figure stands atop cardboard candy box bottom platform which is 2.5" diameter by 1" tall. Underside of removable base has "Walter E. Disney" ink stamp plus German company name. - **$175 $300 $600**

MKY-178

❏ **MKY-178. Mickey Mouse Enameled Brass Comb Holder,** c. 1932. Cohn & Rosenberger Inc. 1x4.5". - **$115 $175 $325**

MKY-179

❏ **MKY-179. Mickey/Minnie Fabric Pillow Cover Front,**
c. 1932. Unmarked 15x15.75" but item is known to be German-made. - **$150 $275 $550**

MKY-180

❏ **MKY-180. Mickey And Minnie Mouse Rug,**
c. 1932. Unmarked, likely German. 24x39".
- **$95 $190 $375**

MKY-181

MKY-182

❏ **MKY-181. Mickey Mouse United Kingdom Stickpin,**
c. 1932. 1-1/8" tall silvered brass figure marked "All Rights Reserved." - **$45 $85 $150**

❏ **MKY-182. Mickey Mouse German China Bridge Set,**
c. 1932. "Koenigszelt Germany." Marked on underside of each piece. Set consists of 5.75" diameter by 1.75" deep dish and four 3.5" diameter individual serving plates, all have scalloped edges with bright gold trim. One example shown. Dish - **$200 $400 $750**
Each Plate - **$50 $100 $200**

MKY-183

❏ **MKY-183. "Mickey Mouse" Figural China Container,**
c. 1932. German. Marked "Foreign." 5.5" tall. Mickey has five fingers and his head serves as lid. - **$275 $550 $900**

MKY-184

❑ **MKY-184. Mickey And Minnie Glazed China Canister Set,**
c. 1932. Made In Japan. Nine pieces about 3" tall or smaller, most with lids, to hold various substances for kitchen use.
Set - **$500 $1000 $2000**

MKY-185

❑ **MKY-185. Child's Warming Dish,**
c. 1932. Bavarian China. 6" diameter by 2" deep bowl converted into a warming dish by mounting inside of a stainless steel container with American trademark "Excello" on underside. - **$125 $235 $450**

MKY-186

❑ **MKY-186. Mickey Mouse China Egg Timer,**
c. 1932. Unmarked but likely German made. 3.75" tall. - **$275 $550 $900**

MKY-187

❑ **MKY-187. Mickey Mouse China Egg Timer,**
c. 1932. German. 3.5" tall overall. - **$125 $250 $450**

MKY-188

❑ **MKY-188. Mickey Mouse "30 Comics" Litho Button,**
c. 1932. Green Duck. 1-1/8". - **$100 $225 $450**

MKY-189

❑ **MKY-189. "Mickey Mouse Club" Button,**
c. 1932. Rim text copyright "1928-1930 By W.E. Disney." Kay Kamen backpaper. 1.25". - **$65 $125 $200**

MKY-190

☐ MKY-190. "Mickey Mouse Club" Early Cello Button,
c. 1932. 1/2". Likely produced by local theater owner using image from 1932
Exhibitor Campaign book. - **$225 $450
$725**

MKY-191

☐ MKY-191. Mickey Mouse Mask,
c. 1932. Germany. 8.5x9" pressed and
formed paper mache. Inside of mask has
ink stamps including name of "Walter E.
Disney" as well as "Made In Germany." -
$150 $300 $500

MKY-192

**☐ MKY-192. Mickey Mouse Vintage
Homemade Adult Size Head Mask,**
c. 1932. 13x14.5x12.5". Paper mache and
hand painted mask. - **$65 $125 $225**

MKY-193

**☐ MKY-193. Mickey Mouse Hand
Puppet By Steiff,**
c. 1932. 10" tall velvetten puppet with
stuffed head that has felt ears, oilcloth
eyes and pair of string whiskers. Shown
with small "Steiff" metal button in left ear.
Front of pants are complete with pair of
mother-of-pearl buttons. See MKY-150 for
version with no pants.
Without Tag and Button. - **$550 $1350
$2500**
With Tag or Button. - **$700 $1500 $2650**
With Tag and Button. - **$850 $1650 $2800**

MKY-194

❑ **MKY-194. Mickey Mouse Flat Figural Ceramic Ashtray,**
c. 1932. Germany. Incised under base #6584 and stamp "Germany" 5x5.25x2" deep. - **$275 $550 $1100**

MKY-196

❑ **MKY-196. Puzzle Set,**
1933. Features the whole gang, except Donald who didn't arrive until the following year. Four different puzzles in a box with lid repeating one scene.
Each - **$55 $90 $165**
Box (not shown) - **$75 $150 $300**

MKY-195

❑ **MKY-195. Bagatelle Featuring Mickey Mouse And Felix The Cat,**
c. 1932. Italian by "Bottega Lithografica Muller And Brescia." 11.5x19.25x1.25" deep. - **$115 $235 $450**

MKY-197

❑ **MKY-197. "The Art Of Mickey Mouse And His Creator Walt Disney" Booklet,**
1933. "College Art Assn." 5x6.5" eight-page glossy paper publication, probably issued for the first animation art exhibit. Contents include three Mickey short scenes, illustration of Mickey and Minnie ice skating, photo of Walt and Mickey. Film scene on back is from "Ye Olden Days." Text includes detailed information on Walt's career up to this point. - **$85 $150 $250**

MKY-198

❏ **MKY-198. Pencil Drawing,**
1933. Animation paper is 9.5x12" centered
by 3x3.75" image for 'Puppy Love' cartoon
short. No. "524" from a numbered
sequence. - **$125 $250 $475**

MKY-199

❏ **MKY-199. Mickey And Minnie Mouse
Pencil Drawing From Mickey's
Mellerdrammer,**
1933. Animation paper is 9.5x12" with 4x6"
image. Depicts Mickey in blackface as
Uncle Tom and Minnie as Little Eva
dancing. - **$150 $300 $550**

MKY-200

❏ **MKY-200. Ethnic Pencil Drawing,**
1933. Animation paper is 9.5x12" centered
by 3x4.5" drawing for 'Mickey's
Mellerdrammer' short. Mickey is depicted
as African American caricature with black
face, braided hair with bows, tattered outfit.
Margin has "155/357," one being a
sequence number. - **$150 $300 $550**

MKY-201

❏ **MKY-201. Minnie Mouse Pencil
Drawing From Building A Building,**
1933. Sheet of animation paper is 9.5x12"
with 2x3.5" image in lead/blue/red pencil.
- **$125 $250 $400**

MKY-202

❏ **MKY-202. Mickey Mouse Pencil
Drawing From Giant Land,**
1933. 9.5x12" sheet of animation paper
with 2.75x2.75" image. "153" from a numbered sequence. - **$100 $200 $350**

MKY-203

□ **MKY-203. "Lumar Mickey Mouse Jig-Saw" Boxed English Puzzle,**
1933. Boxed puzzle is 6.5x9.5x1" deep titled "Mickey's Circus." Box underside has paper label for puzzle completion contest and a related leaflet entry form is enclosed. - **$50 $100 $175**

MKY-204

□ **MKY-204. "Confectioner's Journal" With Mickey Candy Ad,**
1933. Ad is 8.5x11.5" in "The World's Oldest Candy Paper." Contains full page ad for "Mickey Mouse Nibbles" candy that includes photo with full display box. - **$15 $35 $75**

MKY-205

□ **MKY-205. "Confectioners Journal" With Mickey Mouse Ad,**
1933. Volume 59, #699 from April 1, 1933 with 68 pages. Features a one-page ad for "Mickey Mouse Nibbles" including photo of candy display box picturing Mickey. - **$15 $35 $75**

MKY-206

□ **MKY-206. Mickey/Minnie Mouse Premium Masks With Envelope,**
1933. Einson-Freeman Co. 10x12" brown envelope contains eight stiff paper masks, seven for Mickey and one for Minnie. Masks were given one per package in Quaker Crackels.
Envelope - **$60 $125 $250**
Mickey Mask - **$40 $75 $150**
Minnie Mask - **$40 $75 $150**

MKY-207

□ **MKY-207. "Wrights Mickey Mouse Biscuits" Wrapper,**
1933. English by L. Wright & Son. 10x11.5" flattened wrapper was originally wrapped around a cardboard box. - **$85 $165 $285**

MKY-208

□ **MKY-208. "World Flight Of Mickey Mouse" Premium Game,**
1933. Australian by John Sands Ltd./R.M. Osbourne Ltd. for Woodson's tea and "Anchor Brand Groceries." Also issued in USA. Australian - **$350 $650 $1250** USA - **$600 $1200 $2000**

MKY-209

□ **MKY-209. Mickey Mouse Wood Plaque,**
1933. A Fine Art Picture. 4x5.5x.25" thick with image on front that is described on reverse as "Hand-Printed In Oil Colors/ Washable." - **$50 $85 $150**

MKY-210

□ **MKY-210. Chicago World's Fair Bank,**
1933. Bank is 2.25x4.25x2" tall metal formed as replica chest overlaid by lightly embossed oilcloth fabric with brass-plated side panels. Oilcloth body is designed as a brick building. There are two versions of this bank and this world's fair variety has a number of differences to the standard "Mickey Mouse Bank." Text on top reads "Mickey And Minnie At The World's Fair" with images of them plus text "1933 Chicago 1934." - **$125 $250 $450**

MKY-211

MKY-214

❏ **MKY-211. Mickey Mouse Club Password Pinback,**
1933. The words and letters meant "Things are swell." Given away at clothing stores and theaters. This pinback was only produced for two months - January and February of 1933. - **$85 $190 $375**

MKY-212

❏ **MKY-212. "Mickey Mouse And Minnie's In Town" Sheet Music,**
1933. Irving Berlin Inc. 9x11.75" with eight pages. - **$40 $90 $150**

MKY-213

❏ **MKY-213. "Mickey & Minnie Mouse Coloring Book,"**
1933. Saalfield. 10.75x15.25" with 28 pages. Illustrations throughout by Disney Studio staff including 16 example pictures printed in full color. - **$95 $250 $500**

❏ **MKY-214. "Mickey Mouse" First Big Little Book,**
1933. Whitman. Book #717. First ever Mickey Big Little Book with first edition cover design. This cover features a more primitive-looking Mickey on the front cover and has Walt Disney signature at lower left. - **$356 $1068 $2850**

MKY-215

❏ **MKY-215. "Mickey Mouse" First Big Little Book Variety,**
1933. Whitman. Big Little Book #717, the first Mickey Big Little Book but the second version as cover art was altered. On the first version Mickey has more of a rat-like appearance and illustration on back is Mickey and Minnie hugging. This cover has the classic Mickey image on front; on back he is depicted giving Minnie a flower. The first cover also had Walt's signature whereas it is removed on this edition. - **$188 $564 $1500**

MKY-216

❑ **MKY-216. "Mickey Mouse The Mail Pilot" Rare Variety,**
1933. Whitman. Apparently Whitman was ready to publish Mickey's second story before new cover art was ready. This copy has cover from the first Mickey Big Little Book #717 (second edition) with the second title added to front cover. The back cover has black overprint of first story designation "No. 717" with "No. 731" printed next to it. - **$2500 $5000 $10000**

MKY-219

MKY-217

❑ **MKY-219. "Mickey Mouse The Mail Pilot" BLB,**
1933. Whitman. No number. Softcover version unusual format with size of 3.5x4.75" rather than 4x4" size. - **$43 $129 $300**

❑ **MKY-217. Mickey Mouse, The Great Big Midget Book,**
1933. England version of 1st book. Scarce. - **$168 $504 $1350**

MKY-218

MKY-220

❑ **MKY-218. "Mickey Mouse The Mail Pilot" Premium Big Little Book,**
1933. Whitman. (Un-numbered). Soft cover issued by American Oil Co. Also issued as standard hardcover Whitman #731. Either Version - **$43 $129 $300**

❑ **MKY-220. "Mickey Mouse Sails For Treasure Island" Big Little Book,**
1933. Whitman. Book #750. Also issued as un-numbered premium without ads or with Kolynos Dental Cream ad. Numbered Edition - **$43 $129 $300**
Un-numbered Edition - **$51 $153 $360**

MKY-221

MKY-223

❑ **MKY-221. "Mickey Mouse Sails For Treasure Island" English Book,**
1933. Dean & Son, England. "The Great Big Midget Book." - **$131 $393 $1050**

❑ **MKY-223. "Mickey Mouse" Reprint Book,**
1933. Whitman. 8.5x10" edition #948 with dual copyright 1932-1933. Content is 34 pages of full color Sunday strip reprints. Cardboard covers have identical art front and back. A similar book was published by David McKay titled "Mickey Mouse Book No. 3." - **$165 $325 $650**

MKY-222

MKY-224

❑ **MKY-222. "Mickey Mouse Annual,"**
1933. The Musson Book Co. Ltd., Toronto 6.75x9x2" thick hardcover with 246 pages. - **$165 $325 $650**

❑ **MKY-224. "Mickey Mouse Adventures" Canadian Book Condensed Version,**
1933. Musson Book Co. Ltd. 6.25x8.5" cardboard covered 36 pages. One page features four-panel story "Ear-Ear" in which Mickey tries to use his ear as a coin for a chocolate vending machine. - **$125 $250 $500**

MKY-225

❏ **MKY-225. "Mickey Mouse Adventures" Standard Version Book,**
1933. Canadian by Musson Book Co. Ltd. 6.25x8.5" with 64 pages. - **$100 $200 $400**

MKY-226

❏ **MKY-226. "Mickey Mouse Story Book" Canadian Printing,**
1933. Musson. 6.25x8.5" with 64 pages. Soft cover version. - **$70 $135 $250**

MKY-227

❏ **MKY-227. English Magazine With Mickey Mouse Contest,**
1933. Amalgamated Press Ltd. "Film Pictorial" 8.5x11.5" Vol. 4 #2 weekly issue for November 25. Content includes photo features on many U.S. movie stars plus a one-page "Mickey Mouse Cut-Out Puzzles" contest including four different numbered cut-outs of Mickey, each with slightly different body parts. Object was to make a complete Mickey figure using one or more of the cut-outs. Front cover has small Mickey image at top left corner pointing to title "New Mickey Mouse Contest: Money Prizes." - **$25 $50 $85**

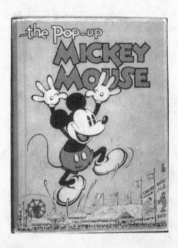

MKY-228

❏ **MKY-228. "The Pop-Up Mickey Mouse,"**
1933. Blue Ribbon Books. 6.5x8.75" hard-cover with 24 pages and three two-page full color pop-ups. - **$125 $350 $900**

MKY-229

□ **MKY-229. "The Pop-Up Minnie Mouse" Hardcover,**
1933. Blue Ribbon Books Inc. 6.75x8.75" with 28 pages. - **$125 $350 $900**

MKY-230

□ **MKY-230. "Mickey Mouse In King Arthur's Court With 'Pop-Up' Illustrations,"**
1933. Blue Ribbon Books. Hardcover with dust jacket. 7.5x9.5" with 48 stiff cardboard pages. Jacket - **$100 $250 $500**
Book - **$250 $525 $1500**

MKY-231

□ **MKY-231. Mickey/Minnie Mouse Cut Out Doll Book,**
1933. Saalfield. 10x19.25" large format book featuring a cardstock cover and four pages. Outfits including cowboy and drum major for Mickey, Chinese costume and Dutch dress for Minnie. - **$550 $1050 $1750**

MKY-232

❑ **MKY-232. Mickey, Minnie and Pluto Marionettes,**
1933. Made By Hestwood Marionette Studio, Glendale Calif. Made of wood, composition and cloth. Each figure about 12".Each came in a yellowish fabric bag with drawstring.
"Bullocks Wilshire" Decorated Box - **$300 $750 $1500**
"Bullocks" Undecorated Black Box - **$100 $200 $400**
Mickey - **$1000 $2000 $4000**
Minnie - **$800 $1750 $3500**
Pluto - **$600 $1500 $2500**

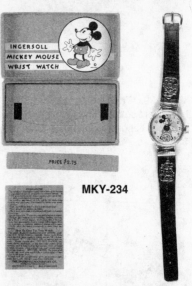

MKY-234

MKY-233

❑ **MKY-233. Mickey Mouse Electric Clock,**
1933. Ingersoll. 4.5" square by 2.25" deep. Mickey's body revolves each minute. Paper band around three sides of the case. Clock - **$450 $1050 $2000**
Box With Pop-Up Mickey Flap - **$675 $1400 $2250**
Price Tag - **$35 $65 $125**

❑ **MKY-234. First Variety of First "Mickey Mouse Ingersoll" Wristwatch,**
1933. Sold at Chicago World's Fair and distinguished from second variety introduced in the Fall, 1933 by: wider image of Mickey, different typeface for numerals, number "5" positioned above Mickey's knee on dial, Art Deco geometric design on bezel, wire lugs on case to hold either metal links or leather strap band.
Box (and Insert) with 1933 Exposition Logo Sticker - **$600 $1800 $3500**
Box (and Insert) without Sticker - **$300 $600 $1200**
Cardboard Strip with $2.75 price designated - **$40 $75 $125**
Guarantee Insert paper - **$20 $35 $65**
Watch with Metal or Leather Band - **$450 $900 $1800**

MKY-235

☐ **MKY-235. Mickey Mouse Ingersoll Silvered Brass Link Straps,**
1933. Two-piece strap 5.75" long has clasp and each piece consists of four links including a pair with Mickey image. For first watch. - **$60 $125 $200**

MKY-237

MKY-236

☐ **MKY-236. "Mickey Mouse Ingersoll" First English Watch,**
1933. 1-1/8" diameter with earliest Mickey image on the celluloid dial. The large image was later changed to the more tra-ditional portrait with blush color on the face. - **$1100 $2150 $3650**

☐ **MKY-237. Second and Later Varieties of First Wrist Watch Design,**
Fall 1933 through 1939. Ingersoll. Re-designed 2.5x4.5x1" deep hinged lid box. To be complete, all versions through Spring/Summer 1935 contain box insert, cardboard strip with text specifying retail price and "Guarantee" paper. All versions were avalable with metal bands (seven links plus two with Mickey image) or leather bands with two metal die-cut Mickeys attached. Bands are now held to watch case by pins rather than wire lugs. Second variety (shown in photo) has same dial as Chicago World's Fair variety, but no designs on the bezel. The watch for 1934 has a newly designed dial with thinner Mickey, different typeface for the numerals and number "5" is below Mickey's knee. Beginning Fall 1935, the caption "Made in U.S.A." now appears on dial to the left of Mickey's pants. A larger blue box was introduced for Fall/Winter 1935 containing box insert, four-page guarantee folder and small slip telling dealer how to display the boxed watch. This watch design and box

(with minor changes) were used through 1939, athough newly designed rectangular case watches were introduced in Spring 1937 (for girls) and Fall 1937 (for boys). Second Variety Watch With Either Band - **$225 $450 $900**
Second Variety Box Complete - **$225 $450 $900**
Round 1935 - 1939 Watch With Either Band - **$175 $350 $650**
Blue 1935 - 1939 Box Complete - **$175 $350 $650**

MKY-239

MKY-238

❑ **MKY-238. "Mickey Mouse Ingersoll Pocketwatch" Complete Boxed Set,** 1933. Ingersoll. 2.5x4.75x.75" deep box contains complete and earliest issue. Box is scarcer style with large image of Mickey on lid and inside of lid rather than repeated pattern of small characters. Box has two-piece cardboard insert that holds the fob in place. The silvered brass fob with incised image of Mickey has black leather strap. Watch is earliest style with longer stem. Metal case has incised image of Mickey on back which matches design on the fob.
Box Complete - **$350 $700 $1500**
Watch - **$350 $700 $1500**
Fob - **$60 $110 $250**

❑ **MKY-239. "Mickey Mouse Ingersoll Pocketwatch" Complete In Second Issue Box,** 1933. Ingersoll. 2.5x4.75x.75" deep box contains complete issue. Box has two-piece cardboard insert that holds fob in place. The silvered brass fob with incised image of Mickey has black leather strap.
Box Complete - **$275 $550 $1200**
Watch - **$325 $650 $1300**
Fob - **$60 $110 $250**

MKY-240

❑ **MKY-240. First English "Mickey Mouse Ingersoll" Pocket Watch,** 1933. Watch is 2" in diameter with silvered metal case. Second hand disk has three small Mickey images. - **$400 $850 $1700**

MKY-241

MKY-243

❑ **MKY-241. Mickey Mouse Musician Miniature Metal Figure,**
c. 1933. Unmarked. Likely Austrian. From a series known to include violinist, bass fiddle, bass drum. Each - **$150 $300 $600**

❑ **MKY-243. Mickey Camping Out Scene Reliance Art Glass Framed Picture,**
c. 1933. Reliance Picture Frame Co. 7.75x10.75" wood frame holding glass with bright enamel picture on reverse of glass. Titled "The Joys Of Camping." - **$165 $350 $700**

MKY-242

MKY-244

❑ **MKY-242. "Mickey Mouse Bank,"**
c. 1933. Zell Products Corp. 2.25x4.25x2" tall metal bank designed like a chest overlaid by lightly embossed oilcloth fabric with brass-plated side panels. This is the non-1933/1934 Chicago World's Fair variety with text "Mickey Mouse Bank Be Thrifty-Save Your Coins." - **$85 $165 $300**

❑ **MKY-244. Birthday Card,**
c. 1933. Hall Brothers Inc. Closed 4x4.25" folder card. - **$30 $60 $90**

MKY-245

❑ **MKY-245. English Ingersoll Clock Variety,**
c. 1933. English version 2x4x4" tall wind-up clock differing in several aspects from its U.S. Ingersoll counterpart of same production era. Both have painted metal case but English version decal around one side across the top to opposite side has different images of Mickey, Minnie, Pluto, Horace, Clarabelle. English clock face design differs by a running pose by Mickey rather than standing pose. Similar pose variations are on the inset second timer wheel.
Clock - **$325 $650 $1350**
Box - **$325 $650 $1350**

MKY-246

❑ **MKY-246. "Sincerely Yours-Mickey Mouse" Celluloid Button,**
c. 1933. Button is 3.5". Worn by toy store employees. - **$325 $1300 $2600**

MKY-247

MKY-248

❑ **MKY-247. Mickey Mouse Celluloid On Tin Litho Wind-Up Tricycle,**
c. 1933. Made in Japan. 4.5" Mickey on 5.5" long tricycle. - **$275 $550 $1000**

❑ **MKY-248. "Mickey Mouse" Fountain Pen,**
c. 1933. Inkograph Company. Screw-on cap has pocket clip with "Mickey Mouse" name and around bottom edge are three decals, two of Mickey and one of Minnie. Body of pen has full figure Mickey decal and metal pen point has small Mickey portrait and copyright symbol. - **$65 $135 $275**

MKY-249

❏ **MKY-249. Mickey Mouse And Donald Duck Pencil Drawing From The Dognapper,**
1934. Animation paper is 9x12" with 4x4.5" image. #134 of a numbered sequence. - **$150 $300 $500**

MKY-250

❏ **MKY-250. Lot Of Original Licensing Correspondence Including Kay Kamen Signed Letter,**
1934. Artists 4-page letter proposing a lamp design, sketch of lamp and refusal letter from Kamen. Unique Near Mint - **$465**

MKY-251

❏ **MKY-251. "Mickey Mouse Choral Top" With Box,**
1934. Box is 8.75" square holding very large tin lithographed top with 10" diameter by 11" tall. Top features great character images of Mickey, Minnie, Pluto, Three Little Pigs and Big Bad Wolf. Bottom half has text reading "Exclusively For Geo. Borgfeldt Corp./Made by Lackawanna Mfg. Co. Box - **$265 $625 $1200**
Top - **$225 $425 $750**

MKY-252

❏ **MKY-252. Film Directory Annual With Mickey And Others,**
1934. "Film Daily Production Guide and Directors Annual" 6x9.25" hardcover, 368 pages. Content overall is an encyclopedia of movie information including full-page Walt Disney ad with illustrations of Mickey and Minnie, smaller images of Silly Symphony characters, mention that cartoons will be in Technicolor "For The First Time." - **$45 $90 $150**

MKY-253

❑ **MKY-253. Mickey And Minnie Metal English Car Mascot,**
1934. Desmo Corporation. Paint over chromium plating. Mickey is 4-3/8" tall, Minnie is 4-1/8" tall. Both are attached to 4.5" wide metal base which is mounted on a lucite base for display. - **$3150 $7850 $13750**

MKY-254

❑ **MKY-254. Mickey Mouse Metal English Car Mascot,**
1934. Desmo Corporation, England. 4.25" tall chromium with over-paint (displayed on plastic base). - **$2350 $4750 $9250**

MKY-255

❑ **MKY-255. "Post Toasties" Shipping Carton Panel With Mickey,**
1934. Panel is 14.75x16" with 4" tall image of Mickey plus his name below in large letters. Panel was cut from a carton of "Double-Crisp Corn Flakes." - **$35 $65 $115**

MKY-256

84

❏ **MKY-256. Mickey Mouse Glazed Ceramic Perfume Bottle,**
1934. 4" tall with removable hollow head and tin lithographed movable ears. Hole in nose for perfume. Missing rubber cover on back of head. Has 1934 Chicago World's Fair foil sticker. - **$225 $450 $900**

❏ **MKY-258. "Folio Of Songs From Walt Disney's Famous Pictures Mickey Mouse And Silly Symphony,"**
1934. Irving Berlin Inc. 9x12" with 32 pages. Includes illustrations and words and music to eleven different songs. - **$65 $135 $265**

MKY-259

MKY-257

MKY-260

❏ **MKY-257. Mickey Mouse Jointed Wood Figure,**
1934. Made in Italy by Peri with Walter E. Disney copyright. 5-7/8" tall. - **$250 $500 $1000**

❏ **MKY-259. "Mickey Mouse Merchandise" First Catalogue,**
1934. Kay Kamen Inc. 9x12" With 76 pages of Disney licensee product photos and information. 25,000 produced. - **$2100 $3700 $6800**

❏ **MKY-260. Mickey Mouse Store Display Standee,**
1934. Made By Old King Cole, Distributed By Kay Kamen. Molded 'laminite' 11x15.5x1.5" deep. - **$600 $1150 $1850**

MKY-258

MKY-261

MKY-262

❑ **MKY-261. "Mickey Mouse The Detective" Big Little Book,**
1934. Whitman. Book #1139. - **$58 $174 $410**

❑ **MKY-262. "Mickey Mouse In Blaggard Castle" Big Little Book,**
1934. Whitman. Book #726. - **$43 $129 $300**

MKY-263

❑ **MKY-263. "Mickey Mouse And Minnie Mouse At Macy's" Premium Book,**
1934. Whitman. No number. Christmas give-away 3.25x3.5" softcover with 148 pages. - **$400 $1200 $3200**

MKY-264

❑ **MKY-264. "Mickey Mouse Stories,"**
1934. David McKay Co. 6.25x8.5" stiff cover Book #2 with 62 pages. Has illustrations taken directly from Mickey's earliest cartoons including Pioneer Days, The Delivery Boy, The Castaway and The Moose Hunt. - **$85 $165 $385**

MKY-265

MKY-266

❏ **MKY-265. "Mickey Mouse In 'Giant Land',"**
1934. David McKay Co. 6.25x8.25 hardcover with 48 pages. - **$85 $165 $385**

❏ **MKY-266. "Mickey Mouse Movie Stories Book 2" Hardcover,**
1934. David McKay Co. 6.75x8.5" with 200 pages. Includes art taken from Mickey's earliest cartoons. - **$165 $335 $825**

❏ **MKY-267. "Mickey Mouse Wee Little Books" Boxed Set,**
1934. Whitman. Set of six 3x3.5" books with 1.5x3.75x2" deep box. Each book has 40 pages. Box - **$55 $125 $250**
Each Book - **$12 $36 $85**

❏ **MKY-268. "Mickey Mouse In Giant Land" English Hardcover,**
1934. William Collins Sons & Co. Ltd. 7.25x10" with 96 thick paper pages. - **$75 $150 $325**

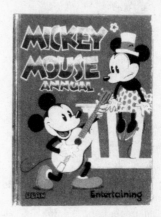

MKY-267

MKY-269

❏ **MKY-269. "Mickey Mouse Annual" English Hardcover,**
1934. Dean & Son Ltd. 6.5x8.5x2" thick with 124 thick paper pages. - **$125 $275 $550**

MKY-268

MKY-270

❏ **MKY-270. "Mickey Mouse Waddle Book" Wrapper Strip,**
1934. Stiff paper band is 4.25x10.5" that originally went around the 1934 Waddle Book by Blue Ribbon Books. Band was usually disposed of and is extremely rare.
- **$125 $335 $650**

MKY-271

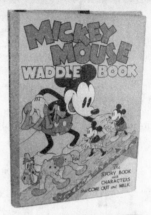

❏ **MKY-271. "Mickey Mouse Waddle Book" With Dust Jacket And Set Of Waddles,**
1934. Blue Ribbon Books. 7.75x10.25" hardcover with 28-page illustrated story and two instruction pages. Characters are designed to walk downward on a stiff paper ramp also included in the book but not pictured. Cover Slip Band - **$125 $335 $650**
Jacket Only - **$90 $250 $550**
Book Only - **$85 $225 $450**
Each Assembled Waddle - **$335 $650 $1100**
Each Unpunched Waddle - **$550 $1300 $4250**
Ramp - **$200 $400 $1100**
Near Mint, Complete - **$19750**

MKY-272

☐ **MKY-272. "Mickey Mouse Book No. 4" Early Reprint Book,**
1934. David McKay Co. 9.75x10" with 48 pages reprinting Floyd Gottfredson 1931 daily comic strips. - **$150 $550 $1050**

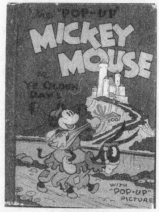

MKY-273

☐ **MKY-273. "The 'Pop-Up' Mickey Mouse In Ye Olden Days" Hardcover,**
1934. Blue Ribbon Press. 4x5" with 60 pages with a number of full page illustrations. Center has full color Mickey pop-up depicting him exiting a castle and preparing for a joust. - **$150 $400 $1200**

MKY-274

☐ **MKY-274. "Mickey Mouse Toy House,"**
1934. O.B. Andrews Co. 13.25x17x.25" deep box holds parts for assembly of large cardboard house. - **$175 $300 $600**

MKY-275

❏ **MKY-275. "Mickey Mouse Animated Circus,"**
1934. Norwich Knitting Co. 4.5x5" cellophane envelope contains 19 cellophane strips, 10 featuring Disney characters and 9 featuring circus animals and a clown. - **$115 $225 $450**

MKY-276

❏ **MKY-276. "Mickey Mouse Circus Game,"**
1934. Marks Brothers Co. 9.5x20x2" box contains stiff cardboard panel that attaches to wood base of box bottom and separate cardboard panel with four 2.5x4.5" sections - two of Mickey and two of Minnie each with wood cup attached to top. Game also came with generic marbles and instruction sheet. Object was to place marble in top cup which caused panels to tip over dropping the ball down which strikes a bell before ball rolls into bottom insert to land in one of the various point value die-cut holes. - **$325 $650 $1350**

MKY-277

❏ **MKY-277. "Mickey Mouse" Activity Box,**
1934. Marks Brothers. 7.5x11x1" deep box contains a total of 12 items. Some of the images on the items in this set also appeared on other products by Marks Brothers Co. but we have never seen any of these images used in the manner that they are with this set. Boxed - **$275 $550 $1100**

MKY-278

❏ **MKY-278. Mickey Mouse Sectional Plate,**
1934. Rare in high grade. Salem China Company. - **$60 $125 $375**

MKY-279

❏ **MKY-279. "Mickey Mouse Hoop La Game,"**
1934. Marks Brothers Co. 10.75x18.5" thick die-cut cardboard. Comes with three generic rings. - **$250 $375 $750**

MKY-280

❏ **MKY-280. Mickey Mouse Greeting Cards,**
1934. Hall Brothers. First is 4x5" folder. Second is 4x4" folder. Each - **$25 $45 $70**

MKY-281

MKY-282

❏ **MKY-281. Mickey Mouse Emerson Radio,**
1934. Solid wood with pressed wood composition panels on four sides measures 5x7.25x7.25" tall. Front bottom has metal plate with raised text "Emerson Mickey Mouse." - **$800 $1600 $3200**

❏ **MKY-282. Mickey Mouse Painted Variety Radio,**
1934. Emerson. 5x7.25x7.25" tall solid wood radio with pressed wood composition panels on four sides. This painted version is much scarcer than the unpainted version. - **$1150 $2250 $3850**

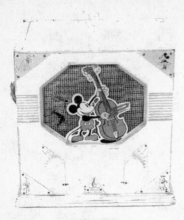

MKY-283

❑ **MKY-283. Mickey Mouse Emerson Radio,**
1934. Emerson. 5.5x7.25x7.25" tall. Radio came in two different colors, black or cream. On the front at each corner are attached aluminum triangular pieces, each with different character image of Minnie, Pluto, Horace and Clarabelle. Bottom center attachment reads "Emerson Radio And Television" with Walt Disney copyright. Has aluminum grill plate depicting Mickey playing a bass. Back of radio has serial number plate.
Cream - **$1200 $2300 $4000**
Black - **$1400 $2800 $4500**

MKY-284

❑ **MKY-284. "Mickey Mouse Scatter Ball Game,"**
1934. Marks Brothers Co. 11.5x11.5x2" deep box contains cardboard insert playing surface with die-cut holes, a top and ten wooden balls. Balls are placed in the center and top is spun causing balls to scatter and land in holes with different point values. - **$150 $300 $650**

MKY-285

MKY-286

❑ **MKY-285. "Mickey Mouse Bagatelle,"**
1934. Marks Brothers. 12x23.5x1" wood toy with paper label. - **$200 $450 $850**

❑ **MKY-286. "Mickey Mouse Ingersoll" English Wrist Watch,**
1934. Celluloid dial in 1.25" case. - **$600 $1200 $2400**

MKY-287

MKY-289

❑ MKY-287. "Mickey Mouse" Second Version English Pocket Watch,
1934. Ingersoll. 2" diameter silvered brass case with glass dial cover. - **$375 $700 $1250**

❑ MKY-289. Minnie Mouse And Pram Tin Wind-Up,
1934. Wells, England. 7" long lithographed tin with 3.5" composition Minnie. - **$875 $1650 $3800**
Box Marked #146 (not shown) - **$650 $1100 $3250**

MKY-288

MKY-290

❑ MKY-288. Mickey Mouse And Pram Tin Wind-Up,
1934. Wells, England. 7" long lithographed tin with 3.5" composition Mickey. A second version has Mickey pushing the pram with his mouth.
Pictured Version - **$1100 $2200 $4400**
Second Version - **$1650 $2750 $4950**
Box Marked #146 (not shown) - **$650 $1100 $3250**

❑ MKY-290. "Mickey Mouse" Large Celluloid Wind-Up Boxed,
1934. Made in Japan for U.S.A. distribution by George Borgfeldt. Known as 'Rambling Mickey.' 8" tall with wire tail. Box is 4.5x7.75x3.5" deep.
Box - **$350 $675 $1350**
Toy - **$550 $1100 $2250**

MKY-293

MKY-291

☐ **MKY-291. "Mickey Mouse No. 2 Paddle Boat" Boxed Tin Lithographed Wind-Up,**
1934. Licensed by Walt Disney Enterprises. Box is 2.25x4x12" long with "Macy's Transatlantic Tunnel And Magic Carpet" sticker on one side. 11.25" long wood boat has 2.25" tall Mickey Mouse holding 8.75" wide wire oars. Front has wire crank to activate Mickey as rower.
Box - **$550 $1100 $1650**
Toy - **$1650 $3300 $5000**

☐ **MKY-293. "Lionel Mickey Mouse Hand Car" Wind-Up,**
1934. Lionel Corporation. Box holds 27" diameter circle of track for the 2x7.5x5.5" tall metal car with 4.5" composition figures to travel on. Minnie has red wood hat. Both have rubber legs and rubber-coated wire tails. Car body in green or red versions. Box And Track - **$350 $700 $1500**
Hand Car - **$325 $675 $1400**

MKY-292

☐ **MKY-292. Mickey Mouse Tricycle,**
1934. The Colson Co. Elyria, Ohio. 18x34x27" tall. Company was licensed for only one year. - **$1000 $2000 $4500**

MKY-294

❑ **MKY-294. Mickey And Minnie Boxed Wind-Up "Playland" Toy,**
1934. Copyright Walt. Disney Enterprises Ltd. Borgfeldt. Box is 5.5x10.5x1.75" deep. Toy is 9" wide by 10.5" tall overall with thin cardboard canopy and pair of 3.5" celluloid figures. Mickey holds ring and Minnie has bell. Box - **$800 $1600 $3200**
Toy - **$1600 $2700 $4250**

MKY-296

❑ **MKY-296. "Mickey Mouse Soldier Set,"**
1934. Marks Brothers Co. 8.25x18.5x1" deep box contains eight 2.25x6" cardboard targets with wood bases. Four are of Mickey, four are of Donald. Both are depicted in soldier attire with rifles. Box included generic pop-rifle and corks.
Boxed Set - **$275 $550 $875**
Single Figure - **$20 $40 $60**

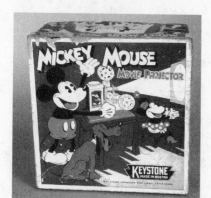

MKY-295

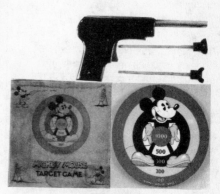

MKY-297

❑ **MKY-295. "Mickey Mouse Movie Projector,"**
1934. Keystone Mfg. Co., Boston. Large graphic box holds electrically operated 16mm projector to show "Mickey Mouse Cine Art Films" and others. Box lid served as screen. Box - **$450 $800 $1600**
Projector - **$275 $550 $1100**

❑ **MKY-297. "Mickey Mouse Target Game" Boxed Set,**
1934. Marks Brothers. 18x18x1" deep box contains 17.5" diameter cardboard target (largest of two sizes issued by Marks), metal gun and pair of darts.
Box - **$115 $225 $450**
Target - **$110 $225 $350**
Gun - **$15 $25 $60**

MKY-298

MKY-299

☐ **MKY-298. "Mickey Mouse Pop Game,"**
1934. Marks Brothers Co. 11x18x1.75" deep box contains graphic target and generic pop gun for corks. - **$175 $375 $750**

☐ **MKY-299. "Mickey Mouse" Blackboard,**
1934. Richmond School Furniture Co. Thick masonite blackboard is 19.5x28". Total height of the piece from top of blackboard to bottom of the attached wood legs is 40". - **$125 $235 $475**

MKY-300

☐ **MKY-300. Mickey Mouse European Postcard,**
1934. 3.5x5.5". - **$20 $40 $65**

MKY-301

☐ **MKY-301. "Mickey Mouse Composition Book,"**
1934. Powers Paper Co. Book is 6.75x8.25". - **$30 $60 $100**

MKY-302

☐ **MKY-302. Mickey/Minnie Large Wood Children's Clothing Rack,**
c. 1934. Kroehler. Figural piece consists of two wooden panels, each 16" wide by 42.5" tall. Image on outer surface of wood shows figures with arms raised as if to hold the bar that runs across top to hold clothing. At lower portion figures are separated by a slanted wooden board with raised edge intended to hold shoes. - **$325 $800 $1600**

MKY-303

☐ MKY-303. Mickey And Minnie Riding Elephant Celluloid Wind-Up,

c. 1934. Borgfeldt. 7.5" tall by 9.75" long. Elephant's head bobs and ears move. Elephant in orange or white versions. - **$1100 $2200 $4500**

MKY-304

☐ MKY-304. Mickey And Minnie Mouse Theater Issued Variety Fan Cards,

c. 1934. Local theater. Pair with identical text on back which reads "Mickey Mouse Presents The Big Bad Wolf And Walt Disney Presents Mickey Mouse In The Orphans' Benefit" with additional ad for non-Disney film The House of Rothschild plus text including "Now Playing At United Artists Theater Broadway At Ninth." Each - **$50 $100 $175**

MKY-305

☐ MKY-305. "Mickey Mouse Toothbrush" With Card,

c. 1934. Henry L. Hughes Co. Inc. 2.5x6" card holds 5.75" toothbrush, however the card is for the toothbrush variety that had a Mickey decal on the handle rather than this brush which has thick die-cut celluloid Mickey figure which were sold on larger cards. Card - **$65 $125 $250** Either Brush - **$40 $85 $175**

MKY-306

☐ MKY-306. Mickey Mouse Cuff Bracelet,

c. 1934. Cohn & Rosenberger. 1" wide by 2.25" diameter enamel paint on brass. Wrap-around design features two separate scenes. One of Mickey as hunter with rifle and Pluto by his side and the other a campfire scene of him and Minnie cooking over an open fire while behind them is tent and Pluto. - **$225 $425 $700**

MKY-307

☐ **MKY-307. Mickey Mouse Silver Plated Cup,**
c. 1934. International Silver Co. 1.75" tall with stamped-in image. From a set of six different. Each - **$50 $85 $150**

MKY-308

☐ **MKY-308. Minnie Mouse Silver Plated Cup,**
c. 1934. International Silver Co. 2.5" tall from a series of six different. Front has nice incised image of Minnie waving a hanky. Each - **$50 $85 $150**

MKY-309

☐ **MKY-309. Mickey Mouse Silver Plated Cup,**
c. 1934. The International Silver Co. 2.5" tall. - **$50 $85 $150**

MKY-310

☐ **MKY-310. Mickey Mouse Napkin Ring,**
c. 1934. International Silver Co. .75" wide with 1.5" diameter. Silver plated. - **$35 $75 $135**

MKY-311

MKY-312

☐ **MKY-311. Mickey Mouse Silver Plated Child's Plate,**
c. 1934. International Silver Co. 7.5x9.25x1" deep. Side handle-like edges are for placement of utensils with incised text "My Mickey Mouse Fork/Spoon Goes Here." Reverse has small incised symbols and "8119." - **$75 $140 $250**

☐ **MKY-312. "Mickey Mouse" Boxed Utensils,**
c. 1934. International Silver Co. 3.5x5x2" deep box contains pair of 4.5" utensils, a Mickey spoon and Minnie fork.
Box - **$65 $125 $250**
Utensil Pair - **$50 $80 $120**

MKY-313

MKY-313. Seiberling Retailers Catalogue/Sales Sheets Featuring Rare Disney Items,
c. 1934. Seiberling Latex Products Co. Four items, each 8.5x10.75". Eight-page catalogue, two one-sided sale sheets and one two-sided sales sheet.
Catalogue - **$115 $225 $350**
Each Sales Sheet - **$30 $60 $110**

MKY-314

MKY-315

MKY-314. "Penney's For Back To School Needs" Celluloid Button,
c. 1934. Backpaper by maker M. Pudlin Co. Inc. NYC. 7/8". - **$45 $70 $115**

MKY-315. "Pin The Tail On Mickey Party Game,"
c. 1934. Marks Brothers Co. 8.25x10x.75" deep box contains 18x22" linen sheet. Photo example shows tails cut from sheet.
Box - **$50 $75 $150**
Uncut Sheet - **$35 $65 $125**
Cut Sheet Complete - **$25 $45 $75**

MKY-316

MKY-316. "Mickey Mouse Composition Book,"
c. 1934. Powers Paper Co. 6.5x8.25". Cover design depicts Mickey and Minnie sliding down a bannister for their breakfast. Photo example includes paste-in clippings. - **$40 $75 $135**

MKY-317

MKY-317. "The Story Of Mickey Mouse Big Big Book,"
1935. Whitman. 7.25x9.25". Book #4062. - **$138 $414 $1100**

MKY-318

MKY-318. "Another Mickey Mouse Coloring Book,"
1935. Saalfield. 10.75x15.25" with 28 pages. Book #2110. One of the scarcest early coloring books. - **$275 $550 $1100**

MKY-319

❏ **MKY-319. "Another Mickey Mouse Coloring Book,"**
1935. Saalfield Publishing Co. 10.75x15" #295. Variety with 32 pages rather than 28 and all art in black and white rather than with some color illustration. - **$225 $450 $900**

MKY-320

❏ **MKY-320. "Mickey Mouse Magic Movie Palette,"**
1935. Premium stiff paper card measures 5x8". Has small die-cut window at top and comes with attached disk with illustrations that can be turned to produce a "movie." Front reads "A Xmas Gift From Mickey Mouse." - **$115 $250 $450**

MKY-321

❏ **MKY-321. Mickey Mouse Pencil Drawing From Mickey's Garden,**
1935. Animation paper is 12x9.5" with 9x5.5" image. - **$250 $500 $1000**

MKY-322

MKY-323

❏ **MKY-322. Mickey Mouse Pencil Drawing From Mickey's Service Station,**
1935. 9.5x12" sheet of animation paper with 3.75x5.75" image. "64" from a numbered sequence. - **$200 $400 $750**

❏ **MKY-323. Mickey "Post Toasties Corn Flakes" Cereal Box,**
1935. Box is 2.5x7.5x11" tall with Mickey at lower right corner. Two side panels have cut-outs, one of "Minnie The Belle Of The Prairie" and one of "Mickey On Paint." Back of box features story of "Two-Gun Mickey, A Wild West Movie."
Complete - **$550 $1500 $2750**

MKY-324

☐ **MKY-324. Post Toasties Corn Flakes Mickey Mouse Picture Panel Set,**
1935. Set of six cards cut from box back panel. This set features stage production of "Uncle Tom's Cabin" performed by and involving Mickey, Minnie, Horace, Goofy and Pluto. Cut Set - **$30 $60 $150**

MKY-325

☐ **MKY-325. Post Toasties Corn Flakes Mickey Mouse Picture Panel Set,**
1935. Set of six cards cut from box back panel. This set is titled "Mickey's Kangaroo" and involves him boxing a baby kangaroo and its mother, other characters involved are Minnie and Pluto.
Cut Set - **$30 $60 $150**

MKY-326

☐ **MKY-326. "Mickey Mouse Lunch Kit,"**
1935. Geuder, Paeschke & Frey Co., Milwaukee. 5x8x5" tall tin lithographed container and lid unit complete with separate inner tray and outer rigid wire carrying grips. - **$850 $1750 $3500**

MKY-327

❏ MKY-327. "Kiddie-Malt" Elaborate Sales Promotion Book With Accessories,
1935. Remarkable and elaborate sales-man's portfolio from archives of premium creators Sam and Gordon Gold. Design intent was to persuade storekeepers to purchase Kiddie-Malt, a product of National Foods Inc. Principal piece is an oversized 12x15" spiral-bound book with woodgrain design front cover accented by an inset foil reflective mirror and actual lock and key. 18 pages including slash pockets holding product photos, "Surprise Stickers" and 16x20" poster. - **$2350 $4650 $8000**

❏ MKY-328. Premium Folder From Mickey Mouse Kiddie-Malt,
1935. 4x5.5" with three panels containing total of eight characters on sixteen stick-ers. - **$135 $275 $550**

MKY-329

❏ MKY-329. "Mickey Mouse Pocket Combs" Framed Ad,
1935. American Hard Rubber Co. Ad is 8.75x11.75". - **$40 $75 $150**

MKY-328

MKY-330

❑ **MKY-330. "Mickey Mouse Flashlight" Advertising Mailer,**
1935. United States Electric Mfg. Corp. 8.5x11" four-page folder for flashlights and batteries. - **$65 $135 $275**

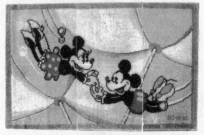

MKY-331

❑ **MKY-331. Mickey/Minnie Fabric Throw Rug,**
1935. Alexander Smith & Sons. 27x42" rug. - **$275 $550 $1250**

MKY-332

❑ **MKY-332. Mickey/Minnie/ Donald Fabric Throw Rug,**
1935. Alexander Smith & Sons. 26x42" with company label on reverse. - **$275 $550 $1250**

MKY-333

❑ **MKY-333. Mickey Mouse Western Theme Rug With Pegleg Pete,**
1935. Alexander Smith & Sons. 27x43". - **$225 $450 $900**

MKY-334

❑ **MKY-334. Mickey Mouse With Donald Duck And Peter Pig Rug,**
1935. Alexander Smith & Sons. 27x43". - **$250 $500 $1100**

MKY-335

MKY-336

❑ **MKY-335. "Mickey Mouse" Framed Picture,**
1935. Reliance Art Glass. Number "D-110" in series. 4.25x5.75x3/8" deep wood frame. - **$65 $135 $185**

❑ **MKY-336. Wallpaper Section,**
1935. Canadian 10x19" single complete panel. - **$200 $400 $800**

MKY-337

MKY-339

❏ **MKY-337. Metal Figures Casting Set Boxed,**
1935. Home Foundry Manufacturing Co. Inc. 11x19x2" deep boxed set of casting molds for 2.5" tall figures of Mickey, Minnie, Pluto, Three Pigs. Accessories include electric casting ladle for molten lead, paint jars and brushes, four-page order blank/instruction folder. - **$350 $675 $1500**

❏ **MKY-339. "Mickey Mouse And The Bat Bandit" Big Little Book,**
1935. Whitman. Book #1153. Also issued as no number premium.
Numbered - **$36 $108 $255**
No Number - **$58 $174 $410**

MKY-340

❏ **MKY-340. "Mickey Mouse And Bobo The Elephant,"**
1935. Whitman. Book #1160. - **$36 $108 $255**

MKY-338

❏ **MKY-338. "Popular Songs" With Mickey Mouse,**
1935. Volume 1, #4. Measures 8.5x11.5" with two pages of words and music for "What! No Mickey Mouse?" by Irving Caesar. - **$35 $65 $125**

MKY-341

MKY-342

MKY-344

❏ **MKY-341. "Mickey Correo Aereo" Spanish Book,**
1935. Spanish reprint of the Big Little Book "Mickey Mouse The Mail Pilot" is 4.75x6.25" with 160 pages. - **$75 $135 $275**

❏ **MKY-342. "Mickey Mouse And The Magic Carpet" Premium Book,**
1935 Whitman. 3.5x4" designed like a Big Little Book with illustrations throughout. - **$114 $342 $800**

❏ **MKY-344. "Mickey Mouse And Minnie Mouse March To Macy's" Premium Book ,**
1935. Whitman. No number. Christmas give-away 3.5x3.5" softcover with 148 pages. - **$275 $825 $2200**

MKY-343

❏ **MKY-343. "Mickey Mouse Sails For Treasure Island" Premium Big Little Book,**
1935. Whitman. Big Little Book imprinted on back cover for sponsor "Kolynos Dental Cream." - **$51 $153 $360**

MKY-345

❑ **MKY-345. First Italian Mickey Mouse Book,**
1935. Grandi Piccoli Libri. 4.75x6" hardcover with 60 pages. All text is in Italian. - **$150 $300 $600**

MKY-346

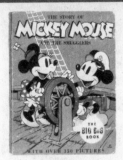

MKY-348

❑ **MKY-348. "The Story Of Mickey Mouse And The Smugglers" Big Big Book,**
1935. Whitman. Big Big Book #4062 with 320 pages and full page illustration on every other page. - **$163 $489 $1300**

MKY-347

❑ **MKY-346. "Mickey Mouse Annual,"**
1935. Dean & Son Ltd. 6.25x8.5x2" thick English hardcover with 124 pages. Has comic panel-style stories, text stories, a few puzzle and game pages including cut-out figure of Mickey riding Horace. - **$125 $275 $650**

❑ **MKY-347. "Mickey Mouse Illustrated Movie Stars" Canadian Hardcover,**
1935. Musson Book Co. Ltd. 6x8" with 40 pages featuring two cartoons "The Firefighters, The Cactus Kid." - **$135 $275 $450**

MKY-349

❑ **MKY-349. King Features Syndicate Christmas Card Folder To Media Customers,**
1935. Hallmark. 5.25x6.25" with nice quality filament paper cover and 24 full color pages of specialty comic strip character art and "Night Before Christmas" text. - **$225 $375 $700**

MKY-350

MKY-350. "Mickey Mouse Old Maid Cards,"
1935. Whitman. 5x6.5x1" deep box contains deck of 35 cards, each 2.5x3.5". - **$40 $85 $165**

MKY-352

MKY-352. "Mickey Mouse" Birthday Card,
1935. Hallmark. 3.5x4.5" glossy paper card. Inside text includes Mickey's name. - **$20 $40 $75**

MKY-351

MKY-353

MKY-351. "Mickey Mouse Funny Facts/Answered By Electricity" Rare Toy,
1935. Einson-Freeman Publishing Corp. 8.5x9.5x2.5" deep battery operated game designed like a large book. Playing area includes black cardboard insert with metal eyelets and pair of fabric-covered wires. Comes with three different two-sided question cards with images of Mickey, Minnie, Pluto, Horace and Clarabell. During play, card is placed on playing surface and one wire is placed on a question while the other is placed on the answer and if answer is correct a bulb was to light. - **$350 $850 $1850**

MKY-353. "Mickey Mouse Circus Train" Boxed Set,
1935. A. Wells & Co. Ltd. England. By Permission Walt Disney Mickey Mouse, Ltd. Consists of wind-up locomotive, "Mickey The Stoker" coal car and three circus cars. Comes with lithographed tin circus tent accented by metal flags. Box is 17x19 by about 3.5" deep. Also issued in one or two car versions in smaller boxes and without the tent. Largest Boxed Set With Tent - **$3250 $6500 $13000**

MKY-354

□ **MKY-354. Promo Folder Featuring Mickey Train/Handcar,**
1935. Lionel Corp. 8.5x11" four-page glossy paper. - **$125 $250 $450**

MKY-355

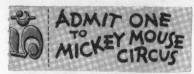

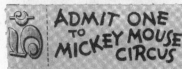

MKY-355. "Lionel Mickey Mouse Circus Train,"

1935. Lionel Corporation. 11.25x17x2.25" deep box holds wind-up gauge O Commodore Vanderbilt engine, tender with moving Mickey shoveling imaginary coal and 3 cars for length of about 30". Included are 84" of track, 5" Mickey circus barker composition figure, 8x18x15" tall paper tent, paper accessories of admission tickets, "To The Circus" sign, Mickey in truck and gasoline station. Complete Boxed Set - **$5000 $10000 $20000**
Engine - **$175 $325 $550**
Tender - **$275 $550 $1100**
Each Car - **$275 $550 $1100**
Barker - **$125 $275 $550**

MKY-356

MKY-356. Mickey Mouse Hairbrush And Comb Boxed Set,

c. 1935. Henry L. Hughes Co. Inc. 4x5.5x1.5" deep box contains two-piece set of comb and brush. Box also includes a fabric lining.
Boxed Set - **$75 $150 $250**
Brush Only - **$35 $60 $125**

MKY-357

MKY-357. "Mickey Mouse Safety Blocks" Set Boxed,

c. 1935. Halsam Co. 5.5x9x1.75" deep boxed complete set of fifteen wood blocks, each 1.75" square. This set is one of eight different boxed sets by Halsam, containing anywhere from six to thirty blocks per set. - **$50 $90 $165**

MKY-358

❑ **MKY-358. Mickey And Minnie Art Deco Tea Set,**
c. 1935. Faiencerie d'Onnaing, France. Teaset with twelve cups and saucers, creamer, covered sugar bowl and covered teapot. All with silver accents. - **$1350 $2700 $4500**

MKY-359

❑ **MKY-359. Mickey And Minnie Tea Set,**
c. 1935. Faiencerie d'Onnaing, France. Teaset with six cups and saucers, creamer, covered sugar bowl and covered 8" tall teapot. All with silver accents. - **$800 $1600 $2800**

MKY-360

❑ **MKY-360. "Mickey Mouse Undies" Box,**
c. 1935 or a few years earlier. 8.25x11.25x2" deep. Features various images of Mickey and Minnie. - **$165 $325 $650**

MKY-361

❑ **MKY-361. "Mickey Mouse Undies" Box,**
c. 1935. Box is 7.25x10.5x2.25" deep. Long-billed Donald on one end panel. - **$150 $300 $600**

MKY-362

❑ **MKY-362. Mickey Mouse Converse Sneakers Celluloid Button,**
c.1935. 1.25" Kay Kamen Backpaper. - **$500 $1500 $3000**

MKY-363

❑ **MKY-363. "Gurd's Mickey Mouse Club" Celluloid Button,**
c. 1935. Issued by Canadian gingerale soda maker. 1.25". - **$275 $550 $1100**

MKY-364

MKY-367

❏ MKY-364. "Mickey Mouse Hose"
Celluloid Button,
c. 1935. Backpaper by M. Pudlin Co. 7/8".
- $65 $115 $165

MKY-365

❏ MKY-365. "Mickey Mouse" Licensed
Product Buttons,
c. 1935. Issued as 1-1/8" litho (pictured)
and 1-1/4" celluloid. Both issued with back
paper reading "Mickey Mouse Gloves and
Mittens."
Litho. - $85 $185 $425
Cello. - $275 $775 $1550

MKY-368

MKY-366

❏ MKY-367. "A Handful Of Fun" Diecut
Booklet,
c. 1935. Eisendrath Glove Co. 5.25x7.75"
stiff paper 12-page premium, die-cut
throughout in the shape of Mickey's gloved
hand. Content includes different image on
every page. Gordon Gold Archives. - $500
$1150 $2400

❏ MKY-366. "Minneapolis Morning
Tribune Times-Tribune Movie Club
Member" Button,
c. 1935. Williamson Stamp Co. 1.25". The
only 1930s button known showing both
Mickey and Donald. - $325 $650 $1100

❏ MKY-368. "Mickey Mouse Circus"
English Book,
c. 1935. Birn Brothers Ltd. 8x10" hardcover, 124 stiff paper pages. - $125 $225
$500

MKY-371

MKY-372

MKY-369

☐ **MKY-369. Post Toasties Box,**
1935. Scarce. Mickey pictured on front.
Several versions. Each Complete - **$550**
$1500 $2750
1934 box complete - **$1000 $2500 $3750**
Rare. Mickey pictured on front. Several
versions. Few known to exist. "Mickey At
The Circus" box back pictured above is
from 1934.

☐ **MKY-371. Mickey And Pluto Small
Wind-Up Cart,**
c. 1935. Made In Japan. Celluloid figures
with tin cart. Toy is 3.25" tall by 5" long.
Paper label reads "By Permission Walt
Disney." Pluto is missing one leg in the
photo example. - **$325 $650 $1300**

☐ **MKY-372. "Mickey Mouse Jolly Cart"
Boxed Wind-Up,**
c. 1935. Made in Japan for English market.
Sold by Paradise Novelty Co. Celluloid fig-
ures with tin cart, 4" tall by 7.5" long. Box
is 2.75x7.5x3.75" deep.
Box - **$225 $450 $875**
Toy - **$350 $700 $1400**

MKY-370

☐ **MKY-370. "The First Step By Mickey
Mouse" Bank,**
c. 1935. Automatic Recording Safe
Company, 3.25x4.75x.75" deep metal
bank designed like a book. - **$175 $350**
$600

MKY-373

❏ **MKY-373. "Mickey Mouse Merchandise" Catalogue With Mailer,** 1936. Kay Kamen Ltd.
Mailer - **$115 $225 $335**
Catalogue - **$800 $1600 $2750**

MKY-376

MKY-374

❏ **MKY-374. "40 Big Pages Of Mickey Mouse,"** 1936. Whitman. Book #945. 10.25x12.5". Features "Stories, Verses, Puzzles, Games, Pictures To Draw & Color." - **$135 $325 $650**

❏ **MKY-376. "Mickey Mouse Big Big Box,"** 1936. Whitman. #2170. Box measures 8.75x12x2.5" deep and features a 5x5" tall separate die-cut cardboard Mickey figure attached to lid. 256 pages to color in format of seven signatures of 32 pages each. Set included crayons. - **$450 $875 $1475**

MKY-375

MKY-377

❏ **MKY-375. "Mickey Mouse Big Little Set,"** 1936. Whitman. 8.25x8.5" display card with attached 4x5.25" 160-page softcover book and box of crayons. Set #3059. Art is based on early Mickey cartoons. Set is usually missing crayons.
Without Crayons - **$1025 $2100 $3750**
Add For Crayons - **$25 $50 $100**

❏ **MKY-377. Mickey Mouse Pencil Drawings From Mickey's Circus,** 1936. Animation papers are 12x9.5" with three separate images measuring 12x6.25",12x7.5", and12x6.75".
Group - **$300 $600 $1200**

MKY-378

MKY-380   MKY-381

MKY-379

❑ **MKY-380. Mickey And Minnie Mouse With Pluto Flashlight,**
1936. U.S. Electric Mfg. Co. Has text "Use Mickey Mouse Batteries." 6-1/8" tall. - **$225 $450 $1000**

❑ **MKY-381. Mickey Figural Lamp,**
1936. Soreng-Manegold Co. 6" diameter painted plaster 6.25" tall to tip of upturned nose and 10.25" tall to top of bulb socket. Image is Mickey seated in armchair and holding a book. - **$550 $1100 $2300**

❑ **MKY-378. "Mickey's Polo Team" Model Sheet Original,**
1936. Three-quarters of the sheet features different sketch designs and views of horses for Will Rogers, Jack Holt, Laurel & Hardy as well as Harpo Marx's ostrich. Bottom quarter features fully detailed images of Mickey, Goofy, Big Bad Wolf, Donald Duck riding horses/donkey. - **$265 $550 $875**

❑ **MKY-379. Mickey Mouse Pencil Drawing From "Alpine Climbers,"**
1936. Animation paper is 10x12" with 2.5x6" image. No. "87" from a numbered sequence. - **$85 $165 $335**

MKY-382

❏ **MKY-382. "Mickey Mouse Tool Chest,"**
1936. Hamilton Metal Products Co. 5.5x19x2.5" deep metal case, the largest of several by this maker, with carrying handle and latch for the hinged lid. Bottom edge has a 12" ruler decal. Sold with or without tools. - **$160 $325 $700**

MKY-383

❏ **MKY-383. Mickey Mouse Ceramic Place Setting,**
1936. Sweden. 2" tall cup, 5" diameter saucer and 7-3/8" diameter plate.
Cup - **$30 $55 $115**
Saucer - **$18 $35 $65**
Plate - **$30 $60 $125**

MKY-384

❏ **MKY-384. Mickey, Minnie, Pluto, Donald, Baby's Bowl,**
1936. Salem China Co. 7.75" diameter with three deeply divided sections.- **$75 $150 $285**

MKY-385

❏ **MKY-385. Mickey & Others China Child's Divided Dish,**
1936. Unmarked but Salem China Co. 7.75" diameter by 1.5" deep with three deeply divided sections. - **$75 $150 $285**

MKY-386

❏ **MKY-386. "Patriot China" Mickey Mouse Mug,**
1936. Salem China Co. 3" tall. - **$65 $135 $225**

MKY-387

❑ **MKY-387. Mickey Mouse Banjo,**
1936. Noble & Cooley Co. 20" long metal. -
$165 $325 $650

MKY-388

MKY-389

❑ **MKY-388. "Mickey Mouse" English Record,**
1936. His Master's Voice/Gramophone Co. Ltd. 10" diameter 78 rpm. Features "Mickey's Grand Opera/The Orphan's Benefit." - **$45 $80 $165**

❑ **MKY-389. "Mickey Mouse's Birthday Party" Sheet Music,**
1936. Music sheet is 9.25x12" with 4 pages. - **$45 $80 $165**

MKY-390

❑ **MKY-390. "Mickey Mouse's Birthday Party" Sheet Music,**
1936. Irving Berlin. 7x10.5". - **$55 $135 $240**

MKY-391

❑ **MKY-391. "Here Comes Mickey Mouse" Big Big Color Set,**
1936. Consists of 224 pages of pictures to color. Pages were reprinted from early Mickey Mouse related movie and strip reprints. With crayons. Rare. - **$475 $1300 $3750**

MKY-392

MKY-393

❏ **MKY-392. "Mickey Mouse Book for Coloring",**
1936. Fourth in a series of coloring books, but the first to be die-cut. Features early Mickey cartoons like *On Ice*, *Band Concert*, *The Pointer* and others. Has many great early pictures of Donald, Horace, Minnie, Tanglefoot, Pluto and the Goof. Usually found colored in. Book is 14" tall.- **$135 $300 $600**

MKY-394

❏ **MKY-393. Catalogue With Classic Disney Merchandise,**
1936. "Morris Struhl Wholesalers Gifts /Novelties." 8x11" annual catalogue with photos and illustrations. Classic Mickey Mouse items include the Emerson radio, Ingersoll pocketwatch, wristwatch, alarm and electric clocks, movie projector, sunglasses display, flashlight and battery, thermometer, book bank and constipated Mickey novelty. - **$80 $160 $275**

❏ **MKY-394. "Mickey Mouse And Pluto The Racer" Big Little Book,**
1936. Whitman. Book #1128. - **$34 $102 $235**

MKY-397

MKY-398

MKY-395

❑ **MKY-395. Spanish Big Little Book Reprints,**
1936. Two Spanish reprints of Big Little Books Mickey Mouse and Bobo the Elephant and Mickey Mouse in Blaggard Castle. Each are 4.75x6.5" with 160 pages. Each - **$75 $135 $275**

❑ **MKY-397. "Mickey Mouse Alphabet Book,"**
1936. Whitman. 6.75x9" with 32 pages. - **$135 $265 $550**

❑ **MKY-398. 'Mickey Mouse Crusoe,"**
1936. Whitman. 7x9.5" with 72 pages. Includes black and white illustrations as well as one color plate. - **$85 $165 $325**

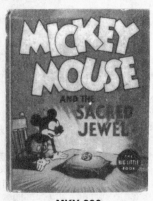

MKY-396

❑ **MKY-396. "Mickey Mouse And The Sacred Jewel" Big Little Book,**
1936. Whitman. Big Little Book #1187 with different art front and back cover. Latter depicts Mickey and Minnie riding a camel. - **$33 $99 $230**

MKY-399

MKY-400

MKY-402

MKY-403

❏ **MKY-399. "Mickey Mouse And Pluto The Pup" Hardcover,**
1936. Whitman. 7.25x9.75" with 68 pages. - **$85 $165 $350**

❏ **MKY-400. "The Mickey Mouse Fire Brigade" Hardcover With Dust Jacket,**
1936. Whitman. 7.25x10" with 68 pages.
Jacket - **$100 $300 $600**
Book - **$75 $150 $400**

❏ **MKY-402. "Mickey Mouse In Pigmy Land,"**
1936. Whitman. 7.25x9.5" with 72 pages. - **$70 $150 $325**

❏ **MKY-403. "Mickey Mouse/A Stand-Out Book,"**
1936. Whitman. 7.25x8.25" hardcover, 32 pages. Title is derived from thick cardboard 5x5" die-cut figure applied on front cover. - **$90 $200 $400**

MKY-401

MKY-404

❏ **MKY-401. "A Mickey Mouse ABC Story" Hardcover,**
1936. Whitman. 7x9.25" with 32 stiff paper pages. Has single page devoted to each letter of the alphabet with art in a music theme of Mickey, Pluto, Donald, Silly Symphony characters, etc. playing musical instruments. - **$115 $225 $450**

❏ **MKY-404. "Mickey Mouse Annual" English Book,**
1936. Dean & Sons Ltd. 6.5x8" hardcover with 2" thickness from 128 stiff paper pages. - **$125 $225 $500**

MKY-405

☐ **MKY-405. "Mickey Mouse And His Horse Tanglefoot" Hardcover With Dust Jacket,**
1936. David McKay Co. 6.5x8.75" with 60 pages. Rare with dust jacket.
Jacket - **$125 $225 $500**
Book - **$175 $350 $950**

MKY-406

☐ **MKY-406. "Mickey Mouse Lights By Noma,"**
1936. Noma Electric Corp. Set consists of eight hard plastic bulb covers with decals and original bulbs. Box - **$80 $165 $325**
Lights - **$70 $135 $225**

MKY-407

☐ **MKY-407. "Mickey Mouse Playing Cards,"**
1936. Whitman Publishing Co. Complete miniature deck comes in 1.5x2.5x.75" deep box. - **$35 $65 $115**

MKY-408

☐ **MKY-408. Valentine Card,**
1936. Hallmark. 3.25x5" die-cut stiff paper folder. - **$30 $55 $85**

MKY-409

☐ **MKY-409. English "Ingersoll Mickey Mouse Pocket Watch" Box/Guarantee,**
1936. Empty box measuring 2.5x4.5x1" deep and originally contained the English pocket watch. Identical to American version but marked on inside "This Box Printed And Made In England."Photo example is missing insert that held watch in place. Comes with original 2x3" folded guarantee. - **$525 $1050 $2100**

MKY-410

❏ **MKY-410. Mickey Mouse Pull Toy,**
c. 1936. N. N. Hill Brass Co.
5.5x9.5x14.25" tall with pair of steel wheels
attached to thick die-cut wood figure which
has two additional wooden wheels. Metal
wheels originally had printed paper disks
with Mickey images. - **$240 $475 $875**

MKY-411

❏ **MKY-411. Italian Mickey/Minnie
Chocolate Bar Display Bin,**
c. 1936. Cirio Topolino. Die-cut cardboard
with flattened size of 15x19.5". - **$210
$425 $850**

MKY-412

❏ **MKY-412. Italian Mickey/Minnie
Chocolate Bar Promotional Pamphlet,**
c. 1936. - **$80 $165 $335**

MKY-413

❏ **MKY-413. "Mickey Mouse Jewelry"
Boxed Pair of Pins,**
c. 1936. Brier Mfg. Co. 2.5x2.5x3/8" deep
box contains pair of 1.25" tall enamel on
brass pins. Box - **$40 $75 $140**
Mickey - **$45 $80 $135**
Minnie - **$45 $80 $135**

MKY-414

❑ **MKY-414. Mickey And Minnie Mouse Wood Wall Plaques,**
c. 1936. Kerk Guild Inc. Each is 5x10.25x.25" thick. Originally sold in boxes marked "Mickey Mouse Art Gallery."
Mickey - **$45 $85 $150**
Minnie - **$35 $75 $125**

MKY-415

MKY-416

❑ **MKY-415. Mickey Mouse Popcorn Popper,**
c. 1936. Ohio Art. 6.25" diameter by 3.75" tall lithographed tin. - **$135 $265 $550**

❑ **MKY-416. Toy Drum,**
c. 1936. Noble & Cooley Co. 6.5" diameter by 3.75" tall toy formed by painted wood body, stiff paper drum heads, painted tin rims, decorative stringing, plus a neck string possibly added. Mickey image on top drum head has "W.D. Ent." marking. - **$275 $525 $850**

MKY-417

❑ **MKY-417. "Mickey Mouse" Store Display Wall Sign,**
c. 1936. Old King Cole distributed by Kay Kamen. Molded 'laminate' in high relief about 24" across. - **$4250 $8500 $17000**

MKY-418

❑ **MKY-418. "Mickey Mouse Racing Car" Boxed Wind-Up,**
c. 1936. Joseph Schneider. 4" long tin litho with nicely illustrated box.
Box - **$275 $550 $1100**
Toy - **$275 $550 $1100**

MKY-419

☐ **MKY-419. "Mickey Mouse Scrapbook,"**
c. 1936. Unmarked but by Whitman.
10.5x15.25". Unused - **$80 $160 $335**

MKY-420

☐ **MKY-420. "Mickey Mouse Circus" Rare English Hardcover,**
c. 1936. Birn Brothers Ltd. 8x10" by 1.25"
thick with 124 pages and four color plates.
- **$135 $275 $550**

MKY-421

☐ **MKY-421. Mickey Mouse Child's Scissors On Store Card,**
1937. Walt Disney Enterprises. Card is
3.5x6" with 3.25" metal scissors which
have 5/8" die-cut tin Mickey figure.
Card - **$110 $225 $450**
Scissors - **$55 $160 $275**

MKY-422

☐ **MKY-422. "Mickey Mouse Annual" English Hardcover,**
1937. Dean & Son Ltd. 6.25x8.5x2". 128
pages features text stories and illustrations, comic panel stories, and several
puzzles. - **$140 $275 $550**

MKY-423

☐ **MKY-423. "A Walt Disney Paint Book,"**
1937. Whitman. 11x14" with 48 pages. -
$75 $135 $285

MKY-424

❏ **MKY-425. Movie Exhibitor Magazine With Mickey And Others,**
1937. "Motion Picture Herald." 9.25x12.25" October 2 weekly for movie theater owners, 94 pages. Content includes two-page ad for Walt Disney/RKO. Front page features Mickey surrounded by photo portraits of other RKO stars, back of page includes list of films plus "Scene From Clock Cleaners" featuring Mickey and Donald. Other prominent movie ads are for Shirley Temple and Lone Ranger. - **$225 $400 $700**

❏ **MKY-424. Movie Exhibitor Magazine With Mickey And Gene Autry,**
1937. "Motion Picture Herald." 9.25x12.25" September 18 weekly for movie theater owners, 108 pages. Content includes two-page ad for Walt Disney cartoons "Now Distributed By RKO-Radio Pictures" and "Mickey Hangs His Hat At RKO." Back of page includes illustration "Scene From Hawaiian Holiday" of Mickey and Minnie. Inside back cover ad is devoted to Gene Autry. - **$165 $325 $550**

MKY-426

❏ **MKY-426. Mickey Mouse Globe Trotters Bread Company Store Sign,**
1937. Paper sign 10.5x23" with 1.5" vertical gummed left and right margins for window display. Illustrates May, 1937 issue of Mickey Mouse Magazine. - **$350 $650 $1300**

MKY-425

MKY-427

☐ **MKY-427. "Mickey Mouse" Globe Trotters Premium Picture,**
1937. Various bakeries and dairies. 4.75x5.75x5" deep wood frame contains 4x5" cardboard picture of Mickey. Back has partial label which reads "To My Dear Friend/For Completing Globe Trotter Map/Sincerely Mickey Mouse." - **$115 $225 $350**

☐ **MKY-429. "Mickey Mouse Cookies" Store Window Sign,**
1937. National Biscuit Co. 9.5x12" glossy paper sign with .5" wide gummed strip on front top and bottom margins for window mounting. - **$650 $1300 $2000**

MKY-430

☐ **MKY-430. "The Mickey Mouse Globe Trotter Weekly,"**
1937. Volume 5, #5. Four-page publication 5x8.5" with continuing "Race 'Round The World" story. Each - **$30 $55 $80**

MKY-428

☐ **MKY-428. "Mickey Mouse Cookies" Box,**
1937. National Biscuit Co. 2x5x2.75" emptied box with string carrier. - **$115 $225 $425**

MKY-431

☐ **MKY-431. Walt Disney Characters "Pepsodent Paste & Powder" Store Display Sign,**
1937. Cardboard sign is 16x20". - **$325 $650 $1300**

MKY-429

MKY-432

❑ **MKY-432. "Minnie Mouse" As Tennis Player Glass,**
1937. Clear tumbler is 5.5" tall with fluted bottom from athletic series, also produced in smaller 4.75" heighth. - **$165 $325 $650**

MKY-433

❑ **MKY-433. "Playthings" Trade Publication Featuring Mickey Mouse,**
1937. Issue of "The National Magazine Of The Toy Trade" for May 1937 is 9x12" with 112 pages. Contents feature toy photos and ads. Includes special eight-page photo feature on the New York toy fair. - **$85 $165 $350**

MKY-434

❑ **MKY-434. "Mickey Mouse Drummer" Pull Toy,**
1937. Fisher-Price. 4x7.5x8.5" tall mostly wood pull toy #795. - **$325 $650 $1100**

MKY-435

❑ **MKY-435. "Mickey Mouse Ingersoll De-Luxe" Boxed Wrist Watch,**
1937. Box variety is 2.5x5x1.5" deep with sloped platform base.
Complete Box - **$425 $850 $1300**
Watch - **$225 $450 $875**

MKY-436

❑ **MKY-436. "Mickey Mouse Club" English Coronation Souvenir,**
1937. 7/8". Features issuer's name "County Cinemas" and bluetone photos of George VI and Queen Elizabeth. - **$110 $225 $425**

MKY-437

☐ **MKY-437. "Mickey Mouse Globe Trotters" Members Celluloid Button,**
1937. Imprints of various bakery and dairy companies. 1.25" with backpaper by M. Pudlin Co. or Kay Kamen Ltd. with Mickey extending left hand image.
Freihofer - **$18 $30 $50**
Others - **$25 $50 $100**

MKY-438

☐ **MKY-438. Mickey Mouse "Wesley's Bread" Button,**
1937. Kay Kamen Ltd. 1.25". Various sponsor imprints. - **$55 $110 $165**

MKY-439

☐ **MKY-439. "Mickey Mouse" The Atlanta Georgian's 1937 Silver Anniversary Button,**
1937. Roy Booker-Atlanta. 1 1/8" litho. from Southern newspaper button set which included other non-Disney characters. - **$225 $450 $900**

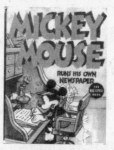

MKY-440

MKY-441

☐ **MKY-440. "Mickey Mouse Runs His Own Newspaper" Big Little Book,**
1937. Whitman. Book #1409. - **$31 $93 $220**

☐ **MKY-441. "Mickey Mouse And His Big Little Kit,"**
1937. Whitman. 4.5x6.5x1.5" deep box contains 384 4.25x6" black and white pages for construction of a customized Big Little Book. - **$225 $550 $1100**

MKY-442

❏ **MKY 442. "Mickey Mouse's Friends Wait For The County Fair,"**
1937. Whitman. 8.5x9.5" "Walt Disney Storybook" #883. 24 pages. - **$115 $225 $450**

MKY-443

MKY-444

❏ **MKY-443. "Mickey Mouse Has A Busy Day,"**
1937. Whitman. Book #1077 from "Picture Storybook" series. - **$115 $225 $450**

❏ **MKY-444. "Mickey Mouse Presents Walt Disney's Nursery Stories" Hardcover With Dust Jacket,**
1937. Whitman. 6.5x9x1.5" thick with 212 pages of stories mostly related to nursery rhyme characters. The only reference to Mickey is the book's title.
Jacket - **$25 $65 $150**
Book - **$35 $85 $200**

MKY-445

MKY-446

❏ **MKY-445. "Mickey Mouse Annual" English Hardcover,**
1937. Dean & Son Ltd. 6.5x8.5x2" thick with 124 thick stiff pages. Along with standard story pages, there is a two-page cutout puzzle. - **$115 $225 $450**

❏ **MKY-446. "Walt Disney Presents The Mickey Mouse Mother Goose" Hardcover,**
1937. Whitman. 6.5x9x1.5" thick with 144 pages. Contents include numerous stories featuring Disney and nursery rhyme characters. - **$135 $275 $600**

MKY-447

❏ **MKY-447. "Mickey Mouse Bedtime Stories" English Book,**
1937. William Collins Sons & Co. Ltd. 7.75x9.5" hardcover, 96 pages. - **$135 $275 $600**

MKY-448

MKY-449

❏ **MKY-448. "Walt Disney's Mickey Mouse Linen-Like" Book,**
1937. Whitman. 9.75x12.5" with 12 pages. Contents are reprints of "Good Housekeeping" magazine pages. - **$75 $150 $300**

❏ **MKY-449. "Walt Disney Silly Symphony Mickey's Magic Hat/Cookie Carnival" Book Abridged Version,**
1937. Whitman. Book #1077. 8.5x9.5" with 16 pages rather than 24 pages in Whitman book #883 with the same title. - **$95 $200 $400**

MKY-450

❏ **MKY-450. "Mickey Mouse Magazine" Gift Subscription Card,**
1937. Stiff paper card is 4x5" sent to child notifying of one-year subscription to the magazine from mother and father. Card has inked "For/From" names on appropriate line. Mickey holds a copy of August 1937, Vol. 2 #11 issue with several other issues trailing behind the plane. - **$275 $625 $950**

MKY-451

❏ **MKY-451. "Mickey Mouse" Christmas Card,**
1937. Hall Bros. 4x5.25" stiff paper card with gold border designed like a movie screen. - **$85 $135 $250**

MKY-452

❏ **MKY-452. Christmas Card,**
1937. Hallmark. 3x5.25" closed folder. - **$30 $55 $85**

MKY-453

☐ **MKY-453. Birthday Card,**
1937. Hallmark. Closed 3.25x5" folder card. - **$45 $85 $150**

MKY-454

☐ **MKY-454. Mickey Pencil Box With Donald And Nephews,**
1937. Textured paper-covered cardboard with snap closure lid is 2.5x8.25x1" deep. - **$55 $110 $175**

MKY-455

☐ **MKY-455. "County Mickey Mouse Club" English Enamel Pin,**
c. 1937. Die-cut Mickey with 1" octagonal border. - **$75 $150 $300**

MKY-456

☐ **MKY-456. Mickey Mouse China Cup/Egg Cup Boxed Set,**
c. 1937. "Limoges France." 4x6x3" deep original but generic pink box with hinged lid contains two-piece set consisting of 2.75" tall cup and 1.25" tall egg cup. Both pieces have gold stamp on underside "Licensed Walt Disney" as well as "Singer" name and Pegasus logo plus "Limoges France." Box - **$15 $25 $50**
Cup - **$80 $135 $250**
Egg Cup - **$75 $125 $225**

MKY-457

❑ **MKY-457. Minnie Mouse Glass From Musical Note Series,**
c. 1937. 4.75" tall. - **$250 $500 $1000**

MKY-458

❑ **MKY-458. French Album Promoting Disney Premium Cards To Retailers,**
c. 1937. 6.25x9.25" with 24 pages. Reproduces 100 numbered cards from "Series A" set. - **$50 $100 $200**

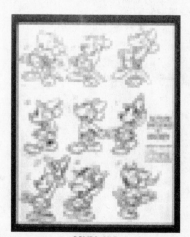

MKY-459

❑ **MKY-459. Mickey Model Sheet,**
1938. 19x15" tall model sheet. - **$75 $150 $250**

MKY-460

❑ **MKY-460. "Mickey Mouse In Numberland" Activity Book,**
1938. Whitman. 8.25x11.25" #745 with 96 black and white pages. - **$65 $150 $325**

MKY-461

❑ **MKY-461. "Mickey Mouse Holiday Special" Publication,**
1938. English by Odhams Press Ltd. 9x12" with 64 pages. - **$85 $165 $350**

MKY-462

❑ **MKY-462. "Mickey Mouse Globe-Trotters" Door Hanger,**
1938. Die-cut 8x11.5" stiff paper. Bottom of piece is application card to be cut out and sent in for "Globe-Trotters Official Membership Button And World Map." - **$115 $225 $350**

MKY-463

❑ **MKY-463. "The Happy Homemakers Weekly/Mickey Mouse Travel Club News" Publications,**
1938. Various bakeries. Six consecutive issues, each 5.75x8" with four pages #3-#8. Each has one or two state-shaped cut-outs for mounting on map that details Mickey and Donald's journey across the USA. At least 22 known. Each - **$20 $30 $60**

MKY-464

❑ **MKY-464. "Mickey Mouse Travel Club" Premium Map,**
1938. Mills Bakery and others. 16.5x24" for mounting cut-outs of states from folders titled "Happy Homemakers' Weekly." - **$125 $325 $700**

MKY-465

❑ **MKY-465. Mickey Mouse Chocolate Candy Box,**
1938. John F. Schoener Inc., Reading, PA. 5.5x11x4.25" deep. - **$85 $165 $335**

MKY-466

MKY-469

❑ **MKY-466. "Mickey Mouse" Lamp,**
1938. LaMode Studios. 4" diameter base and 9.5" tall. Mickey figure is 6.25" tall. - **$275 $550 $900**

MKY-467

❑ **MKY-467. Mickey Mouse Lamp Shade,**
1938. Doris Lamp Shades Co. Inc. 6" tall thin cardboard for use with LaMode Studios lamp. - **$425 $825 $1500**

❑ **MKY-469. "Marks Brothers Co. Games And Toys" 1938-1939 Catalogue,**
1938. Catalogue is 8.5x11" with 16 pages. On one page is the Mickey Mouse Target Game while on another page is Mickey Mouse Jack-In-The-Box and Piano with dancing figures. The final page of catalogue is devoted exclusively to Mickey and Snow White items. The Mickey items are Topple-Over Shooting Game, Rollem Bowling Game, Pin The Tail On The Mickey And Soldier. - **$75 $135 $275**

MKY-468

MKY-470

❑ **MKY-468. "Sunoco Oil" Disney Booklet,**
1938. Sun Oil Co. 4.75x7.25" booklet with 8 pages. - **$50 $100 $175**

❑ **MKY-470. Disney Character Ink Blotter,**
1938. Sherwin Williams Co. of Canada. 3.5x8.75" with title "It's Time To Decorate." - **$110 $215 $325**

MKY-471

❑ **MKY-471. "Kiddies' Christmas Trip To Hollywood" Premium Book,**
1938. Softcover 6x8" with 16 pages issued by Detroit department store. Story plus four full-page illustrations for four film sets including Snow White, Little Tailor, In The Nickel Of Time and Lonesome Ghosts. Also includes four pages of toys and related items. - **$135 $265 $525**

MKY-472

❑ **MKY-472. "Mickey Mouse/The Sheriff Of Nugget Gulch" Fast-Action Storybook,**
1938. Dell Publishing Co. 4x5.5" with 192 pages. Similar to Big Little Book with illustrations. - **$51 $153 $360**

MKY-473

❑ **MKY-473. Die Cut Standee,**
1938. From "The Mickey Mouse Theatre of the Air" program (NBC), sponsored by Pepsodent. 32" x 31". Rare. - **$2650 $6000 $9000**

MKY-474

❑ **MKY-474. "Mickey Mouse In The Race For Riches" Big Little Book,** 1938. Whitman. Book #1476. - **$31 $93 $220**

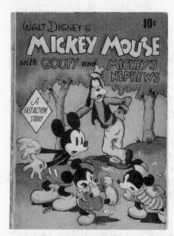

MKY-475

❑ **MKY-475. "Mickey Mouse With Goofy And Mickey's Nephews" Fast Action Storybook,** 1938. Dell. 4x5.25" softcover. Unusual variety with ads on both inside covers and back cover for Johnson Smith & Co. products. - **$51 $153 $360**

MKY-476

❑ **MKY-476. "Mickey Mouse Has A Party,"** 1938. Whitman. 7.25x10" with 48 pages. A "School Reader" book #798. Has thin cardboard covers. - **$85 $165 $325**

MKY-477

❑ **MKY-477. Mickey Mouse Tenth Birthday Envelope,** 1938. 3.75x6.5" envelope. Has September 29, 1938 postmark from Los Angeles, California. - **$25 $45 $75**

MKY-478

MKY-481

❏ **MKY-478. "Walt Disney's Brave Little Tailor,"**
1938. Whitman. 9.5x13" stiff cover with 24 pages. - **$75 $140 $275**

❏ **MKY-481. "Mickey's Hawaiian Holiday" English Hardcover,**
1938. Dean & Son Ltd. 7.2x9.75". 80 pages. - **$100 $200 $450**

MKY-479

❏ **MKY-479. "A Mickey Mouse Alphabet/ABC" Book,**
1938. Whitman. 9.5x13" linen-like book with 16 pages of Disney characters representing different letters of the alphabet. - **$115 $250 $450**

MKY-482

❏ **MKY-482. Radio Magazine With Mickey,**
1938. "Radio Guide" 10.5x13.5" weekly for January 8 published by Regal Press Inc. Front cover pictures him at radio microphone and content includes half-page article about his radio debut, a 13-week series for NBC. Information on radio stars and programs such as "The Inside Story Of The Mae West-Charlie McCarthy Broadcast" with photos. - **$30 $60 $125**

MKY-480

❏ **MKY-480. "Mickey Mouse Annual" English Hardcover,**
1938. Dean & Son Ltd. 6.5x8.75x2" thick with 124 stiff paper pages. - **$115 $250 $550**

MKY-483

MKY-483. Disney Characer Sand Pail,
1938. Ohio Art. 8" tall with 8.25" diameter tin litho with attached carrying handle. - **$275 $550 $1100**

(DECAL ON BACK)

MKY-484

MKY-484. Mickey Mouse 'Lapel' Pocketwatch,
1938. Ingersoll. 2" diameter. Reverse case features Mickey decal. Came with cord and brass button to fasten in lapel hole.
Box - **$425 $850 $1350**
Watch - **$550 $1100 $2250**
Cord - **$60 $115 $225**

MKY-485

MKY-485. "Walt Disney Handkerchiefs" Boxed Set,
c. 1938. Maker Unknown. 7x7x.25" deep box contains complete and unused set of three different fabric hankies.
Boxed Set - **$85 $165 $275**

MKY-486

MKY-486. Largest "Mickey Mouse Printing And Colouring Outfit,"
c. 1938. English. A "Pingo" set by P.R.S. Co. Ltd. Box is 14.25x14.25x 1.25" deep. This set has 27 different ink stamps ranging in size of 1x1.5" to 1.75x2.5". Four of the ink stamps are generic as issued and feature a tree, grass, house and light house. All of the others feature one or more Disney characters per stamp. Characters and number of different stamps per character are Pluto, Donald, Clarabelle and Horace each with one, Snow White 3, Three Little Pigs 4, Minnie Mouse 4, Mickey Mouse 8. - **$125 $275 $550**

MKY-487

MKY-490

☐ **MKY-487. "Mickey Mouse Paint Box,"**
c. 1938. Made In England. 2.5x6.25x.25" deep lithographed tin. - **$65 $135 $225**

☐ **MKY-489. "Mickey Mouse Weekly" Club Member Enamel On Brass Pin,**
c. 1938. United Kingdom. Issued by weekly publication. 1" with slogan "Mickey Mouse Chums." - **$70 $115 $235**

MKY-488

☐ **MKY-488. Exceptional Walt Disney Character Rug With Tag,**
c. 1938. Large 21.5x45" rug with velvet-like nap. Has small tag marked "Made In Italy" and an additional 2.5x4" stiff paper tag with full color illustration of Snow White and four Dwarfs with text "By Permission Walt Disney." - **$265 $525 $1250**

☐ **MKY-490. Mickey Mouse Composition Bank With Movable Head,**
c. 1938. Crown Toy Mfg. Co. 6" tall. - **$115 $225 $450**

MKY-491

☐ **MKY-491. "Mickey Mouse Toy Chest,"**
c.1938. 12x28" cardboard chest. Depicts various Disney characters on panels.
- **$225 $450 $850**

MKY-489

MKY-494

MKY-492

❏ **MKY-492. "Mickey's Fun Fair Card Game" Boxed Double Deck,**
c. 1938. Castell Brothers Ltd., England. .75x4.75x3.5" tall box contains two complete decks of cards and instruction book. Each deck consists of 44 cards, identical in design with only difference being the color of the card backs. - **$160 $325 $550**

❏ **MKY-494. "Mickey Mouse Good Teeth" Celluloid Button,**
c. 1938. Button is 1.25" with backpaper "Distributed By The Bureau Of Public Relations American Dental Association 212 E. Superior St. Chicago, Ill." - **$65 $135 $200**

MKY-495

❏ **MKY-495. Mickey Mouse Catalin Plastic Pencil Sharpener,**
c. 1938. 1.75" tall. - **$55 $110 $165**

MKY-496

❏ **MKY-496. "Mickey Mouse Magic Painting Book,"**
1939. Birn Brothers Ltd. 8.5x10.75" with 48 pages. Designed to be used with a wet brush to bring out color on pages. - **$200 $325 $650**

MKY-493

❏ **MKY-493. "Mickey Mouse Health Brigade" Pin,**
c. 1938. 1.25" tall die-cut brass pin. - **$110 $225 $335**

MKY-497

❑ **MKY-497. "Hankyventures By Walt Disney" Book,**
1939. Playtime Hankies. 7x9" cardboard hanky book with eight pages. Hankies are incorporated as part of each page design. Complete - **$110 $215 $325**

MKY-498

❑ **MKY-498. "Merry Christmas From Mickey Mouse,"**
1939. K. K. Publications Inc. 7x10" with 16 pages. Contents include illustrations, stories, puzzles, games, pictures to color, etc., much of which is Christmas related. - **$262 $786 $3800**

MKY-499

❑ **MKY-499. Mickey Mouse Pencil Drawing From Society Dog Show,**
1939. Sheet of animation paper is 10x12" with 4x7" image. #45 from a numbered sequence. - **$125 $250 $400**

MKY-500

MKY-501

❑ **MKY-500. Fantasia Concept Sketch,**
1939. Image is 5x6.5". From a numbered sequence and this is "74." - **$225 $425 $650**

❑ **MKY-501. "Mickey Mouse Sugar Wafers" Box,**
1939. National Biscuit Co. 3x8x1" deep. - **$60 $115 $225**

MKY-502

MKY-505

☐ **MKY-502. "Walt Disney All Star Parade" Glass,**
1939. Clear tumbler is 4.75" with wrap-around illustration of Mickey, Minnie, Pluto and a parrot. From a "1939" dated series of glasses featuring various Disney characters. - **$25 $45 $65**

MKY-503

MKY-504

☐ **MKY-503. "Mickey Mouse Dime Register Bank,"**
1939. Lithographed tin bank is 2.75x2.75x.75" deep. - **$185 $315 $625**

☐ **MKY-504. Mickey/Minnie "Blue Sunoco" Ink Blotter,**
1939. Blotter is 4x7.25". - **$40 $80 $135**

☐ **MKY-505. Oil Change Reminder Postcard,**
1939. Sunoco. 3.5x5.5" depiction of Mickey as Pilgrim turkey hunter to illustrate season for changing automobile motor oil to winter grade. Reverse also has small Mickey image with ad text. - **$25 $55 $100**

MKY-506

☐ **MKY-506. Mickey Mouse Sign,**
1939. Sunoco. 19.75x28" cardboard with glossy outdoor protective coating. - **$225 $450 $900**

MKY-507

❑ **MKY-507. "Mickey's And Donald's Race To Treasure Island" Premium Map,**
1939. Standard Oil Co. 19.5x27" map of United States. Has designated areas to paste pictures cut from "Travel Tykes Weekly." Reverse has text on obtaining stamps. - **$165 $325 $650**

MKY-508

❑ **MKY-508. "Travel Tykes Weekly" Premium Newspaper,**
1939. Standard Oil Co. Of California. 11.5x15" issue on newsprint paper. From series. Content of each includes puzzles, games, cartoons. Back cover has pair of numbered pictures to be mounted on the premium map "Mickey's And Donald's Race To Treasure Island," obtained separately. Each - **$15 $30 $60**

MKY-509

MKY-510

❑ **MKY-509. "Mickey Mouse And The Pirate Submarine" Better Little Book,**
1939. Whitman. Book #1463. - **$31 $93 $220**

❑ **MKY-510. "Mickey Never Fails,"**
1939. D. C. Heath and Co. 6.25x8.5" hardcover with 108 pages including nice color throughout. - **$30 $55 $115**

MKY-511

☐ **MKY-511. "Walt Disney's Storybooks,"**
1939. D.C. Heath & Co. 6.25x8.5" hardcover with 56 pages, designed for use in school. Title is "Here They Are." - **$40 $80 $160**

MKY-512

☐ **MKY-512. "Mickey Mouse Annual" English Hardcover,**
1939. Dean & Son Ltd. 6.25x8.5x2" thick with 124 pages of comic-style stories. Also has one glossy color plate. - **$165 $375 $750**

MKY-513

☐ **MKY-513. "The Mickey Mouse Safety First Book,"**
1939. Dean & Son Ltd. Only issued in England. 7x9" with 62 pages. - **$150 $250 $500**

MKY-514

☐ **MKY-514. Mickey And Friends Get Well Card,**
1939. Hallmark. 3.75x4.75" on textured paper. Card opens to reveal large image of Donald with die-cut body that pops out slightly. - **$40 $80 $125**

MKY-515

☐ **MKY-515. Mickey Mouse Valentine's Day Card,**
1939. Hallmark. 3x5" stiff paper card. - **$30 $60 $90**

MKY-516

❑ MKY-518. Mickey Mouse Wristwatch Boxed,
1939. Ingersoll. 4x6.75x1" deep box containing 1" wide chromed case watch with lady's style links band, one of four band styles offered. Dial is similar to the 1938 Ingersoll but on this version the Mickey second hand disk is replaced by conventional second hand with numerals and the case has fluted accents on sides.
Box Reading "New" - **$185 $375 $750**
Watch - **$175 $350 $675**

❑ MKY-516. Cereal Box,
1939. Mickey not on front. - **$225 $450 $800**

MKY-517

MKY-519

❑ MKY-517. "Ingersoll Mickey Mouse Wristwatch" Box,
1939. 3.75x6.75x1" deep box. - **$165 $335 $650**

❑ MKY-519. Gold Case Variety Wristwatch,
1939. Ingersoll. First time Ingersoll offer of limited edition 14-karat gold plate "Goldtone" case watch for $1 more than the standard silvered brass case variety. Dial face has full figure image of Mickey whose hands point at the numerals. The second hand disk between Mickey's legs features numbers only. - **$200 $400 $800**

MKY-518

MKY-520

❏ **MKY-520. "Detective Adventures By Walt Disney" English Hardcover,**
c. 1939. Juvenile Ltd. Productions. 7.5x10.25" with 96 stiff paper pages. - **$85 $190 $400**

MKY-521

❏ **MKY-521. English Birthday Postcard,**
c. 1939. Valentine & Sons Ltd. 3.5x5.5" gloss stiff paper. - **$25 $45 $80**

MKY-522

❏ **MKY-522. "Mickey Mouse Belt" Box,**
1930s. Hickok. 2x8x2" deep box. Bottom includes four different images of Mickey and two of Minnie. - **$80 $160 $300**

MKY-523

❏ **MKY-523. "Mickey Mouse" Child's Belt,**
1930s. Hickok Mfg. Co. Inc. 1.25x30" leather belt marked on reverse "Mickey Mouse Genuine Cowhide" with size "24." Entire front surface of belt has lightly ridged design with fourteen different images. - **$80 $160 $300**

MKY-524

❏ **MKY-524. "Mickey Mouse Children's Hose Supporters" Empty Box,**
1930s. A. Stein & Co. 3.5x9x2.25" deep which originally held one dozen hose supporters. - **$135 $240 $475**

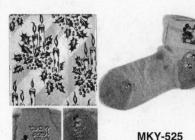

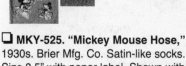

MKY-525

❏ **MKY-525. "Mickey Mouse Hose,"**
1930s. Brier Mfg. Co. Satin-like socks. Size 8.5" with paper label. Shown with vintage generic Christmas box. - **$70 $110 $165**

MKY-526

MKY-528

❑ **MKY-528. Mickey Mouse Metal Shoe Horn,**
1930s. Spanish with no Disney markings. 4" long. - **$80 $160 $325**

❑ **MKY-526. "Converse Mickey Mouse Skoots" Boxed Sneakers,**
1930s. Box is 4.5x10.75x3.25" and contains pair of 9" long sneakers described on one side panel of box as "Misses' Patter White."
Box - **$150 $275 $550**
Sneakers - **$75 $140 $275**

MKY-527

MKY-529

❑ **MKY-527. "Mickey Mouse Slippers" Empty Box,**
1930s. English, maker unknown.
3.25x7x2.75" deep. - **$200 $400 $750**

❑ **MKY-529. "Mickey Mouse" Child's Gloves,**
1930s. Rau F. Company, Prov. R.I. Size 4 gloves each 7.25" long. Outside snap closure. - **$40 $85 $175**

MKY-530

❏ **MKY-530. "Mickey Mouse" Child's Gloves,**
1930s. 6.5x10" with leather hands, cuffs are suede with matching fringe trim. Stitched to the front of each cuff is a 2.5x4.5" felt patch with silk screened design. - **$150 $275 $550**

MKY-531

❏ **MKY-531. "Mickey Mouse Hankies" Boxed Set,**
1930s. Box is 9x9.25x.25" deep and contains seven hankies. Each hanky features a different illustration of Mickey or Minnie along with name of each day of the week.
Box - **$30 $60 $125**
Each Hanky - **$15 $25 $50**

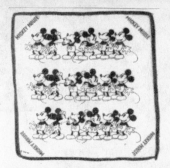

MKY-532

❏ **MKY-532. "Mickey Mouse" Multiple Image Hanky,**
1930s. Hanky is 9.5" square cotton in printed design of three repeated rows of six different Mickey images whose expression changes from happy to angry to sleepy to shocked. At each corner is his name. - **$40 $75 $125**

MKY-533

❏ **MKY-533. "Mickey Mouse Hankies" Boxed Set,**
1930s. Herrmann Handkerchief Co. 7x7x.25" deep box contains set of three cotton hankies. Set - **$75 $135 $275**

MKY-534

❑ MKY-536. Mickey Mouse Hat With Button,
1930s. 8x9" cotton twill hat with attached 7/8" diameter button that has brass rim and fabric center. Hat - **$40 $90 $185**
Button - **$40 $80 $160**

❑ MKY-534. "Walt Disney Handkerchiefs,"
1930s. 7.25x7.25x3/8" deep box contains one 8.5x8.5" hanky of unknown original quantity. Box lid features Mickey, Minnie, Pluto, Donald and two nephews, Elmer Elephant and Dopey. Hanky features Dopey. Box - **$35 $65 $135**
Each Hanky - **$15 $25 $50**

MKY-537

❑ MKY-537. "Mickey Mouse Band-O" Hair Bow On Card,
1930s. 5.5x8" display card holds silk-like hair bow with elastic band. - **$70 $155 $260**

MKY-535

❑ MKY-535. "Mickey Mouse" Hat,
1930s. Cotton twill hat 8x9" with celluloid visor. Outside has attached 7/8" button with brass rim and fabric center with Mickey image.
Hat - **$60 $115 $225**
Button - **$40 $80 $160**

MKY-538

❑ MKY-538. "Mickey Mouse" French Shoe Polish Hat,
1930s. Thin glossy paper hat measures 6x12". Text is in French. Each side has same design of Mickey shining his shoe to see his reflection along with can of shoe polish. - **$25 $50 $90**

MKY-536

MKY-539

MKY-542

❑ **MKY-539. "Mickey Mouse Comic Cookies" Premium Punch-Out Hat,** 1930s. Stiff paper sheet measures 8.25x13". When assembled, image of Mickey would appear on both sides. - **$115 $225 $385**

❑ **MKY-542. "Mickey Mouse Tie Rack,"** 1930s. Wooden rack 5x9" with large image of Mickey and smaller image of Donald. - **$75 $150 $285**

MKY-540

❑ **MKY-540. "Mickey Mouse Comic Cookies" Advertising Poster,** 1930s. 24x18" paper sign offering free hat. - **$325 $650 $1300**

MKY-543

❑ **MKY-543. "Rodeo" Image Necktie,** 1930s. Child's fabric tie with overall 36" length. - **$40 $75 $125**

MKY-541

❑ **MKY-541. "Mickey Mouse Tie Rack,"** 1930s. Rack is 5x8.75". Top has two hanging holes as made, front has attached wood bar for hanging ties. - **$115 $225 $335**

MKY-544

❏ **MKY-544. "Mickey Mouse Tie Rack,"** 1930s. Maker unknown. 4.25x9.5x.25" thick jigsawed wood with silk screened design on front. - **$125 $265 $450**

MKY-545

❏ **MKY-545. Mickey/Minnie Umbrella,** 1930s. Japan. 19" long with diameter of about 23" constructed of wood handle and shaft with metal frame and silk-like synthetic fabric cover. - **$85 $175 $300**

MKY-546

❏ **MKY-546. "Mickey Mouse Muffler" Boxed Scarf,** 1930s. Box is 9.5x9.5x.5" deep containing nice quality all wool "muffler," 8x38". Stitched to one corner of the muffler is 2x2.5" patch with image of Mickey skiing and Pluto running by his side.
Box - **$125 $250 $400**
Scarf - **$60 $110 $165**

MKY-547

❏ **MKY-547. "Mickey Mouse" Sweater,** 1930s. "Murrayknit" small child's wool sweater with body measuring 11x12". On breast pocket is 2x3" emboidered figural patch of Mickey. Stitched inside of collar is 1x1.25" tag for maker with Mickey image and word balloon that reads "It's All Wool." - **$60 $110 $225**

MKY-548

❑ MKY-548. Mickey Mouse Baby Or Toddler Sweater,
1930s. No tags, but authorized. Nice quality wool sweater. - **$60 $115 $225**

MKY-549

❑ MKY-549. Mickey Mouse Tie Clasp,
1930s. Silvered brass 2" long with glass dome at center featuring reverse image with depth. - **$35 $70 $135**

MKY-550

❑ MKY-550. "Mickey Mouse Undies" Clothing,
1930s. Child's four fabric items believed comprising original set consisting of 10x21" sleeveless upper torso garment with button flap on back, size "6" panties, pair of elastic top ankle socks. Each piece is complete with small stitched fabric tag reading "Mickey Mouse Undies" although in two different styles. Group - **$120 $220 $360**

MKY-551

❑ MKY-551. Child's Romper,
1930s. One-piece cotton outfit measuring 13x18" overall. - **$40 $70 $135**

MKY-552

❑ MKY-552. "Mickey Mouse Undies" Sealed Pack,
1930s. Sylcraft. 5x7.75" with single pair. Packaged - **$115 $225 $335**

MKY-553

❏ **MKY-553. "Leader" Printing Set With Mickey Mouse Stamp Pad,**
1930s. Fulton Specialty Co. This is a generic stamp set although includes an official "Mickey Mouse Stamp Pad" with 1.25x2.25x3/8" deep tin case.
Boxed - **$50 $110 $175**
Pad Only - **$35 $80 $135**

MKY-556

MKY-554

❏ **MKY-556. "The Mickey Mouse Counting Book/Paint And Crayon,"**
1930s. English by Collins Clear-Type Press. 10.5x13.5" with 32 pages. - **$135 $275 $550**

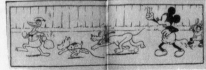

MKY-555

❏ **MKY-554. Picture Printing Set,**
1930s. Fulton Specialty Co. 8.5x11x1" deep boxed "Artistamp Picture Set No. 785" comprised of complete original 15 rubber ink stamps with wood grip handles. One stamp is scene of Mickey and Minnie from Steamboat Willie. - **$85 $200 $375**

❏ **MKY-555. Mickey Mouse Spanish Coloring Booklet,**
1930s. Booklet is 3x4.5" with 12 pages. Title is "El Juicio De Mickey." - **$18 $35 $60**

MKY-557

❏ **MKY-557. "Mickey Mouse Mystery Art Set,"**
1930s. Dixon. 8x11.5x5" deep cardboard unit comes with twelve colored pencils and 7x36" paper sheet with six different "Mystery Drawings," 3" wide illustrated cardboard band that slips over the "easel desk" and an eraser. Easel desk is corrugated cardboard and designed with a cardboard flap that is used to prop it up. - **$150 $300 $650**

MKY-560

❏ **MKY-560. "Mickey Mouse Pantograph,"**
1930s. Marks Brothers Co. 18x18x1.25" deep box contains 17.5" square pantograph board. Boxed - **$200 $400 $800**

MKY-558

❏ **MKY-558. "Mickey Mouse Art Set,"**
1930s. Dixon. 8x13.25x.75" deep box contains six pictures to color, eight colored pencils, eraser, and pair of stencils of Mickey and Minnie. - **$165 $325 $700**

MKY-561

MKY-559

❏ **MKY-559. "Mickey Mouse Drawing Book,"**
1930s. Book is 8.5x11" with 28 blank pages. "Made In Great Britain." - **$30 $65 $135**

❏ **MKY-561 "Mickey Mouse Painting Book,"**
1930s. Dean & Son, Ltd. 8.25x11.25" with 96 pages. Contains great full page illustrations from the earliest Disney cartoons. Title page is marked "For Color Guide See Any Copy Of The Mickey Mouse Weekly." - **$85 $165 $335**

MKY-564

MKY-562

❑ **MKY-562. "Mickey Mouse Poster Colour Painting Outfit,"**
1930s. English. 5.5x7.25x1.75" deep box contains complete amount of five glass bottles of paint plus brush. - **$65 $135 $215**

❑ **MKY-564. Mickey Mouse Puzzle Block Boxed Set,**
1930s. English by Chad Valley Co. Ltd. Set consists of fifteen wood blocks, each 1.5' square with full color paper labels on all sides to form six scenes. - **$165 $325 $650**

MKY-563

MKY-565

❑ **MKY-563. "Mickey Mouse Safety Blocks,"**
1930s. Halsam 4.25x4.25x1.25" deep box contains 9 wooden blocks. Two sides of each block have raised images of Mickey, Minnie or Pluto and other sides have animals or alphabet letters. One of eight different sets with six to thirty blocks per set. Boxed - **$40 $80 $160**

❑ **MKY-565. Mickey Mouse English Pull Toy,**
1930s. Chad Valley Toys. 2.5x3.5x8.75" tall overall. 5.5" tall thin wood figure of Mickey attached to circular wheel base. Figure has pair of separate arms attached to body by rubber strip and fits into slot of a thick wood disk. Disk is contained between pair of outer hard plastic circular sections. Front foot has small hole for string attachment to pull toy. - **$85 $165 $325**

MKY-566

❑ **MKY-566. Minnie Mouse On Scooter Pull Toy,**
1930s. Japan. 3.25" tall celluloid figure is attached to 4" long free-wheeling wood scooter. Attached to the front of the scooter is 19" long string with wood knob on the end. - **$550 $1100 $1650**

MKY-567

MKY-568

❑ **MKY-567. Mickey Mouse And Donald Duck In Boat Pull Toy,**
1930s. English by Chad Valley. 2.75x17x7.75" tall wooden. Photo example missing arms and/or oars. Complete - **$225 $450 $900**

❑ **MKY-568. Walt Disney Character Wood Train Pull Toy,**
1930s. Has Disney name but no maker; possibly Chad Valley. The engine is 3x7x3.5" tall, each of the four cars is 6.5" long. - **$140 $275 $550**

MKY-569

❑ **MKY-569. "Mickey Mouse" Pull Toy,**
1930s. Fun-E-Flex. Free-wheeling painted wood car 3.5x11x2.5" tall with original pull string attached to front. Mickey figure 2.25" tall (missing hands in photo) fits in cylindrical opening above rear spare tire. - **$1050 $2100 $4000**

MKY-570

❑ **MKY-570. "Mickey Mouse Southern Dairies Ice Cream" Decal,**
1930s. "The Palm Brothers Decalomania Co." 4.25x4.25" unused decal. Reverse has maker's name with directions for transferring decal to glass. - **$60 $135 $275**

MKY-571

MKY-574

☐ **MKY-571. Mickey Mouse Southern Dairies Ice Cream Button,**
1930s. Parisian Novelty. 1.25". - **$200 $400 $800**

☐ **MKY-573. "Mickey Mouse" Celluloid Baby Rattle,**
1930s. Marked "Made In Japan/Distributors: Geo. Borgfeldt Corp., New York." 8" long. - **$165 $325 $650**

☐ **MKY-574. Mickey Mouse Celluloid Roly Poly Toy,**
1930s. Toy has height of 3.5" including three-dimensional figure of Mickey with movable arms on top. - **$115 $240 $450**

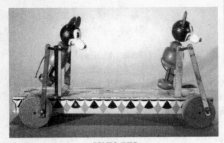

MKY-572

☐ **MKY-572. Mickey And Minnie Circus Pull Toy,**
1930s. By Nifty, distributed by Borgfeldt. Wooden figures swivel as platform moves. Has paper bellows on underside to create squeaking sound. Toy is 4.25x6x11" long. - **$1500 $3000 $6000**

MKY-575

MKY-573

☐ **MKY-575. Disney Character Top,**
1930s. Fritz Bueschel. 7" diameter by 6.5" tall tin litho with wood handle. - **$115 $225 $450**

MKY-576

MKY-578

☐ **MKY-576. Disney Character Balloon Retailer's Catalogue Supplement Folder,**
1930s. Oak Rubber Co. 4x9" four-page glossy paper issued as a "Supplement To Catalogue No. 367." - **$40 $80 $150**

☐ **MKY-578. "Walt Disney Cut-Out Folder Book,"**
1930s. Folder is 6.5x14.5" and opens to 19.25" long. Includes cut-outs for Mickey, Minnie, Goofy, Donna Duck, Dirty Bill and Big Bad Wolf along with accessories and outfits. - **$115 $240 $375**

MKY-577

MKY-579

☐ **MKY-577. "Mickey Mouse Balloon Novelty,"**
1930s. Oak Rubber Co. Two-piece toy comprised of thick 5x7" die-cut cardboard base printed as pair of shoes to hold 6" tall balloon shaped as Mickey figure with large ears. - **$25 $55 $110**

☐ **MKY-579. "Fire Chief Mickey Mouse" Dexterity Puzzle,**
1930s. Cardboard frame puzzle 4x6x.75" deep with clear glass top. Has numerous small ballbearings to be placed in die-cut holes on surface. At least four different. Each - **$75 $135 $225**

MKY-580

❑ **MKY-580. Mickey Mouse With Harmonica Dexterity Puzzle,**
1930s. "Made In Japan". 2.5x5" deep cardboard frame with glass cover. - **$65 $145 $225**

MKY-581

❑ **MKY-581. "Mickey Mouse Picture Puzzles With Trays" Boxed Set,**
1930s. Marks Bros. Co. 11x13.5x1.75" deep box with cellophane display window over complete set of four jigsaw puzzles. Each puzzle is 9.75x11.25" and nestles in individual cardboard tray when completed. The four trays are sized to nest within each other, smaller to larger, for storage in outer box. Near Mint Boxed Set - **$1875**
Each Puzzle or Outer Box - **$115 $225 $375**

MKY-582

❑ **MKY-582. Mickey Mouse/Three Little Pigs English Puzzle,**
1930s. Chad Valley Co. Ltd. 7.25x9.25x.75" deep box contains puzzle with assembled size of 6x8" and consists of jigsawed wood pieces with paper label and same image as 1935 studio Christmas card. - **$115 $225 $450**

MKY-583

❑ **MKY-583. "Mickey Mouse" Large Boxed Jigsaw Puzzle,**
1930s. English by Chad Valley Co. Ltd. Assembled size is 9.75x14". - **$85 $165 $275**

MKY-584

❏ **MKY-584. "Mickey Mouse" With Horn Bisque,**
1930s. From musician set, 3.5" tall. Has incised "C73" on back. - **$40 $70 $145**

MKY-585

MKY-587

❏ **MKY-585. "Mickey Mouse" With Drum Bisque,**
1930s. From musician set, 3-3/8" tall. Has incised "C72" on back. - **$40 $70 $145**

❏ **MKY-587. Mickey With Top Hat And Tuxedo Bisque,**
1930s. Figure is 4" tall. - **$215 $425 $850**

MKY-586

MKY-588

❏ **MKY-586. "Mickey Mouse" With Banjo Large Bisque,**
1930s. Figure is 5.25" tall and has string tail. - **$145 $285 $550**

❏ **MKY-588. "Mickey Mouse" Bisque,**
1930s. Figure is 2.75" tall. - **$35 $65 $115**

MKY-589

MKY-592   **MKY-593**

❑ **MKY-592. Mickey Singer Bisque,**
1930s. Figure is 3.25" tall with string tail.
From set of six. - **$110 $225 $335**

❑ **MKY-593. Mickey With Saxophone Bisque,**
1930s. Figure is 3.25" tall with string tail.
From set of six. - **$110 $225 $335**

❑ **MKY-589. "Micky & Minne" (sic) Boxed Bisques,**
1930s. Geo. Borgfeldt Corp. 3x3x1.5" deep box holds pair of bisques 2.75" tall. Boxed - **$215 $425 $850**

MKY-590   **MKY-591**

❑ **MKY-590. "Mickey Mouse" Large Bisque,**
1930s. Figure is 5.25" marked "Made In Japan" and has incised "A176" on back. - **$95 $185 $350**

❑ **MKY-591. "Mickey Mouse" Conductor Bisque,**
1930s. Figure is 3.5" tall with movable arms. From set of six which included four musicians and Mickey with song book. No incised number. - **$135 $245 $475**

MKY-594

❑ **MKY-594. Mickey With Drum Bisque,**
1930s. Figure is 3.25" tall with string tail.
From set of six. - **$110 $225 $335**

MKY-595

MKY-597   MKY-598

❑ **MKY-595. Mickey And Minnie Unusual Bisque Figures,**
1930s. Figures are bisque with wire legs. Mickey is 3" tall and Minnie is 2-5/8" tall. Marked "Germany" under one foot of each and Mickey has incised "7759" on his rear. Each - **$115 $235 $450**

❑ **MKY-597. "Minnie Mouse" Canadian Glazed Figure,**
1930s. Figure is 4" tall and marked "Made In Japan" and "S763." - **$70 $110 $225**

❑ **MKY-598. "Mickey Mouse" Canadian Glazed Ceramic Figure,**
1930s. Japan. 4" tall distributed in Canada only. Depicts Mickey playing a violin. - **$80 $135 $250**

MKY-596

MKY-599   MKY-600

❑ **MKY-596. Mickey/Minnie Mouse German Bisque Band,**
1930s. Set of six, each marked "Germany." Three wear skirts and three wear pants. Each about 3" tall depicted with five fingers and playing a different instrument. Each - **$85 $165 $275**

❑ **MKY-599. Mickey Mouse Miniature Bisque,**
1930s. Japan. 1.5" tall smallest size of Mickey with one hand raised in the air. - **$30 $45 $85**

❑ **MKY-600. Soldier Mickey With Rifle Bisque,**
1930s. 3.25" tall with "S17" incised on back. - **$55 $110 $165**

MKY-601   **MKY-602**

❑ **MKY-601. Officer Mickey Mouse With Saber Bisque,**
1930s. 3.25" tall with "S16" incised on back. - **$55 $110 $165**

❑ **MKY-602. Mickey Mouse Flag Bearer Bisque,**
1930s. 3.25" tall. #S15 from set of four. - **$55 $110 $165**

MKY-603

❑ **MKY-603 "Mickey/Minnie Mouse" Seated Bisques,**
1930s. Pair of 3" tall figures in seated positions come with pair of chairs and table made of reed/wood with fabric covering. Set issued with a tiny china tea set not shown. Set - **$275 $550 $900**
Each Bisque - **$85 $165 $275**

MKY-604

❑ **MKY-604. "Mickey/Minnie Mouse" Bisque Set,**
1930s. Japan. Matched 4" tall set. Mickey is #S1277, Minnie is #S1276. Each - **$45 $80 $135**

MKY-605

❑ **MKY-605. Mickey Mouse With Drum Large Bisque,**
1930s. Japanese large size 5.25" tall painted bisque likeness with label under base including Mickey and Disney names. - **$210 $415 $675**

MKY-606

MKY-608

MKY-609

☐ **MKY-606. "The Three Pals Mickey, Pluto, Minnie" Bisque Set With Box,**
1930s. 4.25" tall figures with box. "Made In Japan".
Boxed set - **$210 $415 $675**
Minnie "S34" - **$45 $80 $135**
Pluto - **$15 $30 $50**
Mickey "S33" - **$45 $80 $135**

☐ **MKY-608. "Mickey Mouse" Largest Size Bisque Figure,**
1930s. "Made In Japan" 8.5" tall painted bisque on 2.75" square base. Detailing includes two movable arms, string tail, incised name on base front. - **$300 $600 $1250**

☐ **MKY-609. Mickey Mouse Riding Pluto Bisque,**
1930s. Japan. 1x3x2.25" tall. - **$55 $110 $165**

MKY-607

☐ **MKY-607. Mickey And Minnie Mouse Figures,**
1930s. "Germany" matching pair of 1.75" tall painted bisques, each depicted with elongated snouts and wide smiles.
Mickey - **$75 $125 $225**
Minnie - **$65 $100 $200**

MKY-610   **MKY-611**

❑ **MKY-610. "Mickey Mouse" Baseball Player Bisque,**
1930s. Japan. 3-3/8" tall from set of four depicting Mickey in various player positions. With glove and ball. Incised #S65. - **$85 $165 $275**

❑ **MKY-611. "Mickey Mouse" Baseball Player Bisque,**
1930s. Japan. 3-3/8" tall from set of four depicting Mickey in various player positions. In catcher's outfit. Incised #S67. - **$85 $165 $275**

MKY-612   **MKY-613**

❑ **MKY-612. "Mickey Mouse" Baseball Player Bisque,**
1930s. Japan. 3-3/8" tall from set of four depicting Mickey in various player positions. With bat. Incised #S66. - **$85 $165 $275**

❑ **MKY-613. "Mickey Mouse" Playing French Horn Large Bisque,**
1930s. Japan. 5.25" tall. No incised number. - **$210 $415 $675**

MKY-614

❑ **MKY-614. "Mickey Mouse" Playing Accordion Large Bisque,**
1930s. Japan. 5.25" tall. No incised number. - **$210 $415 $675**

MKY-615

❑ **MKY-615. Mickey Mouse Bisque Pin Cushion,**
1930s. "Made In Japan" 4.5" long with felt cushion. - **$215 $425 $850**

MKY-616

❑ **MKY-616. Mickey Mouse And Santa Bisque,**
1930s. Unmarked, likely Japan. 1.25". - **$215 $375 $750**

MKY-617

❑ **MKY-617. Mickey Mouse Bisque Figure,**
1930s. United Kingdom. Dean's Rag Book-style image incised with number that appears to be in the 500 series. 2" tall. - **$45 $80 $135**

MKY-620

MKY-618

❑ **MKY-618. Mickey Mouse Stickpin Figure,**
1930s. Stiff molded spun paper body, pipe cleaner arms, legs and tail with die-cut ears figure is 2.75" tall. - **$55 $110 $165**

❑ **MKY-620. Mickey Mouse Celluloid Place Card Holder,**
1930s. Japan. 2.5" tall. All celluloid including die-cut Mickey. Has tube designed to hold a single flower. - **$145 $285 $550**

MKY-619

MKY-621

❑ **MKY-619. Large "Mickey Mouse" Jointed Celluloid Figure,**
1930s. Figure is 2.75x3x6.25" tall, the largest of three sizes. Has raised name on chest and back is marked "Made In Japan." - **$325 $650 $1300**

❑ **MKY-621. Mickey And Minnie Mouse Celluloid Place Card Holders,**
1930s. Unmarked. Mickey is 1.75" tall, Minnie is 2" tall. Both have small cello tab on back for card. Mickey - **$55 $110 $165** Minnie - **$45 $80 $135**

MKY-622

MKY-624   MKY-625

❏ **MKY-622. Unusual Mickey Mouse Celluloid Figure,**
1930s. Figure is 2.25x2.75x4.25" tall. Eyes are attached to springs and when tapped vibrate feverishly. Marked "Made In Japan" with tax stamp under one foot. - **$145 $285 $550**

❏ **MKY-624. Mickey's Nephew Celluloid Figure,**
1930s. "Made In Japan". 5.25" tall. Depicts nephew in nightshirt and has movable head. Body contains granules so figure can be used as a rattle. - **$165 $375 $750**

❏ **MKY-625. "Mickey Mouse" Celluloid Figure,**
1930s. Maker unknown. 5.75" tall. His name on chest, molded hands at waist and molded tail on reverse. - **$165 $335 $650**

MKY-623

MKY-626

❏ **MKY-623. Mickey Mouse Celluloid Figure,**
1930s. Japan. 3.75" tall holding a flag with raised text that reads "Yusho." Piece is unmarked but probably Japanese made for the European market. - **$70 $110 $225**

❏ **MKY-626. Celluloid Mickey Mouse With Movable Head,**
1930s. Unmarked, likely Japanese. 3.5x3.5x4.5" tall. - **$265 $525 $1000**

MKY-627

MKY-630

❏ **MKY-627. Mickey And Minnie Celluloid Squeaker Toys,**
1930s. Made In Japan. Mickey is 5.5" tall, Minnie is 6.25" tall. Each - **$215 $425 $850**

❏ **MKY-630. Mickey Mouse In Bathing Suit Celluloid Figure/Rattle With Life Preserver,**
1930s. Japan. 4.25" tall figure with 3" diameter life preserver. Mickey filled with granules and serves as a rattle. - **$1100 $2150 $3650**

MKY-628   MKY-629

MKY-631

❏ **MKY-628. Mickey Mouse Celluloid Squeaker Figure,**
1930s. "Made In Japan". 6" tall. Celluloid body with felt pants with buttons and string tail. - **$265 $550 $1100**

❏ **MKY-629. Mickey Mouse Dean's Rag-Style China Figure,**
1930s. Figure is 2-1/8" tall. Back of base is marked "Reg." and underside has incised number. Made in Japan for the English market. - **$40 $75 $125**

❏ **MKY-631. Mickey Mouse Grinning Glazed Ceramic Figure,**
1930s. Looks identical to 3.5" porcelain figure by Rosenthal and has their incised #551, but this is 4" and glazed ceremic. Also has gold foil sticker in German that translates to "Mickey Mouse Brings Luck To The Home." - **$165 $335 $650**

MKY-632

MKY-633

❑ **MKY-632. Mickey Mouse With Saxophone China Figurine,**
1930s. Germany. 3.25" tall. #6592. Each In Series - **$135 $245 $475**

❑ **MKY-633. Mickey Mouse In Chair English Ceramic Figurine,**
1930s. 2x2x3.75" tall marked on underside "British Maker." - **$110 $225 $335**

MKY-634

❑ **MKY-634. Mickey Mouse German Musician China Figurines,**
1930s. Each is 1.5" tall. Each - **$55 $110 $165**

MKY-635

❑ **MKY-635. Bath Salts Figural Container,**
1930s. "Imex Bath Crystals." 3x3x6.5" tall figure "Made In Japan" for English market. Reverse of base is simulated tree stump. Back has registration number and "By Special Permission Walt Disney Enterprises." - **$525 $1050 $1600**

MKY-636

❑ **MKY-636. Mickey Mouse China Figural Bottle Stopper/Pourer,**
1930s. Germany. 3" tall. - **$70 $110 $225**

MKY-637

❑ **MKY-637. Mickey Mouse Large China Ashtray,**
1930s. Dutch by "Mosa Maastricht." 3.5x3.5x7.5" tall with five-fingered Mickey. - **$550 $1350 $2850**

MKY-639

❑ **MKY-639. Mickey Mouse Seated Glazed Ceramic Figure,**
1930s. United Kingdom. Dean's Rag Book doll image marked "Foreign 2205." 1.25" tall. - **$35 $65 $115**

MKY-638

❑ **MKY-638. Mickey Mouse Golfer Tootbrush Holder Ceramic Figure,**
1930s. S. Maw Son & Sons. Ltd., London. 4" tall. - **$250 $550 $1100**

MKY-640

❑ **MKY-640. Mickey Mouse Figural Ceramic Pitcher,**
1930s. Large size 4x7.5x6.75" tall painted and glazed ceramic. Incised markings underneath including number which appears to be "5028." - **$70 $110 $225**

MKY-641

❑ **MKY-641. Unauthorized Mickey Mouse Composition Figure,**
1930s. Figure is 4.25x4.75x10.25" tall composition. - **$55 $110 $165**

MKY-642

❑ **MKY-642. Minnie Compo/Wire Figure,**
1930s. Figure is 7.5" tall ornament dancer formed by painted composition body, hands and feet jointed by coil spring arms and legs. Top of head has metal loop for string or rubber band attachment. - **$165 $335 $650**

MKY-643

❑ **MKY-643. "Mickey Mouse" Painted Lead Figure,**
1930s. Three-dimensional figure 2.5" tall with name on base. - **$135 $245 $475**

MKY-644

❑ **MKY-644. Mickey/Minnie/Pluto Painted Lead Figures,**
1930s. Set of three 2.25" tall semi-flat lead figures, all neatly painted as issued. Each - **$18 $35 $70**

MKY-645

❑ **MKY-645. Miniature Solid Bronze Mickey Mouse Figure,**
1930s. Vienna by Fritz Bermannwien with initials under base "FBW." 1.75" tall depicting a five-finger Mickey. - **$165 $335 $650**

MKY-646

❑ **MKY-646. Mickey Mouse Car Radiator Ornament,**
1930s, England. Maker unknown. 5.75" tall stamped brass originally finished in black paint and silver luster. Pair of long thin mounting wires on reverse. - **$165 $335 $650**

MKY-647

❑ **MKY-647. Mickey Mouse Playing Mandolin Pewter Figure,**
1930s. Figure is 1.75" tall. No markings. - **$175 $300 $600**

MKY-648

❑ **MKY-648. Mickey Mouse Cast Aluminum Doorstop,**
1930s. Maker unknown, three examples known to exist. Unusual design features include over-sized shoes and, although his head is turned to the right, his ears remain in frontal view. One leg is slightly bent at the knee and his chest protrudes. 7" tall. - **$6500 $17500 $30000**

MKY-649

MKY-651

❑ **MKY-649. Mickey Mouse Store Display Standee,**
1930s. Made By Old King Cole, Distributed By Kay Kamen. Molded 'laminite' 11x17.5x1.5" deep. - **$600 $1200 $2000**

❑ **MKY-651. "Mickey Mouse" Jumping Jack Fun-E-Flex Toy,**
1930s. George Borgfeldt. 12" tall wood toy which moves arms and legs when bellows are operated. - **$550 $1100 $2200**

MKY-650

❑ **MKY-650. Mickey, Minnie And Pluto Wood Sled,**
1930s. Fun-E-Flex. Toy is 1.75x4.25x10" long. - **$600 $1200 $2400**

MKY-652

□ **MKY-652. Mickey And Minnie Fun-E-Flex Figures,**
1930s. Wooden figures with wire arms and legs measures 3.75" tall. Decals on chest. Each - **$55 $110 $165**

MKY-654

□ **MKY-654. English Mickey Mouse Band Member Wood Figures,**
1930s. Each is 2.75" tall, similar in design to Dean's rag dolls. Each - **$55 $110 $165**

MKY-653

□ **MKY-653. "Mickey Mouse Fun-E-Flex" Figure,**
1930s. Figure is 3x6.5x7" tall with wood body and metal cable arms and legs, cardboard ears and fabric-covered wire tail with wooden tip. Has Mickey decal on chest and Fun-E-Flex decal under foot. - **$215 $425 $850**

MKY-655   MKY-656

□ **MKY-655. Unlicensed Mickey Mouse Wood Jointed Figure,**
1930s. Unmarked but by Jaymar. 5.75" tall with elastic string attached to head. This particular toy was never sold in a box. - **$60 $120 $175**

□ **MKY-656. Mickey Mouse Folk Art Two-Sided Display Figure,**
1930s. Jigsawed plywood is 7x15". Maker is unknown. Similar - **$70 $110 $225**

MKY-657

❑ **MKY-657. Mickey Mouse Skier Articulated Wood Figure,**
1930s. Italian by Peri. 2.75" tall with 4" long skis. - **$210 $415 $675**

MKY-658

❑ **MKY-658. Boxed Mickey Mouse Wood Jointed Figure,**
1930s. "Patent Tokyo." 4" tall. Wooden body while arms, legs and tail are coated wire. Insert card 2x4" with images and Japanese text roughly translated to "Fun To Play With."
Box Or Card Each - **$20 $40 $65**
Figure - **$150 $300 $600**

MKY-659

❑ **MKY-659. Mickey Mouse On Scooters Wood Jointed Pair,**
1930s. Unmarked but from Czechoslovakia. 3" tall and 1.75" tall.
Large - **$30 $65 $100**
Small - **$25 $45 $65**

MKY-660

❑ **MKY-660. Unusual Wood/Metal Mickey Mouse Figure,**
1930s. Homemade. 1.5x4x4" tall with painted wood body parts and poseable metal rod arms and legs.
Unique, Very Fine - **$225**

MKY-661   **MKY-662**

MKY-661. Unauthorized Mickey Plaster Figure,
1930s. Solid plaster carnival statue 4.5x4x10.5" tall marked on back of one foot "Nunak." - **$30 $60 $100**

MKY-662. Mickey Mouse Painted Plaster Statue,
1930s. Carnival statue 9.75" tall, the only one we know of which closely resembles 1930s studio images. Maker is unknown. - **$55 $110 $165**

MKY-663

MKY-663. "Mickey Mouse" Bread Promotion Display Sign,
1930s. 8x19.5" tri-fold die-cut cardboard. Advertises the premium scrapbook for collecting picture cards that were issued with loaves of bread. - **$275 $550 $1100**

MKY-664

MKY-664. "Mickey Mouse Bread" Store Sign, 1930s. 9-7/8x16-3/4". Bottom has unused area for bakery imprint. - **$325 $800 $1350**

MKY-665

MKY-665. "Mickey Mouse Scrapbook" Advertising Paper,
1930s. Waxed paper strip 2x9" that was part of a bread loaf packaging. - **$80 $135 $250**

MKY-666

MKY-666. "Mickey Mouse Recipe Scrapbook,"
1930s. Book is 4.25x6.25" with 48 pages. Issued by various bread companies. Inside has many character designs around recipe areas where picture cards were to be attached. Empty Book - **$55 $110 $165**

MKY-667

❑ **MKY-667. "Mickey Mouse Recipe Scrapbook" Display Sign,**
1930s. 6x9.75" die-cut cardboard with blank reverse. Depicts Mickey reading the scrapbook. - **$550 $1250 $2000**

MKY-668

❑ **MKY-668. "Mickey Mouse" Bread Picture Card Store Sign,**
1930s. Sign is 18x25". - **$725 $1600 $2750**

MKY-669

❑ **MKY-669. Mickey And Minnie Mouse Butter Nut Bread Store Sign,**
1930s. 10x17". - **$350 $750 $1500**

MKY-670

❑ **MKY-670. Earliest Version "Mickey Mouse Scrapbook,"**
1930s. Armstrong's Bread. 4-1/8x7.25" album with 28 pages and 24 glued in superb color 3.25x5" paper pictures which illustrate a paragraph of text printed below the picture. See next item. Preceded similar but smaller "Recipe" album.
Complete - **$350 $700 $1400**
Album Only - **$95 $185 $350**

MKY-671

MKY-672

❏ **MKY-671. "Mickey Mouse" Bread Loaf Band,**
1930s. 2x19.5" complete waxed paper band with perforated top and bottom edges. - **$80 $135 $250**

❏ **MKY-672. Mickey Mouse Large Size Recipe Cards,**
1930s. Issued by various bakeries. Complete set of 24 stiff paper recipe cards, each 3.25x5". This is a totally different set than those mounted in previous item. Thus, there is an unknown 24-card album or, less likely, a 48-card album. Each - **$12 $25 $40**

MKY-673

❑ **MKY-673. "Mickey Mouse Magic Show" Candy Wrapper,**
1930s. A. McLean & Son. 5x5" one-cent wrapper from a series of 24 different riddles. On this one, Donald is asking a question and the answer is to appear on the movie screen when wrapper is wet. - **$30 $60 $110**

MKY-674

❑ **MKY-674. "Mickey Mouse Chocolate Bar" Candy Box,**
1930s. William Patterson Ltd., Canada. 1.5x4x1.25" deep waxed cardboard box originally held a "Caramel Nougat Chocolate Bar." Photo example ironically has mouse-chewed hole. - **$110 $225 $335**

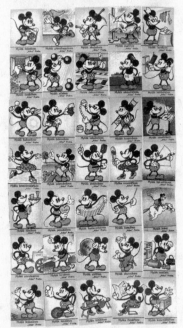

MKY-675

❑ **MKY-675. Rare Mickey Mouse Picture Cards From Prague, Czechoslovakia,**
1930s. Large group of 41, each 1.75x2-3/8" glossy thin paper. Each is marked "Atlas Praha." Six feature Minnie Mouse. All others feature Mickey. Each - **$5 $10 $15**

MKY-676

☐ MKY-676. Dutch Chocolate Tin,

1930s. Lithographed tin canister with lid is 2.25" diameter by 4.75" tall. Design is circular brick building with total of thirteen windows and a door on front with simulated sign "Simon De Wit's Gestampte Muisjes" translating as Chocolate Mice. At each window is a totally different image of either Mickey or Minnie. An additional image of him on the lid is peeking out of a skylight window. - **$165 $375 $700**

☐ MKY-677. Mickey Mouse French Chocolate Card Set,

1930s. Set of sixty each 1x2" card has black and white advertising "Chocolaterie Rubis Berbiers." Cards essentially feature just Mickey although one is of him with Minnie and another is of him washing Pluto. Each - **$5 $10 $15**

MKY-678

☐ MKY-678. "Mickey Mouse" Complete Set of Licorice Flip Cards,

1930s. Likely English or Australian issue. Giant Brand licorice. Set of 24 numbered cards, each 1-3/8"x2.5". Cards are designed to be held at bottom and flipped to view sequence. Set - **$225 $450 $625**

MKY-677

MKY-679

❑ **MKY-679. Mickey Mouse and Donald Duck General Foods Breakfast Cereal Display Sign,**
1930s. General Foods. 10x14" cardboard sign. - **$600 $1600 $2750**

MKY-680

❑ **MKY-680. "Post Toasties" Stationery,**
1930s. Paper is 8.5x11" with design at top advertising Post Toasties that feature "Mickey Mouse And Other Walt Disney Cut-outs On Back And Sides of Package." - **$70 $110 $235**

MKY-681

❑ **MKY-681. Mickey Mouse Boxed Plastic Cereal Bowl,**
1930s. No maker name, just "Cat. No. 705" on box. Box is 5.5x5.5x1.75" deep and bowl is 1.5" deep by 5.25" diameter.
Box - **$85 $165 $275**
Bowl - **$25 $50 $75**

MKY-682

❑ **MKY-682. "Mickey Mouse Picture Card Album" With Revised Cover Art,**
1930s. Gum Inc. Cover features more traditional looking Mickey Mouse image on the front. Version also has "Property" owner's name line at lower left.
Album Only - **$115 $235 $450**

MKY-683

Back Cover Detail

❑ **MKY-683. "Mickey Mouse Picture Card Album,"**
1930s. Volume 1, 6x10" for card series "No. 1 to No. 48." Has 16 pages for mounting cards. First version with primitive Mickey on front cover. - **$115 $235 $450**

MKY-684

❑ **MKY-684. "Mickey Mouse Picture Card Album" With Cards,**
1930s. Gum Inc. 6x10" 16-page album "Vol. 2" with complete set of 48 cards numbered 49-96. Album very fine, cards average fine to very fine. Set - **$2000**
Empty Album - **$150 $300 $600**

Mickey Mouse with the Movie Stars—No. 100

MKY-685

❑ **MKY-685. "Mickey Mouse With The Movie Stars" Gum Card,**
1930s. Gum Inc. 2.5x3-1/8" from second series #97-120. Card #100 showing Will Rogers. Each - **$100 $200 $400**

MKY-686

❑ **MKY-686. "Mickey Mouse" Canadian Gum Card,**
1930s. O-Pee-Chee Co. Ltd. Card #33, identical to American "Gum Inc." issue, except for company name on reverse. - **$18 $35 $60**

MKY-687

❑ **MKY-687. "Mickey Mouse Bubble Gum" Wrapper,**
1930s. Gum Inc. 5x7" waxed paper. Five character illustrations at top and includes ad for Mickey Mouse picture card album available with five wrappers and five cents. - **$80 $135 $275**

MKY-688

❑ **MKY-688. "Mickey Mouse Bubble Gum" Wrapper Variety,**
1930s. Gum Inc. 4.5x6" waxed paper design variation of character illustrations at top of just Minnie, Pluto and Horace rather than the five character variety that also featured Mickey and Clarabelle. This version also has thin blue border around center art and has no text "Save The Wrappers" which appears on the five-character variety. - **$100 $200 $400**

MKY-689

❑ **MKY-689. "Mickey Mouse With The Movie Stars" Gum Card Wrapper,**
1933. Gum, Inc. 4.5x6" waxed paper. - **$175 $350 $750**

MKY-690

❑ **MKY-690. "Mickey Mouse" Ice Cream Cup Lids,**
1930s. Australian by "Peter's Ice Cream" Melbourne. Each is 2.25" diameter. 50 lids needed for prize. Each - **$30 $45 $85**

MKY-691

❑ **MKY-691. "Mickey Mouse" Drink Coaster,**
1930s. Coaster is 4.25" diameter with advertising for dairy glasses "Drink Meadow Gold Milk In 'Mickey Mouse Glasses,' They Come With Our Cottage Cheese." - **$30 $60 $100**

MKY-695

MKY-696

MKY-692   **MKY-693**

☐ **MKY-694. "Mickey Mouse Beverages" Hat,**
1930s. Felt 4.75x10.25" hat with same design on both sides. Band has designated areas for mounting the six different bottle caps, two per character that were issued with brass pins. - **$95 $185 $350**

☐ **MKY-692. Mickey Mouse Soda Bottle,**
1930s. 9.5" tall. 12 oz. Glass bottle. By Ludford Fruit Products Inc. Example shown likely missing a smaller label from bottle neck. Complete - **$225 $400 $750**

☐ **MKY-693. "Rochester Healthful Beverages Minnie Mouse" Bottle,**
1930s. Heavy glass bottle is 9" tall with 2x2.5" silk screened label on front. - **$210 $335 $525**

☐ **MKY-695. Mickey Mouse Jam Jar/Bank,**
1930s. Clear glass jar with tin lid measures 2.5x2.5x6" tall. Came with paper label not shown on this example. Sides of jar have raised full figure images of Mickey, Minnie, Pluto and Horace. Lid has Mickey portrait with die-cut coin slot across his mouth.
With Label - **$100 $200 $400**
No Label - **$55 $110 $165**

☐ **MKY-696. Disney Characters Gelatin Mold,**
1930s. "Made In England" 6.5x7x3.25" deep five-sided aluminum mold with relief character images on outside of Mickey, Minnie, Pluto, Horace, Clarabelle. Top surface has different Mickey image. - **$110 $225 $335**

MKY-694

MKY-697

☐ **MKY-697. Mickey Mouse Occupational Brass Badges,**
1930s. Each is 1-5/8" tall. Series includes "Aviation Dept.", "Fire Chief" (Mickey in fire truck), "Fire Dept." (Mickey with fire hose), "U.S. Navy" (Mickey with ship in background) and "Police Dept."
Each - **$275 $550 $1100**

MKY-698

☐ **MKY-698. "Mickey Mouse Soap" Celluloid 1.25" Button,**
1930s. Reverse has union bug backstamp and name of maker Bastian Bros. with curl text "The Leo Hart Co. Rochester, N.Y." - **$1000 $3000 $5250**

MKY-699

☐ **MKY-699. "Mickey Mouse Club Safety First" Celluloid Button,**
1930s. Issuer Unknown. 7/8". - **$175 $425 $850**

MKY-700

☐ **MKY-700. "Mickey Mouse Evening Ledger Comics" Celluloid Button,**
1930s. Philadelphia newspaper issued set of 14 different characters, each 1.25" and including Minnie. Several backpaper designs. Mickey Or Minnie - **$275 $650 $1250**

MKY-701

❑ **MKY-701. "Mickey Promotes "Boston Sunday Advertiser" Comic Section Button,**
1930s. 1 1/8" litho. - **$40 $70 $145**

MKY-702

❑ **MKY-702. Mickey Mouse "RKO Keith Kiddie Klub" Celluloid Button,**
1930s. Rare button from movie theater-sponsored club. 1.25". - **$325 $775 $1600**

MKY-703

❑ **MKY-703. Mickey Mouse Australian Club Button,**
1930s. Vic Jensen, we believe a shoe retailer. The only 1930s button known to us, showing Mickey and Minnie full figure. - **$115 $225 $550**

MKY-704

❑ **MKY-704. Mickey Mouse English Biscuits Button,**
1930s. 7/8". - **$85 $165 $325**

MKY-705

❑ **MKY-705. Mickey Mouse "Good Teeth" Button,**
1930s. Kern County, California Health Dept. 1" cello. - **$225 $450 $900**

MKY-706

❑ **MKY-706. "Milk For Better Health Mickey Mouse" Celluloid Button,**
1930s. Backpaper by Pudlin Co. NYC. 1.25". - **$115 $265 $550**

MKY-707

❑ **MKY-707. "Milk For Better Health Mickey Mouse" Button,**
1930s. Button is 3.5". Worn possibly by either an adult store clerk or milk truck driver. - **$1100 $2250 $2850**

MKY-708

❑ **MKY-708. Mickey, Minnie And Tanglefoot Washington Herald Newspaper Button,**
1930s. Parisian Novelty Co. 1.25". Button from set of 10 characters used to promote comic strips appearing in this newspaper. - **$325 $650 $1350**

MKY-709

❑ **MKY-709. "Mickey Mouse Globe Trotters Map,"**
1930s. Map is 20x26.5" and was issued by various bread companies. Comes with original envelope. Borders have designated areas for pasting pictures found on back covers of Mickey Mouse Globe Trotter weekly publications. Reverse has text on different countries and directions on the "Race 'Round The World" between Mickey and Wolf. Mailer - **$35 $65 $115**
Map - **$60 $150 $325**
Each Picture - **$10 $18 $30**

MKY-710

☐ **MKY-710. Pocket Comb With Case,**
1930s. American Hard Rubber Co. 5" long
comb in two-sided fabric-covered stiff cardboard case. One side of comb has lightly
incised name "Mickey Mouse." - **$165 $275
$550**

MKY-711

☐ **MKY-711. Hair Brush Boxed,**
1930s. "Made In England" 7.25" long brush
in 2.25x7.75x1.25" deep box with hinged
lid. Box inside and out has illustrations of
Mickey and Minnie doing various types of
yard work. Grip of brush is celluloid cover
over metallic image.
Box - **$85 $165 $275**
Brush - **$85 $165 $275**

MKY-712

☐ **MKY-712. "Mickey Mouse" Boxed
Figural Soap,**
1930s. Lightfoot Schultz Co. 4.5" tall
castile soap figure in box.
Box - **$55 $110 $165**
Figure - **$40 $70 $145**

MKY-713

☐ **MKY-713. "Mickey Mouse" Boxed
Soap,**
1930s. Monogram Soap Co. 3x5.75x.75"
deep box contains three bars.
Boxed - **$100 $200 $400**

MKY-714

❏ **MKY-714. Mickey/Minnie/Pluto Toothbrush Holder,**
1930s. Marked "Made In Japan" and 2x4x3.5" tall with incised "S335." - **$135 $275 $450**

MKY-715

❏ **MKY-715. Mickey Mouse And Pluto Bisque Toothbrush Holder,**
1930s. Figure is 4.25" tall. - **$135 $275 $450**

MKY-716

MKY-717

❏ **MKY-716. Mickey And Pluto Toothbrush Holder,**
1930s. Canadian version 2.25x4.4.75" tall glazed china. Back has incised "S870." - **$150 $300 $600**

❏ **MKY-717. Mickey English China Toothbrush Holder,**
1930s. Figure is 2x2.75x4" tall and marked underneath with Disney copyright, registration number and "Foreign." Made by Maw & Sons. - **$225 $450 $675**

MKY-718

❑ **MKY-718. "Mickey Mouse/Minnie Mouse" Bisque Toothbrush Holder,** 1930s. Holder is 1.75x3.25x4.5" tall with incised "C100" on back. - **$110 $225 $350**

MKY-719

❑ **MKY-719. "Mickey Mouse" Non-Movable Arm Toothbrush Holder,** 1930s. Bisque figure is 2.5x2.5x5.25" tall. Pedestal base is marked "Mickey Mouse" on front and "Made In Japan" on back. Has toothbrush opening on left side of body just above his hand and came with string tail. - **$375 $750 $1350**

MKY-720   MKY-721

❑ **MKY-720. "Minnie Mouse" Bisque Toothbrush Holder,** 1930s. Japan. 2.5x2.75x5" tall designed with one movable arm and the other arm serves as holder. - **$150 $300 $600**

❑ **MKY-721. Figural Toothbrush Holder,** 1930s. Unauthorized Japanese for Australian market. 2x2x5.25" tall painted china. - **$85 $165 $275**

MKY-722

❑ **MKY-722. "Mickey Mouse" Bisque Toothbrush Holder,** 1930s. Japan #A567. 4.5" tall. Back bottom of base also has copyright of Percy L. Crosby rather than Disney done in error as the company also produced Skippy bisques. - **$350 $700 $1500**

MKY-723

❏ **MKY-723. Mickey Mouse Toothbrush Holder,**
1930s. English in Dean's Rag Book image style. Incised number on reverse "650611." - **$115 $225 $335**

MKY-727

MKY-724

❏ **MKY-724. Long Soap Holder By Faiencerie d'Onnaing,**
1930s. France. 4x9.25" china designed to hold two soap bars. Also issued in "short version" to hold one soap bar.
Long - **$165 $275 $500**
Short - **$135 $225 $400**

MKY-725   **MKY-726**

❏ **MKY-725. "Mickey Mouse Razor Blade,"**
1930s. British Made. 1x1-7/8" paper wrapper contains actual razor blade authorized by Disney. - **$40 $75 $125**

❏ **MKY-726. Mickey Mouse Bisque Candle Holder,**
1930s. Item is 1-1/8" tall incised with "3761." Also came as Mickey seated with one hand resting on his feet.
Each - **$40 $70 $145**

❏ **MKY-727. Boxed "Infant Mickey Mouse Baby Bottle,"**
1930s. Hot water bottle is 5x10" in 5.5x11.75x1.5" deep box. Maker is unknown. Box - **$115 $225 $450**
Bottle - **$125 $250 $500**

MKY-728

❏ **MKY-728. "Mickey Mouse" Door Knocker,**
1930s. Unmarked but English .75x1.75x3.75" tall solid brass figural knocker with his name incised across bottom. - **$115 $235 $450**

MKY-729

❏ **MKY-729. Mickey Mouse Fireplace Fork,**
1930s. Unmarked but English 17.5" tall brass fork. - **$110 $225 $425**

MKY-730

❏ **MKY-730. Mickey Mouse English Fireplace Brush,**
1930s. Brush is 7.5" tall with 2.5" figure of Mickey in brass. Reverse has incised registration number. - **$135** **$265** **$475**

MKY-732

❏ **MKY-732. Mickey Mouse Wall Lamp,**
1930s. Maker unknown. 4x11x3/8" deep embossed tin lithograph. - **$250** **$500** **$1000**

MKY-731

❏ **MKY-731. Lamp Base,**
1930s. Soreng-Manegold Co. 5" diameter enameled metal 6.75" tall to top of electrical bulb socket. - **$80** **$135** **$250**

MKY-733

❏ **MKY-733. Mickey Mouse English Electric Space Heater,**
1930s. 12x12x5" deep. Made in England. Art Deco style heater. - **$500** **$1500** **$3000**

MKY-734

MKY-735

MKY-736

MKY-737

❑ **MKY-734. Mickey And Friends English Night Light Candle,**
1930s. Price's Patent Candle Co. Ltd. Of London. 1.75" diameter by 1.25" tall wax candle in wrap-around waxed paper design. - **$30 $65 $100**

❑ **MKY-735. Mickey Mouse Ceramic Candle Night Light Holder,**
1930s. Crown Devon, England. Unmarked. 2.5x5.5x4.5 tall. - **$275 $550 $1000**

❑ **MKY-736. Mickey And Minnie Mouse Rare Pillow Cover,**
1930s. Cover is 17x18" with top panel in velvet-like finish with thick nap. Great image of Mickey serenading Minnie. - **$100 $175 $350**

❑ **MKY-737. Mickey And Minnie Mouse Child's Potty,**
1930s. R.G.K./N.Y. Germany, initials are of are importer Richard G. Krueger. 3" tall with 5-5/8" top diameter enameled metal. - **$125 $250 $550**

MKY-738

❑ **MKY-738. Mickey Mouse Rug,**
1930s. Rug is 18.5x33". - **$75 $165 $325**

MKY-739

❑ **MKY-739. Mickey's Nephew With Funny Bunnies Rug,**
1930s. 19x34" fabric with velveteen nap and fringe trim along right and left side edges. Maker unknown. - **$60 $125 $200**

MKY-740

❑ **MKY-740. "Mickey Mouse Yarn Sewing Set,"**
1930s. Marks Brothers. 6.5x10.5x1.25" deep box contains complete set of six cards. Sewing cards are each 4x6.25". Boxed - **$150 $300 $600**

MKY-741

❑ **MKY-741. "Mickey Mouse" English Sweeper Toy,**
1930s. Wells-London. 4x6x1.5" tall tin lithograph with wood wheels. Top is three panels of scenes involving Mickey, Minnie, their nephews, semi-long billed Donald and Pluto, all involving a broom or the sweeper itself. Pictured example is missing the wood push rod and the metal bracket that held it. Complete - **$165 $325 $675**

MKY-742

❑ **MKY-742. English Whisk Brush,**
1930s. Brush is 3.5" tall painted white metal three-dimensional Mickey Mouse figure handle attached atop the brush for total height of 7.5". Marked registration number on rear leg is "75050." Figure is same image as Dean's used for rag dolls and depicts five fingers . Rear has a wire spring tail. - **$165 $325 $650**

MKY-745

❑ **MKY-745. Tea Towel,**
1930s. Linen is 13.25x20.25" with single 3x3" die-cut fabric applique of Mickey leisurely seated at business desk to greet Minnie and Clarabelle. - **$35 $65 $135**

MKY-743

❑ **MKY-743. "Mickey Mouse" Sweeper,**
1930s. Ohio Art. 4x6x2" tall tin litho with wood side panels and wood wheels. Came with red wood rod handle. - **$150 $300 $600**

MKY-744

❑ **MKY-744. Mickey Mouse Bridge Table Cover,**
1930s. Maker unknown. 27x29" with small text "Bridge Lesson Broadcast." - **$50 $100 $150**

MKY-746

❏ **MKY-746. "Mickey Mouse Toy Chest And Children's Seat" Variety With Fabric-Covered Lid,**
1930s. Odora Co. 12.5x26.5x14.5" tall. Has wood frame with cardboard side panels, pair of metal carrying handles. Top is variety that has fabric covering and thin layer of padding over a wood board with cardboard panel on interior. Top depicts Mickey and Minnie holding a slate board with image of Pluto. - **$165 $335 $650**

MKY-747

❏ **MKY-747. "Mickey Mouse Toy Chest And Children's Seat" Variety With Cardboard Lid,**
1930s. Odora Co. 12.5x26.5x14.5" tall. This version has lid comprised of thick cardboard rather than fabric-covered wood. - **$135 $275 $550**

MKY-748

❏ **MKY-748. Walt Disney Character Wallpaper,**
1930s. Section measures 9.75x19.25". Similar Size - **$100 $200 $400**

MKY-749

❏ **MKY-749. "Mickey Mouse" Wash Tub,**
1930s. Ohio Art. 5.25" diameter by 2.25" deep lithographed tin. - **$85 $165 $325**

MKY-750

❑ **MKY-750. "Mickey Mouse Washer,"**
1930s. Ohio Art Co. Child's tin lithographed toy washer is 5" diameter by 7.5"
tall. - **$275** **$550** **$1100**

MKY-751

❑ **MKY-751. "Mickey Mouse"**
Sprinkling Can,
1930s. Ohio Art. 4x8x6" tall lithographed
tin. - **$200** **$400** **$800**

MKY-752

❑ **MKY-752. Mickey Mouse Bracelet,**
1930s. Unmarked, but authorized brass
with image under domed glass. - **$75**
$125 **$225**

MKY-753

❑ **MKY-753. Mickey Mouse Italian Lapel**
Stud,
1930s. F.M. Lorioli Castelli/Milano. 3/4"
enamel on brass lapel stud with Mickey
playing a concertina. - **$60** **$125** **$200**

MKY-754

❑ **MKY-754. Mickey Mouse Enamel On**
Gold Two-Sided Charm,
1930s. Charm is 7/8" tall. - **$200** **$400**
$800

MKY-755

❏ **MKY-755. Mickey And Minnie Mouse English Cinema Club Badge,** 1930s. 3/4x1" silvered brass badge for Kiddies 5 Star Club. - **$30 $60 $100**

MKY-758

❏ **MKY-758. Mickey Mouse Die-cut Tin Lithographed Mechanical Novelty Pin,** 1930s. Unmarked 1.5x2.25" with die-cut arm, rubber band and string which allows Mickey to remove his hat. - **$150 $300 $600**

MKY-756

❏ **MKY-756. Mickey Mouse European Enamel Pin,** 1930s. 1 1/8" tall. Features long nose and five fingered Mickey playing a banjo. - **$55 $110 $165**

MKY-759

MKY-757

❏ **MKY-757. "Mickey Mouse Club" Die-cut English Lapel Stud,** 1930s. Stud is 1.5" tall black enamel on silvered brass. - **$70 $110 $225**

MKY-760

❏ **MKY-759. Mickey With Pluto Painted Composition Wood Pin,**
1930s. Pin is 1.5". - **$90 $185 $325**

❏ **MKY-760. Mickey Mouse With Umbrella Enamel On Brass Pin,**
1930s. No markings. 7/8" tall. - **$75 $125 $225**

MKY-761

❏ **MKY-761. "Mickey Mouse" Boxed Ring,**
1930s. Small 1x1x1" box contains adjustable brass ring with enamel paint. Reverse has small "WD" copyright.
Box - **$115 $235 $450**
Ring - **$115 $235 $450**

MKY-762

❏ **MKY-762. Mickey And Minnie Celluloid Figures Bar Pin,**
1930s. English. .75" tall celluloid figures on bar pin. - **$25 $50 $75**

MKY-763

❏ **MKY-763. Mickey Mouse Sheet Music English Enamel And Brass Pin,**
1930s. 1.5" tall. Pin is titled "The Wedding of Mr. Mickey Mouse." - **$70 $110 $225**

MKY-764   **MKY-765**

❏ **MKY-764. Mickey Mouse China Perfume Bottle,**
1930s. Container is 2"deep, 4" tall and 3.5" in diameter. No Disney markings and piece is marked "Made In Japan." - **$110 $225 $335**

❏ **MKY-765. Mickey Mouse Figural Glass Perfume Bottle,**
1930s. Made In France. Bottle is 2x2x5.25" tall with removable head. Has metal spring legs and long fabric tail. - **$300 $600 $1200**

MKY-766

❏ **MKY-766. "Minnie Mouse" Patriot China Bowl,**
1930s. Bowl is 6" in diameter by 1.5" deep and marked underneath with company name. - **$55 $110 $165**

MKY-767

❏ **MKY-767. Mickey & Minnie Mouse Child's Warming Dish,**
1930s. Marked on underside "Industria Argentina." 8" diameter by 2" deep. The ceramic bowl is mounted inside of a stainless steel container. Metal dish is complete with pair of finger loops and spout has screw cap. - **$80 $135 $250**

MKY-768

❏ **MKY-768. Mickey Cake Plates By Faiencerie d'Onnaing China Co. Of France,**
1930s. Serving plate is 11" and individual plates are 7.25". From a set of fifteen. Pictorial Mickey company trademark on reverse. Serving plate is captioned "Hop-La!" while other plates have "Walt Disney" and plate number. Most plates picture a circus theme. Serving Plate - **$115 $235 $450**
Numbered Plates Each - **$40 $70 $145**

MKY-771

MKY-769

❑ **MKY-769. Pitcher And Wash Basin
By Faiencerie d'Onnaing,**
1930s. France. 9.75" tall pitcher and 4.25"
tall by 13" diameter wash basin. About six
sets are known including one in the Disney
archives which years ago curator Dave
Smith rescued from a movie set at the
Disney Studio where it was about to be
smashed as a meaningless movie prop.
Pitcher - **$550 $1650 $3000**
Basin - **$550 $1650 $3000**

❑ **MKY-771. Mickey And Friends
Chinaware,**
1930s. Wadeheath of England. 6x6"
octagonal plate and 1.75" tall tea cup pic-
turing Mickey, 1.75" tea cup picturing
Donald Duck, plus 1.25" tall open sugar
bowl picturing "Baby Seal."
Plate - **$35 $65 $115**
Each Cup - **$25 $40 $75**
Sugar - **$15 $30 $60**

MKY-770

❑ **MKY-770. Miniature Figural Teapot
And Pitcher,**
1930s. Unmarked but Japanese pair of
glazed ceramics. The teapot is 2x3.5x3"
tall, pitcher is 2.25" tall. Mickey's head
serves as the lid of the teapot and is
removable while his right arm serves as
the spout. Teapot - **$85 $165 $275**
Pitcher - **$55 $110 $165**

MKY-772

❑ **MKY-772. Mickey And Minnie Glazed
Ceramic Condiment Set,**
1930s. Made in Japan. 4.5x4.5" tray holds
3.5" tall figures and 2" tall container with lid
designed as cheese wheel. Example pictured missing generic ceramic condiment
spoon. - **$600 $1100 $2000**

MKY-773

❏ **MKY-773. Mickey And Minnie Mouse China Condiment Set,**
1930s. English or German. 2.5x4.5x3.75"
tall marked with registration number on
underside "750611" plus second number of
"11129." - **$650 $1250 $2500**

MKY-774

❏ **MKY-774. Mickey Mouse German China Condiment Set,**
1930s. Marked on underside "Deutchland."
3x4x3.75" tall. - **$250 $500 $1000**

MKY-775

❏ **MKY-775. Large Mickey/Minnie Foreign Tin,**
1930s. Lithographed tin with hinged lid
measures 8.25x10x7"tall. Made in Belgium
or France. - **$350 $650 $1300**

MKY-776

MKY-778

❑ **MKY-776. Mickey Mouse French Tin,** 1930s. Tin is 7" diameter by 1.75" deep with removable lid. Six different poses of Mickey and Minnie around sides. - **$115 $225 $335**

❑ **MKY-778. Mickey Mouse Tin,** 1930s. France. 5.5x6x2" deep hexagonal-shaped with hinged lid. Lid illustration of Mickey walking with nephew, side illustrations depict Mickey in different sports. - **$135 $265 $550**

MKY-777

MKY-779

❑ **MKY-777. Mickey Mouse French Tin,** 1930s. Tin is 7" in diameter and 1.75" deep. Sides feature Pluto running. - **$115 $225 $335**

❑ **MKY-779. Mickey Mouse Tin,** 1930s. Tin is 6.5" diameter by 2.25" deep with removable lid. Lid features Mickey, Minnie, Donald, Pluto, and Clarabell. - **$150 $300 $600**

MKY-780

❏ **MKY-780. Mickey Mouse China Jam Jar,**
1930s. Maws. 4.5" tall Mickey figure is attached to jar 3.75" tall with 2.75" diameter. Marked underneath with registration number and "By Special Permission Walt Disney Enterprises." Photo example missing lid. - **$225 $450 $800**

MKY-782

❏ **MKY-782. Mickey Mouse Mop Tin,**
1930s. Germany. 5x9.25x3.5" deep. No Disney markings. Photo example missing lid. Complete - **$135 $265 $425**

MKY-781

❏ **MKY-781. Minnie English Jam Jar,**
1930s. "Imex." 4.25" tall china figure and adjoining 3.75" tall jar for preserves. Pictured example underside has Disney markings and registration number. Photo example without lid. - **$200 $350 $700**

MKY-783

❏ **MKY-783. Mickey Mouse Head Ceramic Trinket Box,**
1930s. Japan, likely unauthorized. 3.5x3.5x2.5" tall. - **$115 $250 $400**

MKY-784

□ **MKY-784. "Minnie Mouse" Patriot China Mug,**
1930s. Mug is 3" with text on underside including company name. - **$60 $125 $200**

MKY-785

□ **MKY-785. Mickey/Minnie Mouse Double-Sided French Ceramic Egg Cup,**
1930s. Faiencerie d'Onnaing. 1.75" diameter by 2-1/8" tall with recessed area on both top and bottom so either side could be used to hold egg. - **$135 $235 $375**

MKY-786

□ **MKY-786. Mickey And Minnie French Egg Cup,**
1930s. "Faiencerie d'Onnaing Co. Of France." 2" top diameter by 2.25" tall glazed ceramic. - **$135 $235 $375**

MKY-787

□ **MKY-787. Mickey Mouse Figural Egg Cup,**
1930s. Unmarked. 2.75" tall painted and glazed ceramic. Unusual full figure image depicting Mickey with his hands on hips, tail wraps around to the back. - **$75 $125 $225**

MKY-788

□ **MKY-788. Mickey, Minnie, And Donald Baby's English Bowl,**
1930s. Wadeheath. 6.75" diameter by 1.5" deep. - **$50 $100 $175**

MKY-789

MKY-791

❑ MKY-789. Child's Italian Dish Set Boxed,

1930s. "Laveno/Societa Ceramica/Italiana." 12.5x12.5x3.25" deep boxed complete set of eighteen glazed chinaware pieces comprised of soup tureen with lid, two serving dishes, three serving platters, six plates, six shallow soup bowls. Tallest is 3" tureen, flat pieces are 4" diameter or less. A total of seven different images depict Mickey, Minnie, occasional Pluto. Box pictures total of four different Mickey and Minnie dining activities.
Box - **$225 $425 $650**
China Set - **$350 $800 $1500**

❑ MKY-791. Italian Ceramic Disney Miniature Tea Set,

1930s. Laveno/Societa Ceramica/Italiano. Total of 28 pieces including four 1.25" tall teacups and four 2.75" diameter saucers (probably originally from set of six), six 3.25" diameter plates, six 3.25" diameter soup plates, 3.75" diameter round cake or serving plate, 3.5" long oval platter, 2.25" top diameter bowl and 3-1/8" top diameter either soup tureen or sugar bowl with lid, all about 1" tall. - **$550 $1100 $1800**

MKY-790

❑ MKY-790. Candy Dish,

1930s. "Made In Japan" 5.75" diameter by 1" deep china dish with attached arc wood handle rising 5" at center. - **$85 $165 $275**

MKY-792

☐ **MKY-792. "Mickey Mouse Beetleware" Boxed Child's Dish Set,**
1930s. Bryant Electric Co. Of Bridgeport, Connecticut. 6x6x3.5" deep box contains complete three-piece hard plastic set consisting of 2.75" tall mug, 5.25" diameter bowl and 6" diameter child's feeding dish.
Box - **$100 $200 $400**
Each Piece - **$30 $60 $90**

MKY-795

☐ **MKY-795. Mickey Mouse Fleeing Tiger China Mug,**
1930s. Unmarked but similar to Paragon design. 3.75" tall. - **$75 $150 $300**

MKY-793

☐ **MKY-793. "Mickey Mouse" Glass,**
1930s. Tumbler is 4.25" tall clear depicting him walking and waving above his name. Possible dairy glass although differing in size and design from known sets. - **$45 $80 $135**

MKY-796

☐ **MKY-796. "Mickey Mouse and Pluto" English China Mug,**
1930s. Royal Paragon. 2.75" tall. - **$600 $1200 $1800**

MKY-794

☐ **MKY-794. Mickey Cute Unauthorized Mug,**
1930s. "Made In Japan" 2.75" tall glazed ceramic. - **$30 $65 $100**

MKY-797

☐ **MKY-797. Mickey/Minnie Mouse Napkin Rings,**
1930s. Pair of 2" diameter thick celluloid napkin rings each has attached hollow celluloid figure on front 2.25" tall. Marked "Made In England." Each - **$55 $110 $165**

MKY-798

❑ **MKY-798. Mickey Mouse Catalin Plastic Napkin Ring,**
1930s. 2.5x3x.5" thick with Mickey portrait decal on front. - **$60** **$125** **$200**

MKY-799

❑ **MKY-799. Figural Pitcher,**
1930s. "Made In Japan" 3.5x4.5x4.5" tall painted and glazed ceramic likeness of plump Mickey with curved tail as the handle and open mouth pouring spout. No Disney markings. - **$30** **$60** **$90**

❑ **MKY-800. Mickey Mouse Paragon China "Baby's Plate,"**
1930s. Paragon. 6.5x8.5x2" deep. Depicts scene of Mickey and Pluto hunting a moose. - **$550** **$1100** **$2200**

MKY-801

❑ **MKY-801. "Mickey Mouse" Rare English Serving Tray,**
c. 1930s. St. Dunstan's Veterans Hospital, London. 12.5x18.25x1.5" deep celluloid over wood tray with woven wicker edge. Eight classic black and white images of Mickey, all with titles. In between these images are additional illustrations of him with Kewpie-like baby. Mickey is shown feeding, washing, snuggling and playing with baby. - **$325** **$650** **$1300**

MKY-800

MKY-802

❏ **MKY-802. "Mickey Mouse/Pluto The Pup" Patriot China Plate,**
1930s. Patriot China. 7" diameter plate marked on reverse "Patriot China." - **$75 $135 $225**

MKY-803

❏ **MKY-803. Mickey & Minnie English China "Baby's Plate,"**
1930s. Royal Paragon China . Oval-shaped 5.75x8.25x1.25" deep glazed china plate marked underneath "Mickey Mouse Series." - **$425 $850 $1500**

MKY-804

❏ **MKY-804. "Mickey and Minnie Mouse" English China Sandwich Plate,**
1930s. Royal Paragon. 8.5" square. - **$650 $1250 $2000**

MKY-805

❏ **MKY-805. "Mickey Mouse" Square Format Plate,**
1930s. Patriot China Co. 6.25x6.25" plate with company name in gold on reverse. Image of Mickey is 2.5" tall. - **$60 $110 $225**

MKY-806

❏ **MKY-806. "Minnie Mouse" Square Format Plate,**
1930s. Patriot China Co. 6.25x6.25" plate with company name in gold on reverse. Image of Minnie is 3" tall. - **$50 $100 $200**

MKY-807

❏ **MKY-807. Mickey Mouse Boxing Theme China Plate,**
1930s. Australian. 6.25" diameter. - **$115 $265 $500**

MKY-808

❏ **MKY-808. China Mickey & Minnie "Happy Days" Plate,**
1930s. English by Paragon. 7" diameter. - **$150 $275 $550**

MKY-809

❏ **MKY-809. "Mickey Mouse/ Pluto" Ceramic Plate,**
1930s. Wade. English by Wadeheath Ware. 6" octagonal. - **$55 $110 $165**

MKY-810

MKY-811

❏ **MKY-810. Mickey Mouse Drummer China Shaker,**
1930s. Germany. 2x2x3.5". "6595" incised on back. - **$110 $215 $325**

❏ **MKY-811. Mickey Mouse China Salt & Pepper Set,**
1930s. Germany. Each 2.25" tall. #7733. - **$140 $280 $400**

MKY-812

❑ **MKY-812. Mickey And Minnie Ceramic Salt Shakers,**
1930s. Made in Japan. 3" tall. Set - **$160 $330 $500**

MKY-813

❑ **MKY-813. Mickey Mouse 4 Burner Gas Stove Enameled Metal Cover,**
1930s. Maker Unknown. 17x21x.5" deep burner cover for the top of an actual stove. - **$75 $150 $300**

MKY-815

❑ **MKY-815. "Mickey And Minnie Mouse Toy Tea Set,"**
1930s. Geo. Borgfeldt Corp. 9.25x10.75x2.75" deep box with Mickey and Minnie images holds 15-piece china tea set. The cups, saucers and plates all have matching images - Minnie on fence, Mickey with balloons, Mickey playing hockey and Mickey with serving tray. Tray design also appears on creamer, sugar and teapot. Sugar and teapot have lids.
Box only - **$200 $400 $600**
Set only - **$200 $400 $800**

MKY-814

❑ **MKY-814. Mickey Mouse Boxed China Tea Set,**
1930s. 10x12.5x3" deep original but generic box containing 11 piece china set. - **$250 $500 $1000**

MKY-816

MKY-817

☐ **MKY-816. Near-Complete Japanese Toy Tea Set,**
1930s. "Made In Japan" 10.5x12.5x3" deep boxed with 21 original chinaware pieces comprised of teapot with lid, sugar bowl with lid, creamer, six cups, six saucers, six plates. Tallest piece is 3.5" teapot and each plate is 4.5" diameter, slightly larger than the saucers. Pictured in total are six different images of Mickey and Minnie. Box is original but generic pattern design. Complete Boxed - **$300 $600 $900**

☐ **MKY-817. Mickey/Minnie Mouse And Donald Duck Ceramic Teapot,**
1930s. England. Unmarked but believed to be by Wade. 3.5" tall. - **$60 $110 $165**

MKY-818

☐ **MKY-818. Mickey Mouse Scarce Variety Trivet,**
1930s. Trivet is 5.25" diameter by 2" tall scarce version in solid cast brass, usually found in cast iron. Cut-out design on top features large full figure image of Mickey surrounded by accent rays. Stands on three feet. Brass - **$110 $165 $300** Iron - **$90 $140 $265**

MKY-819

☐ **MKY-819. Mickey And Minnie Mouse Tin Serving Tray,**
1930s. English. Happynak series No. 65. 3.5x6". - **$40 $75 $125**

MKY-820

☐ **MKY-820. "Mickey Mouse Silverplate" Boxed Utensil Set,**
1930s. International Silver Co. 4x8.5x1" deep box contains knife, fork and spoon ranging in size from 5.5" to 7.25". All have incised Mickey image and Mickey Mouse name. Box - **$60 $125 $225** Each Utensil - **$18 $35 $55**

MKY-821

MKY-821. "Mickey Mouse" Fork,
1930s. "Winthrop Silver Plate" 5.75" tall
with design on handle of incised image of
Mickey, his raised name and raised flower
designs. - **$20 $35 $55**

MKY-822

**MKY-822. Mickey And Minnie Knife
Rest,**
1930s. Unmarked but believed German
3.25x1.75" tall glazed ceramic figural of
Mickey at one end holding a flower and
Minnie at opposite end with hands
clenched. - **$85 $165 $275**

MKY-823

**MKY-823. Mickey Mouse Silverware
Caddy,**
1930s. William Rogers & Son. Two-piece
unit comprised of thick layered painted
cardboard while the base has wood
wheels. 2x5.5x5.25" tall. - **$135 $265
$475**

MKY-824

**MKY-824. Mickey Figure With Egg
Timer,**
1930s. "Mickey Mouse/Foreign"
1.75x3x3.5" tall china figure with attached
sand-filled glass timer that rotates manually. - **$225 $425 $700**

MKY-825

**MKY-825. Mickey Mouse China Egg
Timer,**
1930s. 2.75" tall. Marked "Germany." -
$200 $400 $600

MKY-826

❑ **MKY-826. German Toothpick Holder,**
1930s. Figurine is 1.25x1.75x2.5" tall china. Underside has registration number.
- **$85 $165 $275**

MKY-827

❑ **MKY-827. "Mickey Mouse Treasure Chest" Bank,**
1930s. Japan. 2x3x2.5" tin litho. - **$200 $425 $850**

MKY-828

❑ **MKY-828. Mickey Mouse "Book" Bank With Key,**
1930s. Zell Products. 3x4.25x1" thick brass bank formed in image of book overlaid on covers by embossed oilcloth fabric.
- **$85 $160 $240**

MKY-829

MKY-830

❑ **MKY-829. "Mickey Mouse" Bee Hive Tin Bank,**
1930s. German by "Elbezet." 2.5" diameter by 3" tall lithographed tin. - **$125 $275 $550**

❑ **MKY-830. Mickey And Minnie Mouse Ceramic Banks,**
1930s. Faiencerie d'Onnaing. French. Each 6" tall. Underside of Minnie has company's mark while underside of Mickey has "Walt Disney" name. Mickey - **$200 $375 $650**
Minnie - **$175 $350 $575**

MKY-831

❏ **MKY-831. Mickey Mouse Atop Drum Metal Bank,**
1930s. Maker unknown, likely French. 4.75" tall. - **$165 $325 $600**

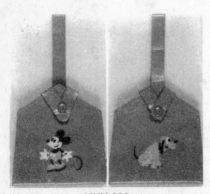

MKY-832

❏ **MKY-832. Mickey Mouse Child's Purse,**
1930s. To the tip of the handle, purse is 4.25x7.5". Leatherette with metal snap closure. - **$50 $100 $200**

MKY-833

❏ **MKY-833. Mickey Mouse Cast Iron French Bank,**
1930s. Maker unknown. 4x6.5x9" tall. Original iron examples are scarce and boldly marked "Depose" on reverse. There are much more common cast aluminum versions of various quality, perhaps made by vocational school students in the 1930s.
Cast Iron - **$1000 $2500 $4500**
Aluminum - **$500 $1000 $2000**

MKY-834

❑ **MKY-834. Mickey And Minnie Metal Change Purse,**
1930s. Enamel on silvered brass purse is 2.25x2.25". - **$200 $400 $800**

MKY-835

❑ **MKY-835. Mickey And Minnie Wallet,**
1930s. Japan. 3x4" leather. Front has coin compartment with snap flap and wallet has attached snap closure. Reverse has clear plastic cover over owner's card. - **$75 $150 $250**

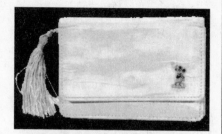

MKY-836

❑ **MKY-836. Mickey Mouse Makeup Kit,**
1930s. 4x3" tall with snap button, metal image of Mickey, and tassel. - **$70 $110 $225**

MKY-837

❑ **MKY-837. Mickey Mouse Bell,**
1930s. Three-dimensional painted cast metal figure of Mickey serving as handle attached to silvered metal bell. Mickey figure is 3" tall, total height is 4.75" with 2.5" diameter opening on bell bottom. Mickey is depicted in early 1930s English style featuring him with teeth and five fingers. A 2" coiled spring tail is on reverse. - **$165 $325 $650**

MKY-838

❏ **MKY-838. "Mickey/Minnie Mouse" Horn,**
1930s. Marks Brothers Co. 6.75" tall with paper label and wood mouthpiece. - **$75 $150 $300**

MKY-839

❏ **MKY-839. Mickey Mouse Drum,**
1930s. Ohio Art Co. 3.5" tall by 7" diameter tin litho. - **$115 $250 $500**

MKY-840

❏ **MKY-840. Mickey Mouse Drum,**
1930s. Ohio Art Co. 4.25" tall by 9" diameter tin litho. - **$135 $265 $575**

MKY-842

❏ **MKY-842. "Mickey Mouse Drum Corps" Tin Drum,**
1930s. J. Chein & Co. 13" diameter by 5.5" deep. - **$800 $1750 $3000**

MKY-841

❏ **MKY-841. Mickey Mouse Drum,**
1930s. Ohio Art Co. 4.25" tall by 9" diameter tin litho. - **$110 $235 $475**

MKY-843

❑ MKY-843. Czech Harmonica,
1930s. "Made In Czechoslovakia" .75x1x4" long instrument formed by wood center reed bar between tin plate top and bottom. Top has incised name "Mickey Mouse Band" with copyright. - **$135 $265 $550**

MKY-844

❑ MKY-844. Box For Large "Mickey Mouse Drum,"
1930s. Box says Nifty, but held 13" diameter drum marked J. Chein & Co. 13.25x13.5x5.5" deep box for "No. 171 Drum." - **$300 $600 $1200**

MKY-845

❑ MKY-845. Mickey Mouse Child's Toy Saxophone,
1930s. Czechoslovakia by "Haro." Imported by Borgfeldt. 16" long tin. Small "W.D." copyright. - **$165 $325 $650**

MKY-846

❑ MKY-846. Mickey Mouse Flute,
1930s. "S.F.C./Made In Italy." 9.75" long lithographed tin. - **$125 $250 $500**

MKY-847

❑ MKY-847. "Mickey Mouse" Wood Piano,
1930s. Made in Japan with copyright "Walt Disney Enterprises, Ltd." 9x11x5.25" tall. - **$250 $500 $900**

MKY-848

☐ **MKY-848. "Mickey Mouse Safe-Toy Music Box" For Projector,**
1930s. English by Ensign. 3.5" diameter by 2" deep tin with cardboard bottom panel, wrap-around paper label for use with Safe-Toy projector. - **$55 $110 $165**

MKY-849

☐ **MKY-849. "Mickey Mouse" Drum,**
1930s. Ohio Art. 6" diameter by 3.75" deep lithographed tin. Has string cross cord around body and stiff paper drumhead with thin mesh fabric covering. - **$165 $335 $650**

MKY-850

☐ **MKY-850. "Mickey Mouse Piano With Dancing Figures,"**
1930s. Marks Bros., Boston. Wood with cardboard figures that dance as keys are struck. Toy is 4.75x9.5x10.25" tall. Box is 5.5x9.75x10.75" tall.
Box - **$400 $800 $1600**
Toy - **$600 $1200 $2400**

MKY-851

MKY-853

❑ **MKY-851. Mickey English Camera Ad Folder,**
1930s. Ensign Ltd. Closed 4.25x5.25" fold-out opens to total size of 8.5x10.5". - **$35 $65 $115**

❑ **MKY-853. Mickey Mouse Movie Club Pennant,**
1930s. 4x9" felt pennant attached to wood rod. An early movie club premium. - **$115 $225 $350**

MKY-854

MKY-852

❑ **MKY-852. "Mickey Mouse Flexible Flyer" Sled Promo Folder,**
1930s. S.L. Allen & Co. Inc. 3.25x6.25" paper opening to 6.25x6.5". - **$115 $225 $450**

❑ **MKY-854. "Mickey Mouse/Thom McAn" Premium Flip Book,**
1930s. Book is 2.25x3" and features "Mickey Takes Minnie For A Ride" on one side and "The Boy In The Thom McAn's Wins" on the other. - **$115 $225 $450**

MKY-855

☐ **MKY-855. "Mickey Mouse Magic Slate,"**
1930s. 2.5x4". Issued as a premium with black and white label on reverse that reads "Compliments Of Mickey Mouse In Gold's Toyland." - **$70 $125 $200**

MKY-856

☐ **MKY-856. Comic Club Birthday Card With Mickey Mouse And Others,**
1930s. Washington Times Adventure Club. 4.25x5.5" stiff paper. Includes illustrations of Mickey Mouse, Popeye, Smitty, Little Annie Rooney and portrait believed to be Kit Carson. - **$30 $60 $100**

MKY-857

☐ **MKY-857. Mickey Premium Picture,**
1930s. "Congoleum Gold Seal Rugs." 9x12" stiff paper image of Mickey signing his name on wall within simulated wood frame. Text includes his name as spelled in various countries. - **$25 $45 $85**

MKY-858

☐ **MKY-858. Congoleum Gold Seal Rug Store Sign Featuring Minnie Mouse,**
1930s. 19.5" diameter die-cut cardboard sign noting 3 store prizes. - **$225 $450 $800**

MKY-859

☐ **MKY-859. Mickey Mouse "Durkee's" Die-cut Sign,**
1930s. San Francisco. 3.5x6" stiff cardboard. - **$40 $75 $150**

MKY-860

❏ **MKY-860. "Toytown" Sign With Mickey And Donald,**
1930s. Possibly Macy's. 7x11" two-sided sign on card stock. - **$125 $265 $425**

MKY-861

❏ **MKY-861. Mickey Mouse "Hallmark" Salesman's Announcement Card,**
1930s. Hallmark. 3.75x5" stiff paper with starched fabric flag attached sent by salesmen to their clientele to announce their upcoming arrival. - **$85 $165 $275**

MKY-862

❏ **MKY-862. "Mickey Mouse Pencil Box" Store Sign,**
1930s. Stiff cardboard sign measuring 5.5x7". - **$40 $75 $145** Smaller 3.5x5.5" size - **$30 $45 $85**

MKY-863

❏ **MKY-863. "Mickey Mouse Pencil Boxes" Ad Card,**
1930s. Dixon. 4x5.25" die-cut cardboard card. - **$75 $150 $250**

MKY-864

❏ **MKY-864. "Mickey Mouse To Color And Draw Big Little Set,"**
1930s. Box is 3.75x5.25x1.5" deep and contains 320 two-sided picture pages to be colored. - **$150 $300 $600**

MKY-865

MKY-867

MKY-868

□ **MKY-865. "The Princess Elizabeth Gift Book" With Disney Color Plates,** 1930s. Hodder & Stoughton of Great Britain 7.5x10" hardcover. 224 pages. Includes superb pair of double page multi-character illustrations. - **$115 $235 $450**

MKY-866

□ **MKY-866. "Mickey Mouse Bedtime Stories" English Hardcover,** 1930s. William Collins Sons & Co. Ltd. 7x9.5" with 96 stiff paper pages. - **$115 $225 $400**

□ **MKY-867. "Mickey Mouse Bedtime Stories" English Softcover,** 1930s. Sunshine Press. 7.25x9.5" with 96 pages. - **$100 $175 $350**

□ **MKY-868. "Micky Maus" Promotional Advertising Flag For Magazines,** 1930s. Switzerland by Bollmann. 8.5x12" two-sided stiff paper. - **$60 $115 $175**

MKY-869

☐ **MKY-869. "Mickey Mouse On Tour" Book,**
1930s. English by Birn Brothers Ltd. 7x9.25" with 28 pages. - **$125 $250 $550**

MKY-870

☐ **MKY-870. "The Mickey Mouse Fun ABC" Book,**
1930s. English by London And Glascow. 7x9.25" with 28 pages. - **$125 $250 $550**

MKY-871

☐ **MKY-871. "Mickey Mouse Stories" Book,**
1930s. English by Dean & Son Ltd. 6x8.5" with 32 pages. - **$175 $375 $750**

MKY-872

☐ **MKY-872. "Mickey Mouse School Bag,"**
1930s. 11x11" velveteen-covered canvas. Maker is unknown. - **$90 $165 $275**

MKY-873

□ MKY-874. Band Leader Mickey Mouse Doll,
1930s. Knickerbocker. 25" tall. Stuffed cloth body with felt ears, felt jacket with brass buttons and braid accents, oilcloth belt with brass snap, plush covered hat with braid chin strap, composition feet, whiskers. - **$1150 $2250 $4500**

MKY-875

□ MKY-873. Boxed "Minnie Mouse Costume,"
1930s. Wornova Play Clothes, N.Y. Five-piece outfit in original 11x12x4" deep box.
Box - **$75 $125 $225**
Costume - **$85 $165 $275**

□ MKY-875. Musical Band Leader Mickey Mouse Doll,
1930s. Knickerbocker. 12" tall. Stuffed cloth body with felt ears, felt jacket with brass buttons and braid accents, oilcloth belt with brass snap, plush covered hat with braid chin strap, wood baton, composition feet, whiskers. Has inner music mechanism. - **$3250 $6250 $12500**

MKY-874

MKY-876

❏ **MKY-876. Cowboy Mickey Mouse 16"
Tall Doll,**
1930s. Knickerbocker. Stuffed cloth body
with felt ears, suede leather/ wool chaps with
metal studs, composition feet, rubber tail,
string whiskers, hat, neck scarf and metal
guns. Doll - **$1000 $2000 $4250**
Tag - **$50 $100 $200**

❏ **MKY-878. Cowboy Mickey Mouse
Doll,**
1930s. Knickerbocker. 5x7.5x12" tall.
Stuffed cloth body with felt ears, suede
leather/wool chaps with metal studs, vest,
composition feet, rubber tail, string
whiskers, hat, neck scarf and metal guns.
Photo example missing parts of outfit.-
$750 $1500 $3000

MKY-877

❏ **MKY-877. Minnie Mouse As Cowgirl
Doll,**
1930s. Knickerbocker. 16.5" tall. Stuffed
fabric body, felt ears, oilcloth eyes, separate string whiskers and painted composition shoes. Outfit consists of removable felt
hat, neckerchief, leatherette skirt and wrist
cuffs accented by metal studs. Underside
of each foot has Knickerbocker label that
includes small Mickey image. - **$900
$1800 $4000**

MKY-879

❏ **MKY-879. Mickey Mouse Cowboy
Jointed Composition Doll,**
1930s. Knickerbocker. 10" tall. - **$1300
$2650 $5500**

MKY-878

MKY-880

❑ **MKY-880. "Mickey Mouse Nursery Set, "** 1930s. Lines Bros. Ltd. England. 9.75x11.75x2.5" deep box contains five pieces of dollhouse furniture: wardrobe, bed, table, rocker and high chair.
Box - **$60 $125 $250**
Set of five - **$300 $600 $1200**

MKY-881

❑ **MKY-881. Mickey Mouse English Doll Bed,**
1930s. Wood-framed bed 10.5x20.5x10" tall. Has 4.5x5" Mickey decal on both headboard and footboard. Fabric covering features non-Disney characters. - **$165 $335 $550**

MKY-882

❑ **MKY-882. Mickey and Minnie Mouse English Doll Bed,**
1930s. 10.5x20x12" tall wood bed with fabric covering. - **$165 $335 $550**

MKY-883

❑ **MKY-883. Knickerbocker Mickey Mouse Stuffed Doll,**
1930s. Stuffed fabric doll 5x6.5x11.5" tall with felt ears, die-cut oilcloth eyes, string whiskers, four plastic buttons and gray rubber tail. Version with felt-covered cardboard feet rather than composition. - **$300 $600 $1200**

MKY-884

❏ **MKY-884. Mickey Mouse Doll,**
1930s. Doll is 4x7x11.5" tall with satin-like covered body, felt ears, hands and shoes and cloth pants with plastic buttons. Has string whiskers, rubber tail and painted facial features. - **$325 $650 $1300**

MKY-885

❏ **MKY-885. Unusual Mickey Mouse Doll,**
1930s. 6x8.5x15" tall with composition head and arms, stuffed fabric body. Probably unauthorized. - **$90 $175 $350**

MKY-886

❏ **MKY-886. Large Composition Mickey Mouse Doll,**
1930s. Knickerbocker. 4x5x9.25" tall painted composition with movable arms and head. - **$500 $1000 $2000**

MKY-887

❏ **MKY-887. Mickey Homemade Doll From Pattern,**
1930s. Large 7x11x18" tall stuffed fabric doll produced from a McCall's pattern. - **$75 $165 $335**

MKY-888

❏ **MKY-888. Mickey Mouse Medium Size Felt/Velveteen Doll,**
1930s. English by Deans Rag Book. 8" tall with wire inserts for posing. Registration number "730811" on neck. - **$225 $450 $750**

MKY-889

❏ **MKY-889. Mickey Mouse Jazzer Boxed Doll,**
1930s. Dean's Rag Book Company Ltd. 6" tall. Has wire attachment to reverse of doll and is designed to be mounted to a record player so that when the record is revolving the figure will dance. Includes 3x3.5" instruction sheet. - **$1100 $2200 $3300**

MKY-891

❏ **MKY-891. Mickey Mouse Largest Steiff Doll,**
1930s. Doll is 18". Near Mint With Metal Ear Button And Tag - **$12000**
With Button Or Tag - **$2250 $4500 $9000**
Without Button And Tag - **$1800 $3250 $7000**

MKY-890

❏ **MKY-890. Mickey Mouse Extremely Large Doll,**
1930s. English by Deans Rag Book. 22" tall mohair and velveteen with wire inserts for posing and a movable head. - **$500 $1000 $2000**

MKY-892

❏ **MKY-892. Mickey Mouse 9" Doll By Steiff,**
1930s. Near Mint With Ear Button And Tag - **$5500**
With Button Or Tag - **$1100 $2200 $4500**
Without Button And Tag - **$825 $1650 $3300**

MKY-893

❑ **MKY-893. Mickey Mouse 12" Doll By Charlotte Clark,**
1930s. - **$2250 $3750 $8250**

MKY-895

❑ **MKY-895. Mickey Mouse Large 20" Heavy Velvet Doll,**
1930s. No markings. Tail is rubber coated wire. - **$1100 $3000 $5250**

MKY-894

❑ **MKY-894. Mickey Mouse Blue Pants Doll,**
1930s. Borgfeldt. 10" tall. - **$825 $1650 $3300**

MKY-896

❑ **MKY-896. Mickey Mouse 12" Doll By Steiff,**
1930s. Has white metal Steiff button in left ear. Walt Disney Mickey Mouse copyright under one foot. With Tag And Button - **$1350 $2850 $5750**
With Tag Or Button - **$1200 $2400 $4500**
Without Tag And Button - **$900 $1750 $3500**

MKY-897

MKY-899

❑ **MKY-897. Mickey Mouse 12"
Borgfeldt Doll,**
1930s. Underside of feet read "Walt
Disney's Mickey Mouse Design Patent
82802 Geo. Borgfeldt & Co. New York." -
$1100 $2200 $4500

❑ **MKY-899. Easter Parade Mickey
Mouse Doll,**
1930s. Knickerbocker. 12.5" tall. Stuffed
cloth body with felt ears and composition
shoes. Elaborate outfit consists of jacket
with plastic buttons, flower on lapel, ascot,
starched felt hat. - **$3250 $6500 $13500**
Tag - **$50 $100 $200**

MKY-898

MKY-900

❑ **MKY-898. Mickey Mouse Large 18"
Doll,**
1930s. No markings. - **$1350 $2750
$5500**

❑ **MKY-900. Easter Parade Minnie
Mouse 12" Tall Knickerbocker Doll,**
1930s. Has rubber tail, composition shoes
and string tag. Doll - **$1000 $3000 $6000**
Tag - **$50 $100 $200**

MKY-901   **MKY-902**

❏ **MKY-901. Mickey Mouse Hanging Marionette Composition Toy,**
1930s. Unmarked. Figure has painted composition head while body is covered by real animal fur, hands and feet are wood pegs. His body has size of 3.5x4.5x7" long with very long tail that is 7.5". Attached to the top of his head is a coil spring and attached to his arms and legs is string used to move these appendages. - **$150 $275 $550**

❏ **MKY-902. Mickey Mouse Jack-In-The Box,**
1930s. Knickerbocker. 6x6.5x6.5" tall wood box with paper labels. Opens to reveal a pop-up Mickey Mouse head 5" tall. - **$1100 $2200 $3300**

MKY-903

❏ **MKY-903. "Climbing Mickey Mouse" Boxed Toy,**
1930s. Dolly Toy Co. 5x9.5x2.25" deep boxed 9" tall diecut cardboard figure toy with wire tail plus length of string with wire finger loop on each end. When string is pulled tightly, Mickey moves up and down.
Box - **$450 $900 $1400**
Toy - **$275 $550 $1100**

MKY-904

❏ **MKY-904. Mickey Mouse Wood Walking Toy,**
1930s. Unmarked but licensed. 13.75" tall with 19.5" black wood rod that fits into hole on back. - **$100 $200 $400**

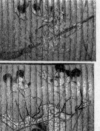

MKY-905

❏ **MKY-905. "Mickey Mouse Garden Roller,"**
1930s. Maker unknown, likely English. Lithographed tin with overall size of 8.5x8.5x4.5" diameter of the roller. Meant to be filled with sand. - **$150 $325 $650**

MKY-906

❑ **MKY-906. "Mickey Mouse" Ashtray,**
1930s. Base resembling stone is
3.25x4x.5" deep with attached 3.25" tall
composition figure.
Complete - **$85 $165 $275**
Figure Only - **$40 $75 $125**

MKY-907

❑ **MKY-907. Mickey Mouse Cigarette
Holder/Ashtray,**
1930s. Marked "Made In Japan" china
ashtray 2.5x4.5x2.5" tall. No Disney copyright. - **$70 $110 $225**

MKY-908

❑ **MKY-908. Mickey And Friends
Figural Ashtray,**
1930s. "Made In Japan" circular 3" diameter by 3" tall china bowl tray with high relief
figures of Mickey with tuba, Minnie with
guitar, Pluto. Bottom edge of base has
their incised names and copyright.
Believed made for Canadian market. -
$175 $350 $650

MKY-909

MKY-910

❑ **MKY-909. Mickey Mouse High
Quality Glass Ashtray,**
1930s. Maker Unknown. 3.5". - **$85 $165
$335**

❑ **MKY-910. Minnie Mouse Bavarian
China Cigarette Holder,**
1930s. White china piece is 1.5x3.25x2.5"
tall and marked "Made In Bavaria." - **$140
$275 $450**

MKY-911

❑ **MKY-911. English Mickey Mouse
Christmas Card,**
1930s. Valentine & Sons. 4x5.25" paper
accordion-fold card that opens to 10.5". -
$25 $45 $75

MKY-912

❏ **MKY-912. Mickey Mouse Christmas Card,**
1930s. Hallmark. 5.25x5.25" eight-page card including cover on parchment-like paper. - **$55 $110 $165**

MKY-913

❏ **MKY-913. Mickey Mouse English Christmas Card,**
1930s. G. Delgado Ltd. 5x5". - **$30 $60 $90**

MKY-914

❏ **MKY-914. Mickey Mouse Christmas Decoration,**
1930s. Japan. 4x7x4.25" tall pressed and formed painted cardboard decoration with 1.75" tall painted composition and wire figure. - **$60 $125 $200**

MKY-915

❏ **MKY-915. "Mickey Mouse Dominos,"**
1930s. Halsam. 2x8.5x1" deep box contains wood dominos. - **$75 $150 $300**

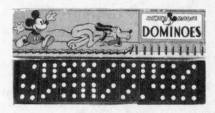

MKY-916

❏ **MKY-916. "Mickey Mouse Ludo" English Game,**
1930s. Chad Valley Co. 6x11x1" deep box. - **$115 $225 $450**

MKY-917

❑ **MKY-917. Mickey Mouse Birthday Card,**
1930s. Hall Brothers Inc. 4x5" on glossy textured paper. - **$30 $55 $85**

MKY-918

❑ **MKY-918. Mickey Mouse "Easter" Card,**
1930s. Hall Brothers. 4.75x6" one-sided card. - **$40 $75 $125**

MKY-919

❑ **MKY-919. Mickey Mouse Die-cut Birthday Card,**
1930s. Hallmark. 4.5x4.5" stiff paper card with Mickey holding die-cut birthday cake. Inside has stove with slot for cake to be inserted. - **$35 $65 $100**

MKY-920

❑ **MKY-920. Mickey Mouse Missing You Card,**
1930s. Hall Brothers Inc. Folded size is 4.75x5.75" and opens a total of four times revealing a different illustration each time for a total size of 18.5x22.5". - **$40 $80 $160**

MKY-921

❏ **MKY-921. Mickey Mouse Christmas Gift Tag,**
1930s. Dennison. 3.5x3.5" stiff paper which opens. - **$20 $40 $65**

MKY-922

❏ **MKY-922. "Mickey Mouse" English Birthday Card,**
1930s. G. Delgado Ltd., London. 4x4" on parchment-like paper. - **$35 $65 $115**

MKY-923

❏ **MKY-923. "Mickey Mouse" Birthday Card,**
1930s. Hall Brothers. 4.25x4.5" die-cut stiff paper. - **$30 $50 $80**

MKY-924

❏ **MKY-924. "Mickey/Minnie Mouse" Birthday Card,**
1930s. Hallmark. 4.5x4.5". - **$30 $50 $80**

MKY-925

❏ **MKY-925. "Mickey" Argentine Radio Front,**
1930s. Heavy cast brass 6x6" originally attached to front of radio. Has "Mickey" name on lower right corner. - **$115 $225 $350**

MKY-926

❏ **MKY-926. Mickey Mouse Radio,**
1930s. Industria Argentina. 7x13x8.75" tall lacquered wood.Mickey image on dial area. - **$550 $1100 $1750**

MKY-927

❏ **MKY-927. Mickey Mouse Silver Plate Prototype Radio,**
1930s. "Wm. Rogers & Son."
4.25x8.75x6.5" tall. This radio is a prototype and we know of only two others and as far as we know, it was never put into production. - **$2750 $5500 $8250**

MKY-928

❏ **MKY-928. Mickey Mouse Valentine's Day Card,**
1930s. Hall Brothers Inc. 5x6" stiff brown paper card that opens a total of four times revealing a different illustration each time for a total of 19x23". - **$60 $120 $175**

MKY-929

❏ **MKY-929. Mickey Mouse Pop-Up Valentine's Day Card,**
1930s. Hall Brothers Inc. 4.75x4.75" on glossy textured paper. - **$125 $250 $450**

MKY-930

❏ **MKY-930. Mickey Valentine,**
1930s. Hall Brothers Inc. 4.75x5.75" die-cut stiff paper. - **$40 $75 $135**

MKY-931

❏ **MKY-931. "Mickey Mouse" Sand Sieve,**
1930s. Ohio Art Co. 8" diameter by 2" deep. Nice beach-related scenes around sides of Mickey, Minnie, Pluto, Horace and Clarabelle. - **$115 $225 $450**

MKY-932

❏ **MKY-932. Mickey Mouse "Atlantic City" Sand Pail,**
1930s. Ohio Art. 4.25" tall lithographed tin pail with handle. - **$275 $550 $1100**

MKY-933

MKY-934

❏ **MKY-933. Mickey Mouse Sand Pail,**
1930s. Ohio Art. 5.5" diameter lithographed tin pail with handle. - **$325 $650 $1300**

❏ **MKY-934. "Mickey Mouse" Sand Pail Shovel,**
1930s. Ohio Art. 1.5x6" long lithographed tin shovel. - **$115 $225 $350**

MKY-935

❑ **MKY-935. Mickey Sand Pail With Shovel,**
1930s. Ohio Art. 3.25" tall lithographed tin pail. Pail - **$190 $385 $675**
Generic Shovel - **$20 $35 $60**

MKY-936

❑ **MKY-936. Mickey Mouse Sand Pail,**
1930s. Ohio Art Co. 4.25" tall by 4.25" diameter tin litho. - **$225 $450 $900**

MKY-937

MKY-938

❑ **MKY-937. Disney Embossed Tin Litho Sand Pail,**
1930s. Ohio Art Co. 6" tall by 5.75" top diameter. Green Water Verision - **$325 $825 $1375**
Yellow Water Version - **$450 $1000 $1650**

❑ **MKY-938. English Sand Pail,**
1930s. "Happynak Seaside Pail No. 12" tin lithographed pail 6.25" tall by 7" top diameter with attached metal carrying bail. - **$135 $275 $450**

MKY-939

MKY-940

❑ **MKY-939. Mickey And Friends Sand Pail,**
1930s. Ohio Art Co. 8" top diameter by 8" tall tin lithographed with wrap-around beach scene. - **$275 $550 $1100**

❑ **MKY-940. "Mickey's Garden" Sand Pail,**
1930s. Ohio Art Co. 5.25" top diameter by 5" tall lithographed tin. - **$200 $375 $750**

MKY-941

❑ **MKY-941. "Mickey Mouse Picnic" Sand Pail,**
1930s. Ohio Art Co. 7" tall with narrow flared-out base. - **$550 $1300 $2500**

MKY-942

❏ **MKY-942. "Happynak" Mickey Mouse Sand Pail,**
1930s. Great Britain. 4.5" tall tin litho. - **$135 $250 $400**

MKY-943

❏ **MKY-943. Mickey Mouse Sand Pail,**
1930s. English. Happynak Seaside Pail No. 7. Lithographed tin pail is 4.25". - **$115 $225 $335**

MKY-944

❏ **MKY-944. Large Sand Pail Featuring Unauthorized Likenesses Of Mickey, Minnie, And Krazy Kat,**
1930s. Marked "Made in U.S.A." 8" tall tin litho. - **$325 $650 $1100**

MKY-945

❏ **MKY-945. Mickey And Minnie Mouse Sand Shovel,**
1930s. Ohio Art. 4.25x5" tin litho. - **$125 $250 $500**

MKY-946

❏ **MKY-946. "Mickey" French Ring Toss Game,**
1930s. "Jeux-Spear." 6.75x8.5x1" deep boxed skill toy game for up to four players. A 4x6.5" die-cut cardboard Mickey figure with paper label inserts into a wood stand. - **$150 $300 $500**

MKY-948

MKY-947

❏ **MKY-947. "Mickey Mouse" Alarm Clock Boxed,**
1930s. Bayard. "Made In France" wind-up alarm in 5x5x3" deep box. Lid side panels picture a sequence of four events related to Mickey and his morning use of the clock. Clock is 4.75" diameter by 2" deep in enameled metal case. Dial face has separate diecut pointer hands and separate diecut tin head that nods as seconds tick. This is an original issue by Bayard, which re-issued this and other character clocks in the 1960s. Box - **$325 $800 $1500**
Clock - **$275 $550 $900**

❏ **MKY-948. "Mickey Mouse" Celluloid Nodder With Box,**
1930s. "Made In Japan" 7" tall. Swinging pendulum rubber-band operating mechanism. Box - **$125 $225 $450**
Nodder - **$225 $450 $900**

MKY-949

❏ **MKY-949. Street Vendor Wind-Up,**
1930s. Lithographed figure is 5.75" tall with built-in key on back. Marked "Made In Germany." When wound, monkeys swing back and forth as vendor raises and lowers his arm and his eyes move. - **$300 $600 $1200**

MKY-950

❏ **MKY-950. "Mickey Mouse" Tin Litho Clickers,**
1930s. 1.5" tall tin litho. Six different each featuring Mickey with a different musical instrument. Each - **$40 $75 $135**

MKY-952

❏ **MKY-952. Mickey Mouse Small Carousel With Original Box,**
1930s. Made In Japan. 7.5" tall with celluloid figure on painted metal base. Box is 3.5x5.5x2.75" deep.
Box - **$325 $650 $1300**
Toy - **$650 $1350 $2000**

MKY-951

❏ **MKY-951. Mickey Mouse Wind-Up,**
1930s. Schuco, Germany. 4" tall. Velveteen-covered body. Does somersaults when wound. - **$165 $275 $550**

MKY-953

❏ **MKY-953. "Mickey Mouse As Cowboy On Pluto" Celluloid Wind-Up,**
1930s. Made In Japan. Celluloid figures, plus paper hat on Mickey, on wood base. Toy is 8" long by 7.5" tall. Box is 5.5x8.25x2.5" deep.
Box - **$800 $1600 $2750**
Toy - **$1250 $2750 $4500**

MKY-954

❑ **MKY-954. Mickey And Minnie See-Saw In Original Box,**
1930s. Made In Japan. Toy is 5" tall by 6" wide with celluloid figures on painted metal base. Operates by means of pendulum and wind-up rubberband mechanism. Box is 2.5x2.5x2.75" deep. Box - **$250 $500 $800**
Toy - **$325 $750 $1350**

MKY-956

MKY-955

❑ **MKY-955. Mickey And Minnie See-Saw With Overhead Umbrella,**
1930s. Made In Japan. Toy stands 7.5" tall. - **$750 $1500 $2250**

❑ **MKY-956. "Mickey & Minnie Mouse Motoring" Wind-Up,**
1930s. Made In Japan. Toy is 2.25" tall by 5.5" long with celluloid figures on painted tin three-wheeled vehicle. Box is 4.75x5.5x2.75" deep.
Box - **$400 $800 $1600**
Toy - **$375 $750 $1500**

MKY-957

❑ **MKY-957. Donald Duck And Minnie Mouse Celluloid Wind-Up,**
1930s. Japan. 2x5x4.75" tall. - **$1100 $2200 $3300**

MKY-958

MKY-959

❑ **MKY-958. Celluloid "Mickey Mouse Whirligig" On Ball Wind-up,**
1930s. Made In Japan. Celluloid toy is 9.5" tall on small wooden base. Box is 2.5x2.75x8" tall.
Box - **$450 $900 $1750**
Toy - **$450 $900 $1750**

❑ **MKY-959. "Mickey Mouse And Minnie Mouse As Acrobats" Boxed Wind-Up,**
1930s. Nifty toy distributed by Borgfeldt. Box is 6.25x13x1.75" deep. Toy consists of 12.5" wire rods with pair of 5" cello figures.
Box - **$425 $850 $1350**
Toy - **$225 $450 $900**

MKY-961

❏ **MKY-961. "Mickey & Minnie Acrobat" Boxed Wind-Up,**
1930s. 8" tall with celluloid figures. Marked "Australia". Box - **$250 $500 $1000**
Toy - **$225 $450 $900**

MKY-960

❏ **MKY-960. "Mickey Mouse On Trapeze" Boxed Wind-Up,**
1930s. Japan. Distributed by Borgfeldt. Mickey celluloid is 4" tall with 6.5" tall trapeze. Box - **$250 $500 $1000**
Toy - **$175 $350 $700**

MKY-962

❏ **MKY-962. "Mickey & Pluto Runabout" Boxed Wind-Up,**
1930s. Borgfeldt. Made In Japan. Walt E. Disney. Box is 5x7.5x3" deep. Toy is 2.5x9x4.5" tall. Box - **$350 $650 $1300**
Toy - **$475 $900 $1650**

MKY-963

❏ **MKY-963. "Mickey & Pluto" Wind-Up Toy With Box,**
1930s. Borgfeldt. 8" long.
Box - **$325 $650 $1300**
Toy - **$475 $900 $1750**

MKY-964

❏ **MKY-964. Mickey Mouse Felt Figure In Wind-Up Car,**
1930s. Schuco, Germany. Copyright Walt E. Disney. 3.75" long by 4.5" tall to top of ball. - **$1650 $3250 $6500**

MKY-965

❏ **MKY-965. Mickey Mouse Carousel Toy Wind-Up,**
1930s. Wheeled tin base holds 5.75" celluloid Mickey. Eight celluloid rods hold celluloid balls and dimensional celluloid figures of Mickey, Minnie, Donald and Pluto.
Toy - **$900 $2200 $4150**
Box (Not Shown) - **$1100 $2200 $4400**

MKY-966

❏ **MKY-966. "Crawling Mickey Mouse" Celuloid Toy With Original Box,**
1930s. Paradise Novelty. 5" tall.
Box - **$550 $1100 $2200**
Toy - **$550 $1100 $2200**

245

MKY-967

☐ **MKY-967. "Mickey Mouse On Rocking Horse" Boxed Wind-Up,**
1930s. Mickey 4.5" celluloid on wood horse and base 3.5x5.75x7.75" long. Box is 6.75x7.75x3.5" deep.
Box - **$1000 $2000 $3000**
Toy - **$1100 $2200 $3300**

MKY-968

☐ **MKY-968. Mickey Mouse Riding Horse Celluloid Wind-Up,**
1930s. 6" tall. "Marked Made In Japan".
- **$650 $1300 $2500**

MKY-969

☐ **MKY-969. Mickey Mouse Cowboy Celluloid On Wooden Horse,**
1930s. Figure (probably missing stiff paper cowboy hat) is 4.75" on jointed horse 4.75" tall by 7" long. - **$700 $1400 $2750**

MKY-970

❑ **MKY-970. Acrobat Toy,**
1930s. Action toy featuring small 1.75" tall celluloid Mickey figure attached to thin metal trapeze unit with overall size of 1.75" wide by 3.5" tall. - **$150 $300 $600**

MKY-972

❑ **MKY-972. "Mickey Mouse" Boxed Films,**
1930s. Keystone Mfg. Co. Each box is 3.75x3.75x1" deep with 16mm black and white film. Films are loops, not on reels, designed to be projected as "Continuous Show." Includes "1050 Oh Suzannah, 1054 To The Rescue, 1055 The Covered Wagon." Each - **$18 $30 $55**

MKY-971

MKY-973

❑ **MKY-971. "Mickey Mouse" Flip Book,**
1930s. Moviescope Corp. 1.75x2.5" with title "Mickey Mouse In Actual Motion Pictures (Series A)." Mickey is playing piano on page fronts, page backs depict Mickey and Minnie dancing. - **$115 $225 $350**

❑ **MKY-973. "Mickey Mouse Movie Jecktor" With Films,**
1930s. The Movie Jecktor Co. 10x10x5" tall tin projector in box comes with original cord with special adapter and original bulb. Has decal of Mickey on top. Boxed paper films on wooden spools included both Disney and non-Disney titles.
Box - **$135 $265 $550**
Projector - **$125 $235 $450**
Boxed Disney Film - **$15 $30 $60**

MKY-974

❑ MKY-974. Mickey English Boxed Projector,
1930s. "Kodak Ltd., London." 8.5x12x13" tall boxed electrical 16mm film projector and accessories. Entire box except label area has repeated images of Mickey and Minnie doing various types of yard work.
Boxed - **$225 $450 $700**

MKY-975

❑ MKY-975. "Mickey Mouse Safe-Toy Cinema" Boxed Electric Film Projector ,
1930s. English By Ensign. 9x10x5" deep illustrated box contains 3x9x6.5" tall metal projector and 9mm film. Box - **$275 $550 $1000**
Projector - **$125 $250 $450**
Boxed Film - **$15 $30 $60**

MKY-976

❑ MKY-976. "Mickey Mouse Lantern Slides" English Set,
1930s. Ensign Ltd., London. 3.5x3.5x1.25" deep boxed single complete set from a series of ten different Mickey sets listed on one side of box label. This example is set "G/The Delivery Boy," consisting of eight different slides produced by arrangement from "The Mickey Mouse Movie Stories Published By Dean & Son Ltd." Slides are comprised of a pair of glass plates with heavy cellophane sheet sandwiched between them and black paper border seal around edges of glass. - **$50 $90 $175**

MKY-977

❏ **MKY-977. "Cine Mickey" Boxed Movie Projector,**
1930s. Made in France. 6.5x9.25x2.25" deep box with paper label on the lid contains 4x6.5x4" tall projector. Boxed - **$165 $325 $600**

MKY-981

❏ **MKY-981. "Mickey Mouse Quoits" Target,**
1930s. Thick wood 18.25" square English toy by Chad Valley Co. Ltd. Board has paper cover target design of Mickey Mouse holding bullseye, also used on circular target boards by this maker. This target is for "Quoits" ring-tossing and has thirteen hook pegs extending outward. - **$165 $325 $650**

MKY-978	MKY-979

❏ **MKY-978. "Mickey Mouse" Pocketknife,**
1930s. Knife is 2.75" long with celluloid grips and single metal blade. One Blade - **$85 $165 $325**
Two Blade Version - **$115 $200 $375**

❏ **MKY-979. Mickey Mouse Four-Blade Pocket Knife,**
1930s. Imperial. 3.75" long. - **$100 $225 $450**

MKY-982

❏ **MKY-982. "Mickey Mouse Thermometer" Variety,**
1930s. Character Art Manufacturing Co. 3.5" diameter by .75" deep metal frame with tin litho thermometer insert. Round case variety rather than octagon. - **$225 $450 $750**

MKY-980

❏ **MKY-980. Mickey Mouse English Target,**
1930s. Chad Valley Co. 10.5" diameter thick cardboard. - **$85 $175 $350**

MKY-983

☐ **MKY-983. Thermometer Plaque,**
1930s. Steel frame is 3.25x3.25x.75" deep
pressed with tin lithograph thermometer
insert under glass. - **$150 $300 $600**

MKY-984

☐ **MKY-984. Mailing Envelope,**
1930s. Paper envelope is 4.75x6.5"
unidentified for original content but
believed to be the mailer for Mickey Mouse
Recipe Scrapbook. - **$15 $30 $50**

MKY-985

☐ **MKY-985. "Dixon's Mickey Mouse
Map Of The United States,"**
1930s. Dixon. 9.75x14.25" came with larger version pencil boxes which had pull-out
drawers. - **$40 $70 $145**

MKY-986

☐ **MKY-986. "Mickey Mouse" Pencil
Box,**
1930s. Dixon. Box is 4x8.25x.75" with
snap closure lid. - **$55 $110 $165**

MKY-987

☐ **MKY-987. "Mickey Mouse" Pencil
Box,**
1930s. Dixon. 5.5x10.5x1" deep stiff cardboard box. Interior has repeated images of
Mickey, Minnie and Pluto. - **$55 $110
$165**

MKY-988

MKY-990

❏ **MKY-990. "Mickey Mouse" Pencil Box,**
1930s. Dixon. 4.25x8.25x.5" deep paper-covered cardboard. - **$65 $130 $200**

❏ **MKY-988. Mickey Mouse Figural Pencil Box Varieties,**
1930s. Dixon 5x8.5x.5" thick. Usual variety has a cream background. Rare variety has an orange background.
Cream Version - **$115 $265 $475**
Orange Version - **$165 $375 $600**

MKY-991

❏ **MKY-991. "Mickey Mouse" Pencil Box,**
1930s. Dixon. 4x8.75x.75" deep cardboard box. - **$55 $110 $165**

MKY-989

❏ **MKY-989. Minnie Mouse Figural Pencil Box,**
1930s. Dixon #2761. 5.75x8.5x.5" thick. - **$135 $275 $525**

MKY-992

❏ **MKY-992. Mickey Mouse Figural Pencil Box,**
1930s. Dixon. 3.25x8.25x5" deep box with stiff cardboard side panels plus die-cut thin cardboard front and back panels. - **$325 $650 $1100**

MKY-993

❏ **MKY-993. "Mickey Mouse" Pencil Box,**
1930s. Dixon. 5x8.5x.75" deep cardboard box with textured paper covering. - **$80 $160 $275**

MKY-994

❏ **MKY-994. "Mickey Mouse" Pencil Box,**
1930s. Dixon. 6x10.5x1.25" deep textured paper over cardboard box #2918 with snap closure. - **$75 $135 $235**

MKY-995

❏ **MKY-995. Figural Compo Pencil Box,**
1930s. Dixon. 5.5x8.5x1.25" deep painted composition box #2770 with details in high relief on both sides. Cardboard storage tray slides out from top of the box. - **$275 $500 $900**

MKY-996

❏ **MKY-996. "Mickey Mouse" Pencil Box,**
1930s. Dixon #2525. 5x8.5x1.25" deep textured paper-covered cardboard box with snap closure. Lid features circus theme illustration with Mickey as ringmaster, Donald riding a seal while dangling a fish in front of its face. Complete With Contents - **$90 $185 $350**
Without Contents - **$55 $135 $265**

MKY-997

□ **MKY-997. "Mickey Mouse/Donald Duck" Pencil Box,**
1930s. Dixon. 4.5x8.5x.75" deep cardboard box with textured paper covering. - **$90 $185 $350**

MKY-998

□ **MKY-998. "Mickey Mouse" Full Color Pencil Box,**
1930s. Dixon, 5x8.5x.75" deep textured paper-covered cardboard box with label on lid. Label notes "Weston's Crackerettes" and box was apparently issued as a premium for them. - **$125 $250 $500**

MKY-999

□ **MKY-999. Mickey Mouse Full Color Pencil Box,**
1930s. "Made in Japan." 9" long. Depicts Mickey and his nephews, Clarabell, and Donald Duck. - **$125 $250 $500**

MKY-1000

MKY-1001

□ **MKY-1000. Mickey Moving Head Celluloid Pencil Holder,**
1930s. Base is 1.75" in diameter by 3" tall with celluloid figure of Mickey. Attached to front of base is crescent-shaped celluloid piece which may serve as a rest for pencil. - **$175 $350 $650**

□ **MKY-1001. Mickey Mouse Pencil Holder,**
1930s. Dixon. 1.25x2.25x4.75" tall painted composition. - **$115 $225 $400**

MKY-1002

MKY-1004

❑ **MKY-1002. Mickey Pencil Holder,**
1930s. Unmarked but Spanish
3.75x4.25x1.5" deep painted jigsawed
wood figure with attachment on back
designed to hold twelve pencils. - **$115
$225 $350**

❑ **MKY-1004. Mickey Mouse Figural
Pencil Sharpener,**
1930s. Celluloid 2.75" tall sharpener. - **$95
$200 $335**

MKY-1003

MKY-1005

❑ **MKY-1003. Mickey Mouse Pencil
Holder,**
1930s. Spanish. 3.75" diameter by 5.25"
tall painted wood. - **$135 $275 $450**

❑ **MKY-1005. "Mickey Mouse" Classic
Pose Catalin Plastic Pencil Sharpener,**
1930s. 1 1/8" diameter. - **$135 $275 $550**

MKY-1006

❏ **MKY-1006. Mickey Mouse Catalin Plastic Pencil Sharpener,**
1930s. One of about eight different designs picturing Mickey or Minnie. 1-1/8x1-1/8" square with beveled corners.
Each - **$70 $135 $200**

MKY-1007

❏ **MKY-1007. "Mickey Mouse Colored Pencils,"**
1930s. Dixon. 2.5x5.3/8" deep box contains set of eight pencils. - **$100 $225 $325**

MKY-1008   **MKY-1009**

❏ **MKY-1008. "Mickey Mouse" Mechanical Pencil,**
1930s. Inkograph Co. 5.25" long with cast metal Mickey head on top plus brass pocket clip. - **$65 $135 $200**

❏ **MKY-1009. "Mickey Mouse Ever-Lasting Soft" True Lead Pencil,**
1930s. "Made In England" Disney copyright 5.5" long solid lead (no wood) pencil with enameled paint covering and silkscreen design including small Mickey image. - **$30 $60 $100**

MKY-1010

❑ **MKY-1010. "Micky-Maus" German Postcard,**
1930s. Stiff glossy paper card 3.5x5.5". -
$40 $80 $135

MKY-1011

❑ **MKY-1011. Mickey Mouse English Postcards,**
1930s. Inter-Art Co. Each is 3x5.5". Series #7087, 7088. Each - **$12 $25 $45**

MKY-1012

❑ **MKY-1012. Mickey Mouse English Postcards,**
1930s. Woolstone Bros. Each is 3x5.5". Series #512, 517. Each **$12 $25 $40**

MKY-1013

❑ **MKY-1013. "Mickey Mouse" English Postcard,**
1930s. G. Delgado Ltd., London. 3.5x5.5". Title is "We're In Luck's Way Down Here." - **$25 $45 $70**

MKY-1014

MKY-1015

❏ **MKY-1014. "Mickey Mouse" English Postcard,**
1930s. G. Delgado Ltd., London. 3.5x5.5". Title is "I Am Glad To Say That We Are 'Jogging Along' As Usual." - **$25 $45 $70**

❏ **MKY-1015. "Mickey Mouse" English Postcard,**
1930s. G. Delgado Ltd., London. 3.5x5.5". Title is "Little Man You've Had A Bee'sy Day." - **$25 $45 $70**

MKY-1016

❏ **MKY-1016. German Postcard,**
1930s. Glossy art depiction is 3.5x5.5". - **$30 $55 $80**

MKY-1017

❏ **MKY-1017. English Postcards,**
1930s. "Inter-Art Company." Four 3x5.5" unused postcards from a numbered series. These examples are 7095-"You're Such A Comfort To Me," 7094-"Now Where Is That Billy Cat?," 7091-"Here's Something To Tickle You," 7085-"I Like What You Like-And You Like What I Like." Each - **$12 $25 $45**

MKY-1018

❏ **MKY-1018. German Postcard,**
1930s. Vertical format card is 3.5x5.5" published for the French market. Front has slightly raised gold text "Bonne Annee," translating literally to Maid Year, apparently for a first anniversary. - **$30 $50 $80**

MKY-1019

❏ **MKY-1019. Mickey Mouse Foreign Postcard,**
1930s. Likely Netherlands. 3.5x5.5" with winter scene on the front plus text "Haad Uut Aastat." - **$25 $45 $70**

MKY-1020

❏ **MKY-1020. "Walt Disney" European Postcard,**
1930s. Unmarked. 4-1/8x5.75". Glossy front and blank back. Walt holds 1932 achievement certificate from Academy of Motion Picture Arts and Sciences. - **$12 $25 $45**

MKY-1021

❏ **MKY-1021. "Mickey Mouse" Stationery,**
1930s Powers Paper Co. 6.5x9.5x1" deep box with 24 sheets of paper and 24 envelopes. Boxed - **$125 $225 $350**

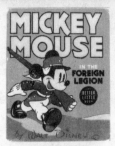

MKY-1022

❏ **MKY-1022. "Mickey Mouse In The Foreign Legion" Better Little Book,**
1940. Whitman. Better Little Book #1428. - **$31 $93 $220**

MKY-1023

❏ **MKY-1023. "Mickey Mouse And The 7 Ghosts" Better Little Book,**
1940. Whitman. Book #1475. - **$31 $93 $220**

MKY-1024

❏ **MKY-1024. "Walt Disney's Wild West" English Hardcover,**
1940. Juvenile Productions Ltd. 8x10x1.25" thick with 128 pages. Has two full color plates. - **$125 $250 $500**

MKY-1025

MKY-1027

MKY-1026

❑ **MKY-1025. "Mickey Mouse Annual" English Hardcover,**
1940. Book is 6.25x8.5x2" thick with 124 pages. Among the scarcest of pre-war annuals. - **$325 $650 $1100**

❑ **MKY-1026. "Mickey Mouse Weekly" Example English Newspaper,**
1940. Volume 5, #232 is 10.5x14" with 8 pages. Original run began February 8, 1936 and continued into the 1950s.
Typical Example Pre-1950 - **$15 $20 $40**
1950's Example - **$8 $12 $20**

❑ **MKY-1027. "Walt Disney's Ski-Jump Target Game,"**
1940. American Toy Works. 13.25x19.5x2" deep box. Cardboard target board is 13x18.5" with paper label on front. Came with gun and darts. - **$185 $375 $800**

MKY-1028

☐ **MKY-1028. "Mickey Mouse Drummer" Pull Toy,**
1941. Fisher-Price. 4x7.5x8.5" tall mostly wood pull toy #476, first introduced in 1941 for five years. - **$125 $225 $400**

MKY-1029

☐ **MKY-1029. Mickey Mouse Pencil Drawing From Canine Caddie,**
1941. 10x12" sheet of animation paper with 4x5" image. "4" from a numbered sequence. - **$125 $250 $500**

MKY-1030

☐ **MKY-1030. "Mickey Mouse Annual" Hardcover,**
1941. English by Dean & Son Ltd. 6.25x8.5x1.75" thick with 128 pages. - **$125 $250 $500**

MKY-1031

☐ **MKY-1031. "Mickey Mouse And The Magic Lamp" Better Little Book,**
1942. Whitman. Book #1429. - **$31 $93 $220**

MKY-1032

☐ **MKY-1032. "Mickey Mouse And Pluto,"**
1942. Dell Publishing Co. 4x5.5" with 192 pages. - **$51 $153 $360**

MKY-1033

☐ **MKY-1033. Mickey "Sunoco Oil" Ink Blotter,**
1942. Blotter is 3.5x6". - **$40 $70 $110**

MKY-1034

☐ **MKY-1034. "Walt Disney Character Plaks,"**
c. 1942. Youngstown Pressed Steel Co. Five 11x14.5" envelopes containing rigid cardboard parts for assembling and coloring dimensional wall plaques picturing Mickey, Donald, Bambi, Thumper, Flower plus Pluto, not shown by example photo. Completed plaques are each 10.5x14". Mickey and Donald Each In Envelope - **$25 $50 $100**
Others in Envelope - **$20 $40 $75**

MKY-1035

☐ **MKY-1035. "Mickey Mouse Annual" English Book,**
1942. Dean & Son Ltd. 6.5x8.5" hardcover with 1.5" thickness from 192 stiff paper pages. - **$135 $265 $550**

MKY-1036

☐ **MKY-1036. "Minnie Shows You The Way To A Lustron Cold Permanent" Beautician Instruction Book,**
1943. Spiral bound hardcover 9x11.5" with 20 pages for "Professional Visual Training Guide" with illustrations by Walt Disney. - **$125 $225 $450**

MKY-1037

❏ **MKY-1037. "Mickey Mouse And The Dude Ranch Bandit" Better Big Little Book,**
1943. Whitman. Better Little Book #1471 version with 352 pages and back cover text on yellow background with list of other Big Little Books. Last two pages also list additional Big Little Book titles. - **$30 $90 $200**

MKY-1038

❏ **MKY-1038. "Mickey Mouse And The Dude Ranch Bandit" Better Big Little Book,**
1943. Whitman. Better Little Book #1471 version with 432 pages. Back cover has color ad for Better Little Books. - **$31 $93 $220**

MKY-1039

❏ **MKY-1039. "Mickey Mouse Annual" English Hardcover,**
1943. Dean & Son Ltd. 6.5x8.75x1.5" thick with 192 pages. - **$115 $225 $400**

MKY-1040

❏ **MKY-1040. "Mickey Mouse On The Cave-Man Island" Better Little Book,**
1944. Whitman. Book #1499. - **$30 $90 $210**

MKY-1041

❏ **MKY-1041. "Mickey Mouse Annual,"**
1944. Dean & Sons Ltd. English hardcover 6.5x8.5" with 192 pages. - **$225 $450 $900**

MKY-1042

❏ **MKY-1044. "Funny Stories About Donald And Mickey By Walt Disney,"**
1945. Whitman. 8.25x10.75" with 128 pages. - **$35 $70 $150**

❏ **MKY-1042. "Mickey Sees The U.S.A." Hardcover.**
1944. D. C. Heath & Co. 6.25x8.25" with 144 pages. From "Walt Disney Storybooks" educational series and this is one of the more advanced reader books. - **$30 $55 $115**

MKY-1045

MKY-1043

❏ **MKY-1043. "Walt Disney 1944 Almanaque" Brazilian Hardcover,**
1944. Book is 8.25x13.5" with 104 pages based on Disney shorts and other stories. - **$115 $225 $400**

MKY-1046

❏ **MKY-1045. "Mickey Mouse Annual" English Hardcover,**
1945. Dean & Son Ltd. 6.5x8.5x1.25" thick with 192 pages. - **$140 $275 $500**

❏ **MKY-1046. "Western Family" Magazine With Mickey Thanksgiving Cover,**
1945. Measures 8.5x11.25" with 32 pages. - **$10 $20 $40**

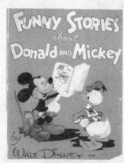

MKY-1044

MKY-1047

❑ **MKY-1047. "Mickey Mouse And The 'Lectro Box'" Better Little Book,**
1946. Whitman. Book #1413. - **$21 $63 $145**

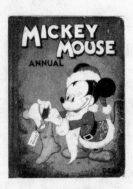

MKY-1048

❑ **MKY-1048. "Mickey Mouse Annual" English Hardcover,**
1946. Dean & Son Ltd. 6.5x8.5x1.25" thick with 192 pages. - **$85 $165 $375**

MKY-1049

❑ **MKY-1049. Mickey Mouse Wristwatch Boxed,**
1946. Kelton/US Time. 2x9.5x1" deep cardboard box with hinge lid containing watch in 1x1.5" 10K gold-plated case with original leather straps plus packaging leaflet and original $12.50 price tag. Dial features separate die-cut tin Mickey head and hands which point at the numerals. His head is on a post and designed to rotate with hour hand. This is the version with all twelve numerals and no Kelton name on the dial, the first post-WWII Mickey watch produced.
Box - **$75 $125 $250**
Watch - **$275 $650 $1500**

MKY-1050

❑ **MKY-1050. Willie The Giant Pencil Drawing.** 1947. Animation paper is 10x12" with large 7x9" image from "Mickey And The Beanstalk." - **$75 $150 $250**

MKY-1051

❑ **MKY-1051. "Mickey And The Beanstalk" Record Set,**
1947. Set comes in 10.5x12" album containing three 78-rpm records on the Capitol label. Has 40-page booklet bound inside. - **$30 $60 $125**

MKY-1052

❑ **MKY-1052. "Walt Disney Character Merchandise 1947-1948" Retailer's Catalogue,**
1947. 9x12" with glossy stiff paper covers and 100 pages featuring black and white photographs. Items include American Pottery figurines, Ben Cooper costumes, Fisher-Price pull toys, Gund stuffed dolls, Jaymar puzzles, Leeds China items, various store displays, Marx wind-up toys, Sun Rubber toys, Transogram paint sets, US Time watch, various books, sheet music, food-related products, clothing, much more. - **$350 $700 $1500**

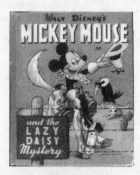

MKY-1053

❑ **MKY-1053. "Mickey Mouse And The Lazy Daisy Mystery" Better Little Book,**
1947. Whitman. Book #1433. - **$21 $63 $145**

MKY-1054

❑ **MKY-1054. "Mickey Mouse Annual" English Hardcover,**
1947. Dean & Son Ltd. 7.75x10" with 128 pages including full color plate of Mickey, Minnie, Goofy and Pluto. - **$30 $60 $125**

MKY-1055

❑ **MKY-1055. "Mickey And The Beanstalk" Hardcover,**
1947. Grosset & Dunlap. 7x8.25" with 32 pages. - **$85 $175 $400**

MKY-1056

MKY-1058

❏ **MKY-1057. "Mickey Mouse Alarm Clock,"**
1947. Ingersoll/U.S. Time 4.75x4.75x3.25" tall box contains 4.5" alarm clock. Comes with generic guarantee paper plus original $2.95 price tag. Box - **$115 $225 $450**
Clock - **$115 $225 $450**

❏ **MKY-1056. "Mickey Mouse Library Of Games,"**
1947. Russell Mfg. Co. 2x5.75x2.5" tall open box with foil label on the front contains complete set of six individually boxed card games. - **$90 $225 $350**

❏ **MKY-1058. Mickey Mouse Wristwatch,**
1947. U. S. Time 1x1.5" silvered metal case marked "Ingersoll/U.S. Time." Has original red leather straps. - **$75 $150 $250**

MKY-1057

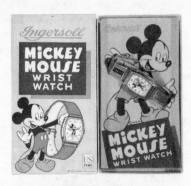

MKY-1059

❏ **MKY-1059. "Mickey Mouse Wristwatch" Box,**
1947. U.S. Time. 4x7x1" deep box with nicely illustrated insert. - **$100 $200 $400**

MKY-1060

❑ **MKY-1060. "Mickey Mouse" Boxed Wrist Watch Variety.**
1947. US Time. 4x7x1" deep box with variety text. The word "New" replaces "Ingersoll" on both box and insert.
Box - **$125 $225 $450**

MKY-1061

❑ **MKY-1061. "Mickey Mouse" Ceramic Cookie Jar,**
c. 1947. Leeds China Co. 5.5x8x11.75" tall Mickey with flowers between his feet. Rare, few known. - **$650 $1350 $2500**

MKY-1062

❑ **MKY-1062. Mickey Mouse Ceramic Bank,**
c. 1947. Leeds China Co. 3x4.5x6.5" tall with over-the-glaze paint accents. - **$30 $60 $100**

MKY-1063

❑ **MKY-1063. "Ritz Theatre Mickey Mouse Club" Button,**
c. 1947. 7/8". Uses same image that appears on the 1947 alarm clock by Ingersoll/U.S. Time. - **$115 $235 $365**

MKY-1064

❑ **MKY-1064. "Mickey Mouse's Summer Vacation" Premium Book,** 1948. Whitman. 4.5x6.25" softcover version from "Story Hour Series," 32 pages. This version was given away with subscriptions to Walt Disney's Comics and Stories. - **$15 $25 $50**

MKY-1067

MKY-1065

MKY-1068

❑ **MKY-1065. "Mickey Mouse In The World Of Tomorrow" Better Little Book,** 1948. Whitman. Book #1444. - **$31 $93 $220**

❑ **MKY-1067. "Mickey Mouse The Miracle Maker,"** 1948. Whitman. 5.25x5.25" hardcover book from "845" series. - **$30 $60 $150**

❑ **MKY-1068. "Mickey Mouse And The Boy Thursday,"** 1948. Whitman. From series #845. - **$30 $60 $150**

MKY-1066

MKY-1069

❑ **MKY-1066. "Mickey Mouse And The Desert Palace" Better Little Book,** 1948. Whitman. Book #1451. - **$21 $63 $145**

❏ **MKY-1069. "Mickey Mouse Annual" English Book,**
1948. Dean & Son Ltd. 7.75x9.75" hardcover, 128 pages. - **$35 $70 $150**

MKY-1070

❏ **MKY-1070. "Mickey And The Beanstalk" Hardcover Premium Issue Book,**
1948. Whitman. 5x6.75" with 32 pages from the "Story Hour Series." Comes with original mailing envelope with illustration of Mickey as Santa marked "Do Not Open Until Christmas." Given as premium for subscription to Walt Disney's Comics & Stories.
Mailer - **$20 $35 $75**
Book - **$20 $35 $75**

MKY-1071

❏ **MKY-1071. Mickey Mouse Luminous Wristwatch,**
1948. Ingersoll (U.S. Time). 3.25x4.25x1" deep box with 3.75" long ballpoint pen which has Mickey decal on cap. One of ten in Mickey's 20th birthday series. Birthday theme lid not shown. Boxed - **$300 $750 $1500**
Watch Only - **$125 $300 $650**

MKY-1072

❏ **MKY-1072. "Mickey Mouse Choo-Choo" Fisher-Price Pull Toy,**
1949. Toy is wood with paper labels measuring 3.5x8.75x7" tall. Toy is #485. - **$80 $165 $350**

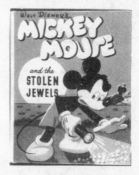

MKY-1073

❏ **MKY-1073. "Mickey Mouse And The Stolen Jewels" Better Little Book,**
1949. Whitman. Book #1464. - **$30 $90 $210**

MKY-1074

❏ **MKY-1074. "Mickey Mouse Annual" English Book,**
1949. Dean & Son Ltd. 7.25x9.75" hardcover, 128 pages. - **$35 $70 $150**

MKY-1077

❏ **MKY-1077. "Walt Disney Character Jewelry" Charm Braclet On Card,**
1940s. Nemo. 3x8.25" die-cut cardboard display card contains 6" long bracelet with five different three-dimensional hard plastic charms .75" to 1" tall.
Card - **$10 $20 $40**
Bracelet - **$15 $30 $50**

MKY-1075

❏ **MKY-1075. Boxed "Mickey Mouse Alarm Clock,"**
1949. Ingersoll/U.S. Time. 2x4x4.5" tall clock with ivory colored plastic case.
Box - **$115 $225 $450**
Clock - **$115 $225 $450**

MKY-1076

❏ **MKY-1076. "Walt Disney's Studio Restaurant" Menu,**
1940s. 9.25x12.5" stiff paper. - **$85 $165 $275**

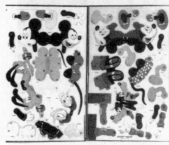

MKY-1078

❏ **MKY-1078. "Mickey Mouse Hingees,"**
1940s. Envelope is 7.5x11.5 and contains unpunched sheet of characters Mickey, Minnie, Donald Pluto and Goofy. - **$50 $100 $200**

MKY-1079

☐ **MKY-1079. "Walt Disney Character Alphabet" Boxed Set,**
1940s. Plane Facts Co. 12x13.25x1" deep box contains two unpunched thick cardboard sheets with 44 punch-out letters for Disney characters and a block of wood where letters can be placed to spell out words. - **$50 $85 $175**

MKY-1080

☐ **MKY-1080. "Walt Disney Jigsaw Puzzle,"**
1940s. Jaymar. 7x10x2" box holds puzzle that measures 14x22" when assembled. - **$20 $40 $75**

MKY-1081

☐ **MKY-1081. "Walt Disney's Parade" Boxed Puzzle,**
1940s. Canadian by Ontex. 6.5x18.75x1" deep box contains complete single puzzle. - **$25 $50 $75**

MKY-1082

☐ **MKY-1082. Mickey As Santa Planter,**
1940s. Unmarked but Leeds China Co. 3.5x6x6" tall glazed ceramic with over-the-glaze paint on face, outfit, sleigh. - **$40 $80 $135**

MKY-1083

☐ **MKY-1083. "Ingersoll" Mickey And Donald Complete Ring Display,**
1940s. Countertop display 8.25x11" with easel back contains twelve sterling silver rings. Ring tops and bands are in various shapes with various designs. Near Mint Complete - **$1300**
Display Card - **$100 $200 $400**
Each Ring - **$25 $40 $75**

MKY-1084

❑ **MKY-1084. "Turnabout Mickey & Minnie Mouse" Cookie Jar,**
1940s. Leeds China Co. 7x7x13" tall with over-the-glaze paint. - **$135 $240 $450**

MKY-1085

❑ **MKY-1085. "Disney Playtime Plastics For The Nursery" Dish Set,**
1940s. John Dickinson & Co. Ltd. 9x15x3.5" deep box contains Gadeware Plastics English set. This is "Set No. 2." Pieces with decals are: Egg cup, small beaker with Mickey, large mug with Elmer, servette ring with Goofy, spoon with Thumper, pusher with Fifer Pig and feeding bowl with Pinocchio. - **$75 $135 $200**

MKY-1086

❑ **MKY-1086. "Walt Disney's Wonder Book" English Hardcover,**
1940s. Mardon Sons & Hall Ltd. 8x10.5" with 80 pages. - **$30 $65 $150**

MKY-1087

❏ **MKY-1087. "Mickey's Very First Book" English Book,**
1940s. Wm. Collins Sons & Co. Ltd. 7.25x9.75" hardcover, 44 pages. Content includes 26 alphabet pages with one letter per page featuring 1930s art including pie-eyed Mickey and other early characters, all with different musical instruments or band-related images. Rest of book is stories and art featuring early 1940s Mickey. End paper design depicts Goofy watching Donald chase after Pluto. - **$275 $550 $1000**

MKY-1089

❏ **MKY-1089. "Mickey's Wonder Book" English Hardcover,**
1940s. William Collins Son & Co. Ltd. 8.5x10.75" clothbound edition, 76 pages. - **$25 $50 $125**

MKY-1090

MKY-1088

❏ **MKY-1088. "Mickey Never Fails" Book Varieties,**
1940s. Two variations under same title but different publishers and a decade apart. Earlier 1939 original edition is 6.25x8.5" hardcover from "Walt Disney Storybooks" series by D.C. Heath & Co., 102 pages. Second 1949 edition is English by London and Glasgow, also 102 pages. Story is identical throughout between the two, and both have same full color story art. Difference is cover art of portrait on 1939 version opposed to full color group scene on front and back on 1949 version.
Earlier - **$35 $60 $125**
Later - **$25 $45 $100**

❏ **MKY-1090. "Walt Disney Designed Ash Tray Set,"**
1940s. Kemper-Thomas Co. 4.75x14x1" deep box contains three different clear glass ashtrays, each 4.5x4.5x1" deep.
Box - **$40 $75 $150**
Each Tray - **$25 $50 $100**

MKY-1091

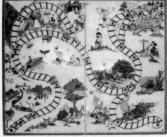

MKY-1092

☐ **MKY-1091. "Walt Disney's Jigsaw Lotto,"**
1940s. Jaymar. 7x10x1" deep boxed game. - **$15 $25 $50**

☐ **MKY-1092. "Journey Through Disneyland" Canadian Game,**
1940s. Ontex Of Canada. 10.75x17.75x1.5" deep boxed game featuring 16x20" railroad route game board plus spinner card and six generic pawns. Board art also relates to Disney film scenes. - **$75 $125 $200**

MKY-1093

☐ **MKY-1093. "The Disney Derby" Game,**
1940s. Australian by Metal-Wood Repetitions Co., Sidney. 10x10x2.25" deep box contains complete game. Boxed - **$75 $135 $250**

MKY-1094

☐ **MKY-1094. Mickey Mouse Trapeze Toy,**
1940s. 8" tall wood frame with 4" long Mickey figure comprised of wood arms and legs, die-cut cardboard body with paper label on each side. This 1940s version is scarcer than the 1930s version. - **$55 $110 $175**

MKY-1095

☐ **MKY-1095. "Mickey Mouse Viewer" English Boxed Set,**
1940s. 2.5x2.75x1.5" deep box contains 2.5" long hard plastic viewer and smaller box containing full color "Film Shots." Each is cut frame of actual 35mm full color film. - **$45 $75 $125**

MKY-1097

MKY-1096

☐ **MKY-1096. "Mickey Mouse Viewer" With Boxed Filmstrips,**
1940s. Craftsmen's Guild. 3" long marbled plastic viewer comes with 3.5x5.25" ad paper/order form and eight 1.75x1.75x.75" deep individually boxed filmstrips. Each is a 16mm strip with "16 Scenes Comprising A Complete Condensed Version Of A Famous Disney Picture" and feature actual film scenes. Films are 1 Brave Little Tailor, 2 Three Little Pigs, 4 Chicken Little, 6 The Ugly Duckling, 7 The Grasshopper And The Ants, 9 The Golden Touch, 10 Little Hiawatha, 11 The Pointer (Pluto).
Paper - **$10 $18 $30**
Viewer - **$15 $30 $60**
Each Box Film - **$8 $15 $30**

☐ **MKY-1097. "Mickey Mouse Movie Fun" Boxed Set,**
1940s. Mastercraft Toy Co. Inc. Consists of black metal "Animator" (zoetrope) which is 4" tall with 7" diameter, complete with wood handle that attaches on underside. The "Animator" is designed with die-cut slots around outer edge and has embossed title "Mickey Mouse Movie-Fun." Ten 2x22" strips are inserted in animator to view movie. Five are Disney: Mickey, Donald, Pluto, Bambi and Pinocchio. Five are non-Disney.
Boxed - **$135 $275 $450**

MKY-1098

☐ **MKY-1098. Mickey Mouse Catalin Plastic Pencil Sharpener,**
1940s. 1" in diameter. - **$45 $75 $125**

MKY-1099

MKY-1101

❏ **MKY-1099. Mickey And Minnie Dolls By Gund,**
1940s. Pair of matching dolls each 4.5x8x14.5" tall with plush bodies, rubber faces, hands and shoes and felt ears with red bows at neck. Mickey has felt pants and Minnie has bow in her hair, cotton skirt and panties. Each - **$135 $250 $500**

❏ **MKY-1101. Mickey Mouse Cookies Box,**
1940s. National Biscuit Co. Box is 5" long with a fabric carrying strap. Mickey pictured on back, Minnie and Pluto on sides. - **$135 $265 $475**

MKY-1102

❏ **MKY-1102. "Playthings November 1950,"**
1950. Volume 48, #11 with 186 pages of toys. Mickey as Santa cover. - **$35 $65 $125**

MKY-1100

❏ **MKY-1100. Mickey Mouse On Train Pencil Sharpener,**
1940s. Item is 1.25" long by 1.25" tall painted white metal. Two similar issued with Donald and Pluto. - **$50 $100 $175**

MKY-1103

❑ **MKY-1103. "Mickey Mouse On The Haunted Island" Better Little Book,** 1950. Whitman. "New Better Little Book" with 3.25x5.5" format, #708-10. - **$14 $42 $95**

MKY-1104

❑ **MKY-1104. "Walt Disney's Hanky Clock,"** c. 1950. English-made 7.5x7.5" die-cut stiff paper clock-shaped folder designed to hold a hanky. Front has a pair of diecut clock hands. - **$50 $85 $150**

MKY-1105

❑ **MKY-1105. Disney Characters Jell-O Comic Molds Original Art Prototype Sign,** c. 1950. 12x17" sheet of crescent art board with diecut design and art done in tempera paint. From Gordon Gold Archives. Unique, Very Good - **$575**

MKY-1106

❑ **MKY-1106. "Mickey Crazy Car" With Box,** c. 1950. Celluloid figure in 4" long tin car with box. "Made In Japan".
Box - **$225 $450 $900**
Toy - **$525 $1050 $1650**

MKY-1107

❑ **MKY-1107. "Walt Disney's Wonder Book" Hardcover,** c. 1951. English by The Sunshine Press. 8x10.75" with 60 pages. - **$25 $50 $100**

MKY-1108

❑ **MKY-1108. "Mickey Mouse Paint Box,"**
1952. Transogram. 4.5x5.75x.5" deep tin litho with hinged lid. - **$15 $25 $50**

MKY-1109

❑ **MKY-1109. "Mickey Mouse Wristwatch" Variety Box,**
1952. US Time. 3x4.25x5" tall display box in rectangular format, the scarcer variation of two designs also offered in oval box format. Sleeve removes to reveal 4.5" tall diecut Mickey figure with slotted hands for strap of watch originally held. Box Only - **$225 $450 $750**

MKY-1110

❑ **MKY-1110. "Mickey Mouse Ingersoll/U.S. Time" Watch With Rare Packaging ,**
1952. Cardboard presentation box is 3.75x5x5.5" tall with die-cut insert containing watch with 7/8" diameter chromed metal case. Packaging - **$225 $450 $750**
Watch - **$40 $70 $115**

MKY-1111

❑ **MKY-1111. "Mickey Mouse Stories" Book,**
1952. English by Dean & Son Ltd. 7.5x9.75" with 44 pages. - **$25 $50 $100**

MKY-1112

❑ **MKY-1112. "Mickey's Wonder Book" English Hardcover,**
c. 1952. Collins. 8x10.75" with 80 pages. - **$25 $50 $100**

MKY-1113

❑ **MKY-1113. "Mickey Mouse Annual" English Book,**
1953. Dean & Son Ltd. 7.5x9.75" hardcover, 96 pages. - **$30 $60 $125**

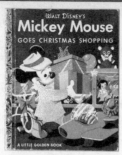

MKY-1114

MKY-1115

MKY-1116

❏ **MKY-1116. "Cheerios" With Disney 3-D Comic Books,**
1954. Box flat is 13.25x20.5" and advertises the three different sets of 3-D comics that were issued one per package. There were eight comics per set. One side panel lists all 24 titles and front of box has attached pair of 3-D glasses to be cut out. Gordon Gold Archives. Box - **$150 $300 $600**

❏ **MKY-1114. "Mickey Mouse Goes Christmas Shopping Little Golden Book,"**
1953. Simon & Schuster. 6.5x8" with 28 pages. 1st printing - **$12 $25 $40**

❏ **MKY-1115. "Tempo" Magazine With Mickey,**
1953. Volume 1, #14. 4.25x6" featuring four-page article titled "The Mouse Who Made Millions" with several pictures of Mickey and one of Walt Disney. - **$12 $25 $40**

MKY-1117

❏ **MKY-1117. "Mickey Mouse" Thermos,**
1954. Adco-Liberty. 8.25" tall metal and red plastic cup. - **$275 $650 $1250**

MKY-1118

❑ **MKY-1118. "Mickey Mouse/Donald Duck" Lunch Box,**
1954. Adco-Liberty Mfg. Corp. 6.5x8.75x3.75" metal box with illustrations on front and back while band has character portraits. - **$125 $275 $650**

MKY-1119

❑ **MKY-1119. "Mickey Mouse Annual" English Book,**
1954. Dean & Son Ltd. 7.5x9.75" hardcover, 96 pages. - **$30 $60 $100**

MKY-1120

❑ **MKY-1120. "Mousegetar" Concept Art,**
c. 1954. Art is 7x13" in pencil by "Disney Legend" toy designer Al Konetzni. Image is titled "Mickey Mouse Ukulele" and was the genesis of toys that came to be produced by Mattel as the Mousegetar and Mousegetar Junior. Original design shows body of ukulele in the shape of Mickey's head. Unique, Fine - **$1200**

MKY-1121

❑ **MKY-1121. "Mousegetar/ Mousegetar Junior" Publicity Photos,**
c. 1954. Pair of glossy photos are 6x8.5" and 7.5x9.5" for final production models of plastic guitars produced by Mattel and originally developed by "Disney Legend" toy designer Al Konetzni. Each - **$12 $25 $40**

MKY-1122

❑ **MKY-1122. "Mickey Mouse Bedtime Stories" Hardcover With Dust Jacket,**
c. 1954. English by The Sunshine Press. 6.75x9.75". Later edition with 96 pages on glossy paper.
Jacket - **$25 $50 $100**
Book - **$60 $135 $275**

MKY-1123

❏ **MKY-1123. "Walt Disney's Sketch A Graph Paint Book,"**
1955. Ohio Art Co. and Whitman. 8x10.75" with 64 pages. - **$20 $35 $75**

MKY-1124

❏ **MKY-1124. Mickey And Friends Candy Box Prototype,**
1955. Original art in ink and color pencil by "Disney Legend" toy designer Al Konetzni consisting of two thin paper sheets, each 6.5x13.5" and overlaid. Nearly the entire top sheet is the proposed box's front, right and left side panels. Mickey is depicted as the store owner pointing to his open door for Donald and his nephews, Minnie, Goofy and Pluto. Sign above awning reads "Mickey Mouse Candy Store" and simulated poster on the wall reads "Try Donald Duck Ice Cream." Unique, Fine - **$1850**

MKY-1125

❏ **MKY-1125. "Mickey Mouse School House" Concept Art,**
1955. Art is 7x9" original in pencil by "Disney Legend" toy designer Al Konetzni for play building to house small character figures and schoolroom accessories. Mickey is pictured as school bell ringer for Pinocchio, Donald Duck and nephews, Minnie, Pluto, Goofy. Unique, Near Mint - **$375**

MKY-1126

❏ **MKY-1126. "Walt Disney Character My First Game,"**
1955. Gabriel, 9.25x14.25x1.25" deep box. - **$15 $25 $45**

MKY-1127

MKY-1129

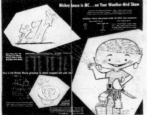

MKY-1128

MKY-1130

❑ **MKY-1129. "Mickey Mouse Circus Cheerios" Box,**
1957. Flattened box is 9x10.5". Ad on front and back for "Mickey Mouse Circus Wiggle Picture Badge" along with six different "Wiggle Pictures." - **$125 $275 $550**

❑ **MKY-1127. "Walt Disney Cartooning Card" Set,**
1956. Set of eighteen numbered stiff paper cards, each 2.25x3.5". Maker unknown. Set - **$200 $400 $600**

❑ **MKY-1130. "Walt Disney/Cheerios" Premium Flicker Set,**
1957. Vari-Vue. 3.5x5.5" mailing envelope contains complete seven-piece premium. Has thin molded plastic badge with opening to hold one of six different flasher inserts. Near Mint Set - **$350**
Badge Only - **$40 $75 $150**
Each Insert - **$10 $20 $30**

❑ **MKY-1128. "Mickey Mouse/Weather-Bird Shoes" Promotional Folder,**
1956. Glossy folder is 8.5x11" and opens to 17x22" with various text and illustrations relating to the Weather-Bird Shoes campaign on the Mickey Mouse Club TV show. - **$25 $45 $85**

MKY-1131

MKY-1133

❑ **MKY-1131. "Mickey Mouse Annual" English Hardcover,**
1957. Dean & Son Ltd. 8.25x10" with 80 pages. - **$25 $50 $100**

❑ **MKY-1133. Mickey Mouse Concept Art For Pull Toy,**
1958. Gong Bell. 12.5x17.5". Three separate art panels glued to a sheet of tissue paper. For a wood pull/riding toy. Art is by Al Konetzni, long-time Disney toy designer. Unique - **$300**

MKY-1132

❑ **MKY-1132. "Mickey Mouse" Boxed Timex Watch With Figure,**
1958. U.S. Time. 4x4.5x5.75" tall box with top that lifts off to reveal display with attached 5" tall hard plastic figure and watch. Near Mint Boxed - **$400**
Figure Only - **$12 $25 $50**
Watch Only - **$40 $70 $115**

MKY-1134

☐ MKY-1134. "Scuffy" Premium Prints With Original Product,
c. 1958. Three different 11.5x14.5" prints with original envelope and bottle of shoe polish in original box. Prints are of Mickey and Donald as they appeared in "Fun And Fancy Free," Snow White and dwarfs with forest animals and picnic scene of "Mickey And His Pals" featuring many Disney characters. Box With Polish - **$25 $45 $80** Print Set - **$50 $100 $175**

MKY-1135

☐ MKY-1135. Mickey Mouse French Magazines Bound Book,
1959. Hardcover 9x12" "Le Journel De Mickey Album No. 16" from a series of bound runs of weekly publication. This volume contains #360-377. Each weekly has 24 pages so book totals 432 pages. Each issue features a combination of Disney and non-Disney stories and features plus comic book-style stories. - **$60 $110 $175**

MKY-1136

☐ MKY-1136. "Mickey Mouse Shoes,"
1950s. Trimfoot Co. 4.5x8x3" deep box contains pair of original but generic "Baby Deer" shoes. Boxed - **$40 $80 $175**

MKY-1137

☐ MKY-1137. "Mickey Mouse Kiddie Hankies,"
1950s. Box is 8.25x8.25x.25" and likely held three 8x8" hankies.
Box - **$20 $40 $75**
Each Hanky - **$8 $12 $25**

MKY-1138

☐ **MKY-1138. "Mickey Mouse Bouncing Ball Target Game" Prototype Box Lid,**
1950s. Konetzni. Original art in ink and color pencil by "Disney Legend" toy designer Al Konetzni on 11x11.75" paper centered by images of a bouncing ball going across the box text, Mickey image at lower left, "Club" emblem at top right. Bottom margin is signed by Konetzni. Unique, Fine - **$250**

MKY-1139

MKY-1140

☐ **MKY-1139. Puzzle Prototype,**
1950s. Paper sheet is 5x8" with pen and ink watercolor art for proposed appliance company jigsaw puzzle premium, probably GE. Image is Mickey fishing although a "No Fishing" sign is behind him. Bottom right corner is an inset image of a stove. Comes with separate acetate sheet of hand-done black outlines of the puzzle pieces which can be placed over top of the art thus showing how completed puzzle would look. Gordon Gold Archives. Unique, Near Mint - **$425**

☐ **MKY-1140. "Mickey Mouse Nestled Rattle Blocks,"**
1950s. Gabriel. Set of five cardboard blocks with paper labels. Largest is 5x5x5.5" while smallest is 3x3x4". - **$15 $25 $50**

MKY-1141

☐ **MKY-1141. Disney Character Fan Card,**
1950s. 8-1/8x10-1/8" stiff paper. - **$12 $25 $50**

MKY-1142

❑ **MKY-1142. Mickey "The 3-Dimensional Jigsaw Puzzle,"** 1950s. Jaymar. 9.75x11.25x2" deep box. Puzzle is 18x18" when assembled and titled "Mickey Mouse-High Diver." Came with 3-D glasses. - **$30 $60 $100**

MKY-1143

❑ **MKY-1143. "Disneyland Ark" English Punch-Out Set,** 1950s. Williams, Ellis & Co. Ltd. Set consists of three colorful thin cardboard sheets with original 3.5x6.25" illustrated paper band used to hold the sheets together. A total of 29 different punch-outs representing 33 different characters. - **$30 $65 $125**

MKY-1144

MKY-1145

❑ **MKY-1144. "Mickey Mouse" As Hunter,** 1950s. Goebel. 3.5" tall. Log has foil sticker and "Mickey Mouse" name. Underside has incised "78" and full bee marking. - **$110 $215 $325**

❑ **MKY-1145. Bandleader Mickey Mouse Ceramic Figurine,** 1950s. Hagen-Renaker. 1.75" tall. - **$65 $135 $235**

MKY-1146

❑ **MKY-1146. Mickey Mouse Small Ceramic Figurine,** 1950s. Shaw. 2" tall. - **$50 $85 $135**

MKY-1147

❑ **MKY-1147. Mickey Mouse with Hat Ceramic Figure,** 1950s. Shaw. 2-5/8" tall. - **$50 $85 $135**

MKY-1148

❏ **MKY-1148. Mickey Mouse Cereamic Potty For Boys,**
1950s. 6" diameter by 5" deep. By Shaw Company. Given as gift from Walt Disney to new parents. - **$500 $1000 $2000**

MKY-1149

❏ **MKY-1149. Mickey Mouse Cereamic Potty For Girls,**
1950s. 6" diameter by 5" deep. By Shaw Company. Given as gift from Walt Disney to new parents. - **$1000 $2000 $3000**

MKY-1150

❏ **MKY-1150. Mickey Mouse Ceramic Figurine,**
1950s. Beswick, England. 3.75" tall. Marked underneath with company mark. - **$165 $325 $550**

MKY-1151

❏ **MKY-1151. Marx Disney Character Figures,**
1950s. Lot of five plastic figures 1.5" to 2" tall. Sold individually as well as included with Marx playset. Each - **$5 $10 $15**

MKY-1152

❑ **MKY-1152. "Mickey Mouse Sugar Babies" Candy Box,**
1950s. Empty box 5.75x9x2.75" that contained 24 packages of candy prices a 5 cents each. - **$25 $50 $85**

MKY-1153

MKY-1154

❑ **MKY-1153. "Comet Candies Inc." Retailers Sales Sheet,**
1950s. Old Dominion Candy Corp. 8.5x11" one-sided sheet. Includes "Mickey Mouse Rave Chocolate Covered Coconut" candy bars as well as "Walt Disney Animated Chocolate," a boxed set of four figural candies of Mickey, Minnie, Donald and Pluto. - **$20 $35 $55**

❑ **MKY-1154. "Mickey Mouse Cookies" Box,**
1950s. Nabisco. 1.75x5x2.75" tall box with front and back panels showing Mickey and Donald while sides are Pluto and Minnie. Top flap is Mickey and Minnie. - **$110 $225 $325**

MKY-1155

❑ **MKY-1155. "Mickey Mouse Cookies" Box,**
1950s. National Biscuits Co. 2x5x2.5" tall cardboard with original string carrier. - **$110 $225 $325**

MKY-1156

❑ **MKY-1156. Disney Character Birthday Party Kit,**
1950s. Rendoll Paper Corp. 9.5x15.25x1" deep illustrated box containing complete, elaborate set of "Over 40 Complete Pieces For 8 Kiddies." Set includes eight colorful stiff paper punch-out party hats and candy baskets, each featuring a different character of Mickey, Minnie, Donald, Daisy, Pluto, Goofy, Dumbo, Pinocchio. Other parts include "Pin The Ear On Pluto" game with eight ears that were to be cut out. - **$30 $60 $85**

MKY-1157

❑ **MKY-1157. "Mickey Mouse" Planter,**
1950s. Leeds. 3x7x7" tall painted and glazed china depicting Mickey in cowboy outfit. - **$25 $55 $85**

MKY-1158

MKY-1159

❑ **MKY-1158. "Disney Candles" Set Boxed,**
1950s. "Made In Japan" 4.25x10x2" deep boxed complete set of 4" tall figural painted wax candles of Mickey, Minnie, Donald, Daisy, Pluto. Boxed - **$20 $35 $70**

❑ **MKY-1159. Disney Characters Ceiling Lamp Boxed,**
1950s. "Globe Product." 13x13x9.5" deep boxed complete ceiling light fixture of 11" diameter painted aluminum mounting base and 8" diameter by 3.25" deep frosted glass bulb cover shade with paint images on inner side. Box - **$10 $20 $30** Fixture - **$60 $110 $165**

MKY-1160

❑ **MKY-1160. "Mickey Mouse Magic Milk Pump,"**
1950s. Morris Plastics Corp. 3.5x3.5x11" tall box contains 11" soft plastic pump designed to be attached to a bottle and pressed down to dispense milk. Plastic top section has raised image of Mickey flexing his muscles. Box - **$12 $20 $40**
Pump - **$12 $20 $40**

MKY-1163

❑ **MKY-1163. Mickey Mouse Boxed (2) Wallpaper Border,**
1950s. United Wallpaper Inc./Trimz Co. Each roll is 12' long. Each with very similar design. Each Boxed - **$20 $35 $65**

MKY-1161

MKY-1162

MKY-1164

❑ **MKY-1164. Mickeypops Club Button,**
1950s. 1.25" button issued by English candy maker. - **$100 $200 $300**

❑ **MKY-1161. Mickey And Thumper Rug,**
1950s. Woven fabric rug is 21.5x41" with fringe trim on right and left margins. - **$50 $85 $150**

❑ **MKY-1162. Mickey Mouse As Hunter Goebel Vase,**
1950s. Figure is 2.75x4.5.25" tall and has full bee marking with incised "DIS 75." - **$115 $240 $385**

MKY-1165

MICKY MOUSE
Key Chain

I STICK OUT MY TONGUE
© W.D.P.

MKY-1165. Mickey Mouse Key Chain On Display Card,
1950s. Maker unknown. 2.25x3.75" card contains 1.25" tall three-dimensional hard plastic Mickey Mouse head with attached brass key chain. Card has small WDP copyright. Additional text including misspelled name reads "Micky Mouse Key Chain/I Stick Out My Tongue." When back plunger is pushed Mickey's nose and tongue extend as ears move forward. Carded - **$25 $50 $75**

MKY-1166

MKY-1166. "Walt Disney Character Party Baskets,"
1950s. Best Hobby Kits. Five 3.5" tall hard plastic baskets in different colors.
Packaged - **$12 $25 $45**

MKY-1167

MKY-1167. "Walt Disney Character Cookie Cutters,"
1950s. Loma Plastics Inc. 4.5x10x1.25" deep box contains complete set of four figural hard plastic cookie cutters, each 4" tall in different color. Includes Mickey, Minnie, Pluto and Donald. Box - **$12 $25 $50** Cutters Each - **$5 $10 $15**

MKY-1168

MKY-1169

MKY-1168. "Disneyland/ Beswick" Ceramic Mug,
1950s. 3" tall. Underside marked "Made In England Expressly For Disneyland By Beswick." - **$30 $50 $80**

MKY-1169. "Mickey Mouse Sunshine Straws,"
1950s. American Sel-Kap Corp. 3.75x8.75x1" deep box contains complete amount of 100 multicolored straws. - **$10 $20 $35**

MKY-1170

MKY-1172

❑ **MKY-1172. Birthday Musical Cake Plate,**
1950s. Authorized "Japan" 7.25" diameter by 1.25" tall tin lithographed plate on wind-up mechanism with on/off switch. - **$30 $50 $75**

❑ **MKY-1170. "Mickey Mouse's Savings House Bank,"**
1950s. Tin litho bank from "The State Savings Bank Of Victoria, Australia." Underside has metal trap. - **$65 $125 $180**

MKY-1171

MKY-1173

❑ **MKY-1171. "Disneyland Melody Player" Musical Toy,**
1950s. J. Chein & Co. 6.x7.5x6.5" tall tin litho. Paper rolls inserted and music produced by cranking. - **$115 $200 $300**

❑ **MKY-1173. Birthday Revolving Carousel,**
1950s. Authorized "Made In Japan" tin lithographed cake decoration on 4" diameter base by 8.5" tall. Base has holders for six candles. Heat from lighted candles causes suspended die-cut metal character figures to revolve slowly while brushing against two metal bell caps to produce delicate chime tones. - **$45 $85 $150**

MKY-1174

MKY-1175

❑ **MKY-1174. Models Catalogue With Mickey And Others,**
1950s. "Model-Craft." 5.5x8.5" catalogue with original mailing envelope. Content is 32 pages devoted to plaster casting sets for various themes but including a Disney set picturing Mickey, Minnie, Donald, Donald's nephew, Mickey's nephew, Pluto. Mailer - **$5 $10 $15**
Catalogue - **$15 $25 $40**

❑ **MKY-1175. "Walt Disney Character And Other TV Toys" Store Sign,**
1950s. Sign is 9.5x18x.25" thick cardboard with same design repeated front and back. - **$30 $60 $90**

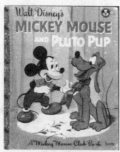

MKY-1176

❑ **MKY-1176. "Mickey Mouse And Pluto Pup,"**
1950s. Simon & Schuster. 6.75x8" with 28 pages. Same as Little Golden Book but this is second edition "Mickey Mouse Club Book." - **$12 $25 $50**

MKY-1177

❑ **MKY-1177. Large Doll House With Disney Character Room,**
1950s. Marx. 8x25x16" tall tin litho. Interior features room depicting wallpaper of Mickey, Minnie and nephews, Donald and his nephews, Pluto and Goofy. Floor shows Donald and corner portraits of Mickey and Donald. - **$75 $135 $275**

MKY-1178

MKY-1180

❏ **MKY-1178. "Walt Disney's Television Playhouse" Playset,**
1950s. Marx. 11x28.5x3" deep box contains set #4349. Has complete set of hard plastic accessories including banquet table, two-story house front, fireman's safety net, treasure map, 38 soft plastic figures 1.25" to 2.25" tall. Includes Snow White and The Seven Dwarfs, five Alice characters, five Pinocchio characters, four Dumbo characters, Mickey, Minnie and nephews, Donald, Daisy and nephews, Pluto. - **$225 $450 $900**

❏ **MKY-1180. Mickey Mouse Ramp Walker,**
1950s. Marx. 3.25" tall hard plastic. - **$18 $35 $65**

MKY-1181

❏ **MKY-1181. Mickey And Donald Ramp Walker,**
1950s. Marx. 4" long hard plastic. - **$40 $70 $125**

MKY-1179

MKY-1182

❏ **MKY-1179. Large Mickey As Clown Squeeze Toy,**
1950s. Soft vinyl figure 10.5" tall made by "Viceroy/Made In Canada." - **$20 $35 $75**

❏ **MKY-1182. Mickey/Minnie Ramp Walker,**
1950s. Marx. 3" tall hard plastic. - **$40** **$70** **$125**

MKY-1183

❏ **MKY-1183. Hunter Mickey With Pluto Ramp Walker,**
1950s. Marx. 3.25" hard plastic. - **$30** **$55** **$110**

MKY-1184

❏ **MKY-1184. Mickey Mouse Figural Christmas Ornament,**
1950s. 2.5x4.25" two-sided embossed diecut tin. Maker unknown. - **$8** **$15** **$25**

MKY-1185

❏ **MKY-1185. "Mickey And Minnie Mouse In Rumba Rhythm" Magnetic Toy,**
1950s. Masco Corp. 1x1.5x2" deep box contains pair of 1.5" tall plastic figures attached to magnet bases. - **$15** **$30** **$60**

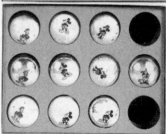

MKY-1186

❏ **MKY-1186. Walt Disney Characters Boxed Christmas Balls,**
1950s. American Glass Corp. 7.5x10x2.5" deep cardboard box has twelve glass ball tree ornaments. Complete Boxed - **$45** **$80** **$160**

MKY-1187

MKY-1188

MKY-1189

MKY-1190

❏ **MKY-1189. Mickey And Friends Sand Pail,**
1950s. Chein. 5.25" tall lithographed tin with carrying handle. - **$65 $135 $250**

❏ **MKY-1190. Mickey Mouse Sand Pail,**
1950s. Chein & Co. 5.25" tall by 5" diameter with attached handle. - **$65 $135 $250**

MKY-1191

❏ **MKY-1187. English Pop-Up Game Board,**
1950s. Chad Valley Co. Ltd. Stand-up board only from amusement park themed game. Board assembles to 10x12x9.5" tall and has cardboard easel on reverse of upright panel. Pop-up elements include game path and staircase. - **$25 $45 $80**

❏ **MKY-1188. "Mickey Mouse 2 Transistor Radio,"**
1950s. Hard plastic figural radio measures 5x5x1" deep. Has thin metal Mickey image on front. Ears serve as on/off knobs. Small sticker on reverse "Gabriel Industries/ Japan." - **$40 $85 $135**

❏ **MKY-1191. "Mickey Mouse Sand Set,"**
1950s. Eldon. 5x6x17.5" set includes soft plastic bucket, sprinkling can, shovel and sand mold attached to cardboard insert and wrapped in yellow string mesh "beach bag." - **$12 $25 $45**

MKY-1192

❏ **MKY-1192. "Mickey Mouse Sand Set,"**
1950s. Eldon. 5x6x17.5" with soft plastic sprinkling can, bucket, shovel, rake, scoop and red string mesh "beach bag." - **$12 $25 $45**

MKY-1193

❏ **MKY-1193. Disney Characters Australian Pail,**
1950s. "A Willow Production." 6.75" top diameter by 6" tall tin lithographed sand pail with wrap-around beach scene involving Mickey, Donald and his nephews, Pluto, Goofy. - **$115 $225 $335**

MKY-1194

❏ **MKY-1194. "Mickey The Magician" Battery Operated Boxed Toy,**
1950s. Line Mar. Lithographed tin with felt cape and starched felt hat. 10" tall on 5-3/8x7" base. Mickey reveals and then makes disappear a tin chick. Box is 6.75x10.5x7.5" deep. Box - **$175 $325 $650**
Toy - **$325 $650 $1350**

MKY-1195

❏ **MKY-1195. "Walt Disney Friction Delivery Wagon" Boxed Toy,** 1950s. Line Mar. 2.5x5x4.25" toy consists of tin lithographed three-wheeled wagon with attached figure of Mickey who has tin lithographed body and feet, celluloid head and legs. Box - **$125 $250 $400** Toy - **$125 $250 $400**

MKY-1196

❏ **MKY-1196. "Line Mar Toys" Disney Friction Airplane,** 1950s. Tin lithographed toy 6x7.5x2" tall. Sides have images of Mickey while Pluto appears on tail fins. Wings have illustrations of Pluto, Goofy and Donald. - **$275 $550 $1100**

MKY-1197

❏ **MKY-1197. Mickey Friction Motorcycle By Line Mar,** 1950s. Marx. Toy is 1.25x3.5x3" tall. - **$115 $225 $450**

MKY-1198

MKY-1199

❏ **MKY-1198. Mickey Mouse Friction Truck,**
1950s. Marx. Hard plastic truck measures 1.75x3.75x2.75" tall. Unmarked. - **$35 $70 $125**

❏ **MKY-1199. "Whirling Tail Mickey Mouse" Boxed Wind-Up,**
1950s. Line Mar. 2x2.75x5.5" tall toy with built-in key. Box - **$135 $265 $525**
Toy - **$135 $265 $525**

MKY-1201

MKY-1200

❏ **MKY-1201. "Mickey Mouse" Dipsy Car Wind-up,**
1950s. Marx. Version with 3.5x5.5x5.75" tall lithographed tin car with hard plastic Mickey. Box - **$235 $425 $750**
Toy - **$175 $275 $500**

MKY-1202

❏ **MKY-1200. "Mickey The Driver" Boxed Wind-up,**
1950s. Marx. 3x7x4.25" tall lithographed tin with built-in key.
Box - **$225 $425 $750**
Toy - **$165 $275 $500**

❏ **MKY-1202. "Mickey Mouse Roller Skater" Boxed Wind-Up,**
1950s. Line Mar. Box is 4.5x6.75x2.5" deep. Tin figure is 6-3/8" tall with fabric pants and rubber ears.
Box - **$275 $550 $1000**
Toy - **$265 $525 $900**

MKY-1203

❑ **MKY-1203. "Disney Parade Roadster" Boxed Wind-Up Car,**
1950s. Marx. 4.75x11.5x3.25" deep box contains 11" long car with built-in key.
Box - **$225 $450 $900**
Toy - **$225 $450 $900**

MKY-1204

❑ **MKY-1204. "Mickey Mouse Mouseketeers Moving Van" Friction Powered,**
1950s. Line Mar. 15" long tin toy with box.
Box - **$225 $450 $900**
Toy - **$325 $550 $1100**

MKY-1205

❑ **MKY-1205. "Mickey Mouse Express" Windup,**
1950s. Line Mar. 9" tin. Box - **$85 $165 $275**
Toy - **$75 $150 $250**

MKY-1206

❑ **MKY-1206. "Disneyland" Marx Wind-Up Train,**
1950s. Toy is 1.5x12.5x2.5" tall. Engine has built-in wind-up key. Engine made either of single color plastic or illustrated litho. tin.
Plastic engine - **$45 $85 $145**   Litho. Tin engine - **$55 $110 $165**

MKY-1207

MKY-1207. "Marx" Wind-Up Mickey Mouse Tricycle,
1950s. Lithographed tin toy is 2.5x3.5x3.5" tall. - **$110 $235 $350**

MKY-1208

❑ **MKY-1208. Mickey Mouse On Scooter Wind-Up By Line Mar Toys,**
1950s. Marx. Lithographed tin 2.5x3.5x4.25" tall. When wound, toy travels in a circle. - **$265 $625 $1100**

MKY-1209

❑ **MKY-1209. "Mickey Mouse Scooter Jockey" With Original Box,**
1950s. Marco. 7" tall plastic toy.
Box - **$30 $60 $90**
Toy - **$40 $80 $150**

MKY-1210

❑ **MKY-1210. Mickey And Minnie Mouse With Street Organ Metal Figure Set,**
1950s. Sacul, England. 1.75" tall figures of Mickey and Minnie and 2.25" tall freewheeling street organ. When organ is cranked it produces musical notes. - **$125 $265 $450**

MKY-1211

MKY-1212

MKY-1213

❑ **MKY-1213. "A Walt Disney Flip Book" Featuring Mickey,**
1950s. Disneyland Art Corner. 3x3.5" featuring illustrations of Mickey as a cowboy performing tricks with his lasso. - **$12 $25 $40**

MKY-1214

❑ **MKY-1211. "Mickey's Air Mail" Airplane,**
1950s. Hard rubber vehicle 5x6.25x3.5" tall with three-dimensional figure of Mickey. Rare color variety and Canadian version by "Sunruco." Has raised "Mickey's Air Mail" on each side. - **$80 $160 $275**

❑ **MKY-1212. "Mickey Mouse The Old Fashioned Car Driver,"**
1950s. Elm Toys. 2" long free-wheeling hard plastic "Stutz Bearcat" comes in colorful box.
Box - **$10 $20 $30**
Car - **$10 $20 $30**

❑ **MKY-1214. "Mickey Mouse 3D Viewer" Set,**
1950s. English by Martin Lucas Ltd. 2x5.5x1.75" tall box contains 4" long hard plastic viewer and includes raised image of Mickey holding "3-D" sign. Comes with 1x5.5" full color cardboard sleeve containing one of two full color filmstrips titled "Mickey's Picnic." Boxed Viewer - **$45 $80 $135**
Boxed Strip - **$15 $25 $35**

MKY-1215

☐ **MKY-1215. "Mickey Mouse School Tablet,"**
1950s. Tablet 8x10" by ample 1" thick. -
$18 $30 $50

MKY-1216

☐ **MKY-1216. Mickey Mouse Desk Letter Holder,**
c. 1960. MPFL Co. 1.25x4x4" tall solid brass with high relief design. - **$20 $35 $65**

MKY-1217

☐ **MKY-1217. "Mickey Mouse Annual" English Hardcover,**
1961. Dean & Son Ltd. 8x10" with 96 pages. - **$25 $55 $100**

MKY-1218

☐ **MKY-1218. "Mickey Mouse World Reporter Kit" Complete Premium,**
1961. "Vicks Medi-Trating Cough Syrup."
7x10" mailing envelope contains complete 3-piece kit consisting of 1.75" button, 2.5x3.5" World Reporter Press Card, 25.75x35" map by Rand McNally.
Button - **$35 $70 $150**
Card - **$15 $25 $40**
Mailer - **$15 $25 $40**
Map - **$35 $65 $100**

MKY-1219

❑ **MKY-1219. Mickey And Donald Floating Soap Raft,**
c. 1961. Dell. 5x6.5x4.25" tall soft vinyl squeaker toy. - **$20 $35 $60**

MKY-1222

MKY-1220

❑ **MKY-1220 "Mickey Mouse" Ceramic Figurine,**
1963. Dan Brechner. 5" tall with "WD 25" under base. - **$20 $40 $75**

❑ **MKY-1221. "Mickey Mouse And Friends Kaboodle Kit,"**
1963. 7x9x4" deep vinyl lunch box. Maker unknown. - **$85 $165 $350**

❑ **MKY-1222. "Mickey And The Beanstalk" Record,**
1963. Disneyland label 12.25x12.25" cardboard album cover containing 33-1/3 rpm recording. - **$8 $15 $25**

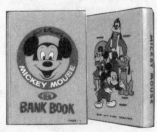

MKY-1223

❑ **MKY-1223. "Mickey Mouse Bank Book,"**
1964. Ideal Toy Corp. 4.5x6x1" deep hard plastic designed like a book. - **$25 $50 $90**

MKY-1221

MKY-1224

❏ **MKY-1224. "Mickey Mouse Annual" English Book,**
1964. Dean & Son Ltd. 8x10.25" hardcover, 96 pages. - **$25 $45 $100**

MKY-1225

❏ **MKY-1225. Mickey Mouse Drawing By Andy Engman With Autograph,**
c. 1965. 12.5x15.5" sheet with 7x13.5" illustration of Mickey in tuxedo raising a glass of champagne. Engman was the president of Walt Disney Animation from 1949-1966. Near Mint Same or Similar - **$275**

MKY-1226

❏ **MKY-1226. "Nabisco Puppets Wheat Puffs Cereal" Container,**
1966. 4.5x5x9.5" tall soft plastic. Also designed as a bank with coin slot on back. - **$15 $25 $50**

MKY-1227

❏ **MKY-1227. Mickey Mouse 3-D Picture,**
1966. W.C. Jones Publishing Co. 10.5x13.5" plastic. - **$25 $45 $65**

MKY-1228

❏ **MKY-1228. Mickey Mouse 3-D Picture,**
1966. W. C. Jones Publishing Co. 8x10" rigid plastic. - **$15 $30 $45**

MKY-1229

MKY-1231

❏ **MKY-1229. Australian Rugby Tray With Disney Characters,**
1966. "Walt Disney Productions." Licensed 12" diameter by .75" deep tin lithographed "Rugby Tour Souvenir Tray" picturing rugby game between "Black Petes" and "Beagle Boys." Goofy is shown scoring a goal and Mickey is pictured as referee. - **$25 $50 $75**

❏ **MKY-1231. Mickey "Bendiface" Toy,**
1967. Lakeside Toys. 6x9" blister card containing 5" tall bendable foam rubber face. Reverse of face has open slot/holes for placement of fingers to change his facial expressions. Near Mint Boxed - **$35**

MKY-1230

MKY-1232

❏ **MKY-1230. "Mickey Mouse Kookie Kamper,"**
1966. Multiple Toymakers. 4x13.5x7" tall boxed 6" long "Putt Putt Motor Sound" friction camper vehicle. Box - **$15 $25 $50** Toy - **$25 $50 $100**

❏ **MKY-1232. Boy Scout "World Jamboree" Song Booklet,**
1967. 7Up. 4x6.75" with 32 pages issued for the 12th World Jamboree held in Idaho. - **$8 $15 $25**

MKY-1233

❑ **MKY-1233. Disney College Homecoming Ashtray,**
1967. 4x4.75" smoked glass. Issue for University of Pittsburgh. - **$12 $25 $35**

MKY-1235

❑ **MKY-1235. Mickey Mouse 40th Birthday Publicity Stills,**
1968. Each is 8x10". Each - **$4 $8 $12**

MKY-1234

❑ **MKY-1234. "Mickey Mouse Surprise Party" Production Letter And Photostats,"**
1968. Colorforms archives. Four items relating to "Free Trips To Disneyland Sweepstakes Promotion." Group - **$30 $55 $80**

MKY-1236

❏ **MKY-1236. Mickey Mouse Gumball Machine Bank,**
1968. Hasbro. 4x4.5x9" tall hard plastic.
Box - **$10 $20 $40**
Bank - **$10 $20 $35**

MKY-1238

❏ **MKY-1238. Mickey Mouse 40th Birthday/GE Nitelite Press Release,**
1968. 8.25x10.75" paper with attached 8x10" glossy photo. The "Picture Caption" text notes the discussion of "Mickey Mouse's 40th Birthday And GE's Mickey Mouse Nitelite Line At The National Hardware Show" between account executive Al Konetzni and GE employee. - **$20 $35 $55**

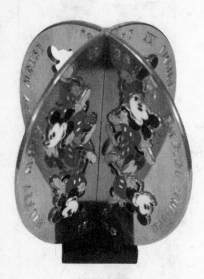

MKY-1237

❏ **MKY-1237. Mickey Mouse 40th Birthday Sculpture By Ernest Trova,**
1968. From a numbered edition of fifty originally sold for $350 each by Ernest Trova, noted contemporary sculptor and collector of Disneyana. Has a 4" diameter and height of 3.5". Sterling silver with embossed text and enameled metal Mickey figural appliques. Four segments with repeated text around rims reading "Mickey Mouse/Empire Builder/1928-1968." Includes 12 Mickey appliques, each 1" tall. Two segments have cut-out image. Stamped-in edition number. Sits atop small black plastic base. Mint As Issued - **$1500**

MKY-1239

❏ **MKY-1239. "American Heritage" Hardcover Magazine,**
1968. 8.5x11" with 112 pages for April. Feature article for Mickey's 40th birthday. - **$12 $25 $35**

MKY-1240

MKY-1242

❏ **MKY-1240. Mickey Mouse "Magnetic Buckle Belt" Display,**
c. 1968. Pyramid Belt Co. 11x12.5" die-cut cardboard. Complete - **$40 $65 $110**

❏ **MKY-1242. Disney Cartoons Song Folio,**
1969. Bourne Co. 9x12" compilation titled in full, "Song Highlights From Walt Disney's Famous Cartoons/Mickey Mouse And Silly Symphony," 60 pages. Content is reprint collection of 1930s material including 19 songs. Cover art is 1930s style, picturing different Mickey image front and back. - **$25 $45 $80**

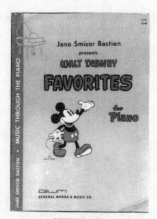

MKY-1241

MKY-1243

❏ **MKY-1241. "Walt Disney Favorites For Piano" Song Folio,**
1969. Bourne Co. 9x12" with 16 pages. Lyrics and music for The Three Little Pigs, Lullaby Land, Pinocchio and Snow White along with several character illustrations. - **$20 $40 $60**

❏ **MKY-1243. "Walt Disney Character Firefighters" Lunch Box With Thermos,**
c. 1969 Aladdin Industries Inc. 7x9x4.25" deep. Underside has three-panel cartoon of safety tips with Donald and his nephews. Thermos is 6.75".
Box - **$60 $120 $250**
Bottle - **$25 $45 $90**

MKY-1244

❑ **MKY-1244. "Parade Of Values" Shelf Display,**
c. 1969. Nabisco. Thin 6x8" flexible die-cut plastic sheet with overhang figure of Mickey as band drummer that wobbles when sheet is mounted on shelf edge. - **$12 $25 $40**

MKY-1245

❑ **MKY-1245. Shoe Holder With Slippers,**
1960s. Soft vinyl hanger rack is 8x35" reinforced by cardboard inserts top and bottom depicting Mickey's head and feet. Center section is elongated body designed to pocket three pairs of shoes and/or slippers. Child's slipper sets of Mickey and Donald are likely not original to the holder.
Holder - **$12 $25 $50**
Slipper Sets Each - **$8 $15 $25**

MKY-1246

MKY-1247

❑ **MKY-1246. "Walt Disney Studios" Licensee Character Guide,**
1960s. 8.5x11" with stiff paper cover plus 12 slightly textured paper sheets. Eleven have character designs, the twelfth has copyright information. - **$35 $65 $100**

❑ **MKY-1247. Daily Comic Strip Original Art Autographed By Gottfredson,**
1960s. Sheet is 6.25x19". Publication date indicated is January 30, 1967.
Same or Similar - **$225 $450 $700**

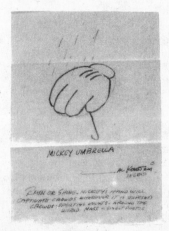

MKY-1248

❑ **MKY-1248. Concept Art For "Mickey Umbrella,"**
1960s. Paper is 7x9" sheet of tracing paper with inked art, text and signature by Al Konetzni, "Disney Legend" toy and merchandise designer. At center is 3x3.25" sketch of an umbrella with entire top designed like Mickey Mouse's hand. Text below this is "Mickey Umbrella/Rain Or Shine-Mickey's Hand Will Captivate Crowds Wherever It Is Exposed/Crowds-Sporting Events- Around The World. Mass & Single Photos." Art was for Disney park use. Unique, Near Mint - **$75**

ONE ROUGH COVER FOR CHILDRENS BOOK '60s

MKY-1251

❑ **MKY-1251. Al Konetzni Concept Art For Disney "School Bus Book,"**
1960s. Sheet of paper measuring 5.25x5.25" mounted to slightly larger 7x7.25" art board featuring art in lead and colored pencil. Unique, Near Mint - **$125**

MKY-1249

❑ **MKY-1249. Mickey Hair Clip,**
1960s. 1.5" brass clip with enameled and silvered brass Mickey at center. - **$10 $15 $30**

MKY-1250

❑ **MKY-1250. "Mousekamagic" Prototype Item,**
1960s. Hand-made prototype measures 1x3" by Al Konetzni, long-time Disney toy designer. Outer sleeve is thin cardboard plus separate die-cut Mickey head image. Also has separate cardboard insert with die-cut diamond opening around drawing of Donald Duck. Object was to hold left end and pull on right to see Donald and then reverse and reinsert to see Mickey. Unique, Very Fine - **$100**

MKY-1252

❑ **MKY-1252. Mickey Mouse Plaster Crib Toy,**
1960s. Enesco. 4" tall. - **$10 $15 $30**

MKY-1253

❑ **MKY-1253. "Mickey And His Friends" Publicity Folder With Photos,**
1960s. Buena Vista Distribution Co. Inc. 8.5x11" folder contains six different 6.75x9.25" glossy publicity photos. - **$25 $45 $70**

MKY-1254

❑ **MKY-1254. Mickey Mouse Nodder,**
1960s. Marx. 2.25" tall hard plastic figure. - **$12 $25 $40**

MKY-1255

❑ **MKY-1255. Mickey Mouse/Donald Duck Poseable Figures,**
1960s. Marx. 5.5" tall figures with hard plastic bodies plus vinyl-covered wire arms and legs for posing. Each wears a fabric outfit. Each - **$10 $20 $40**

MKY-1256

❑ **MKY-1256. Mickey With Goofy And Pluto Ceramic Figurines,**
1960s. Dan Brechner. 1.5x4x5.25" tall Mickey attached by a pair of metal link chains to 3.75" tall Goofy and 2.5" tall Pluto. - **$55 $110 $165**

MKY-1259

MKY-1257

❑ **MKY-1257. Mickey Figurine,**
1960s. Japanese 6.25" tall painted and glazed ceramic. - **$15 $25 $40**

MKY-1260

MKY-1258

❑ **MKY-1258. Mickey Mouse Figurine,**
1960s. Painted and glazed ceramic figure 2.25x3x4.75" tall. Has foil "Enesco" sticker. - **$15 $25 $40**

❑ **MKY-1259. Disney Characters South American Lunch Box,**
1960s. "El Trigal/Uruguay." 3.5x9x3.5" deep metal box designed like suitcase with simulated travel stickers on all sides for Disney characters, different hotels, cruise ships, airlines, e.g. "Grand Mickey Hotel, Pluto Airlines." - **$100 $200 $400**

❑ **MKY-1260. "Mickey And The Band Leader" Soaky,**
1960s. Soft vinyl body and hard vinyl head figure is 9.5" tall. - **$12 $25 $50**

MKY-1261

❏ **MKY-1261. "Soaky" Picture Sheet With Soap Bars,**
1960s. Picture sheet is 12x12" and three bars of soap are each 1.5x2" with picture to cut and mount. Map - **$15 $30 $60**
Each Uncut Wrapper - **$3 $6 $10**

MKY-1262

❏ **MKY-1262. "Walt Disney Character Ex-Pan-Dees Sponge Toy,"**
1960s. James. 11x12x1" deep box contains printed sponge cut-out pieces to form six different "Expanding Characters" for Mickey, Minnie, Donald, Daisy, Pluto and Goofy. Boxed - **$8 $18 $35**

MKY-1263

MKY-1264

❏ **MKY-1263. "Mickey Mouse" Ceramic Lamp Base,**
1960s. Dan Brechner. 8" tall. Socket rod gone from photo example. - **$50 $100 $175**

❏ **MKY-1264. Mickey Mouse Planter,**
1960s. Painted and glazed ceramic 5.25x6.5x4.25" tall. Underside has copyright and "Japan." - **$30 $60 $90**

MKY-1265

MKY-1266

☐ **MKY-1265. "Mickey Mouse" Ceramic Planter,**
1960s. Unmarked. Likely by Enesco. 6" tall. - **$20 $35 $75**

☐ **MKY-1266. "Mickey Mouse Planter,"**
1960s. Painted and glazed ceramic 3.25x5.5x5" tall comes in cardboard box with color label on lid "An Original Dan Brechner Exclusive." Box - **$20 $30 $60** Planter - **$30 $60 $90**

MKY-1267

☐ **MKY-1267. Mickey Mouse Rug,**
1960s. Rug is 20.5x36" fabric with thick cotton nap centered by large image of mod Mickey without name or text. - **$20 $35 $65**

MKY-1268

MKY-1269

☐ **MKY-1268. Mickey Mouse Ceramic Cookie Jar,**
1960s. Enesco. 7.5x12.5x8.25" tall. Unusual design with large pair of die-cut vinyl ears attached to his head. - **$115 $225 $335**

☐ **MKY-1269. Mickey/Minnie Ceramic Mug,**
1960s. Enesco. 4.5" tall. - **$20 $40 $65**

MKY-1270

❑ **MKY-1270. Mickey and Minnie English Button,**
1960s. 2.25". - **$25 $45 $95**

MKY-1271

❑ **MKY-1271. "Disney Cartoon Mug,"**
1960s. Eagle Products. 3.5" tall hard plastic. - **$10 $18 $30**

MKY-1272

❑ **MKY-1272. "Mickey Mouse" Ceramic Salt & Pepper Set,**
1960s. Painted and glazed figures are 4.75" tall. One has foil sticker on reverse "Original Dan Brechner Exclusive." - **$25 $50 $100**

MKY-1273

MKY-1274

❑ **MKY-1273. "Mickey/Minnie Mouse" Ceramic Salt & Pepper Set,**
1960s. Dan Brechner. Each is 5.25" tall. Ink stamp number on underside "WD-52." - **$30 $60 $110**

❑ **MKY-1274. Mickey And Minnie Salt & Pepper Set,**
1960s. Painted and glazed 4" tall shakers on 2x4x2.5" wooden bench. Complete with stopper, foil copyright sticker and small "Japan" sticker. - **$50 $100 $150**

MKY-1275

❑ **MKY-1275. Mickey Mouse Composition Bank,**
1960s. 3x4x6" tall. - **$12 $25 $45**

MKY-1276

☐ **MKY-1276. French Disney Character Bank,**
1960s. Bank is 2.5x5x5.25" tall and lithographed tin. Underside has Disney name and manufacturer "Gulliver-Lyon/Made In France." - **$75 $135 $240**

MKY-1277

☐ **MKY-1277. "Walt Disney Christmas Parade Giant Comic,"**
1960s. Gold Key Series. Issue #5 featuring reprints copyright 1949, 1950, 1952. Has 24-page Christmas story by Carl Barks. - **$10 $30 $100**

MKY-1278

☐ **MKY-1278. "Mickey Mouse" Record Player,**
1960s. Unit is 9x14x5.5" deep with plastic case and carrying handle. Case opens to turntable and figural plastic tone arm in the shape of Mickey's arm and hand with his index finger pointing forward. Canadian issue from the "Sears Electronics" line made for Simpsons-Sears, Toronto, Canada. - **$85 $165 $250**

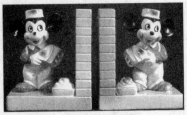

Compliments of your
MICKEY MOUSE SHOE DEALER

GEORGE LEATHERS
CHILDRENS SHOELAND
2947 FIRST ST.
WYANDOTTE, MICH.

MKY-1279

□ MKY-1281. "Mickey Mouse Springees" Boxed Band Set,
1960s. Multiple Toymakers. The unusual 4" tall figures have hard plastic bodies with wire arms and legs for posing, bodies are in a variety of colors and each plays a different instrument. Boxed - **$25 $45 $75**

MKY-1280

MKY-1282

□ MKY-1279. "Mickey Mouse" Premium Picture,
1960s. 5x7" glossy stiff paper featuring the classic official Mickey Mouse 25th birthday portrait by John Hench from 1953. Reverse is marked "Compliments Of Your Mickey Mouse Shoe Dealer" with inked stamp imprint for Wyandotte, Michigan store. - **$12 $25 $50**

□ MKY-1280. Mickey Mouse Ceramic Bookends,
1960s. Dan Brechner. "WD19." Each is 4.5" tall. Set - **$40 $75 $140**

□ MKY-1282. "Mickey's Haunted House" Game With Original Box,
1960s. 15x22" wood with glass cover battery operated game.
Box - **$25 $50 $75**
Toy - **$30 $60 $115**

MKY-1283

MKY-1281

□ MKY-1283. Mickey Mouse Bobbing Head Figure,
1960s. Japan. 6" tall painted composition. - **$25 $50 $75**

(Box)

MKY-1284

❏ **MKY-1284. Mickey "Rolykins" Figure Toy,**
1960s. Marx. Boxed 1.25" tall hard plastic figure with ball bearing insert and foil sticker. Box - **$3 $6 $10**
Toy - **$4 $8 $15**

MKY-1285

MKY-1286

❏ **MKY-1285. Mickey Mouse Alarm Clock Distributed In France,**
1960s. Bayard. 2x4.5x4.75" tall in metal case. Mickey's head nods as seconds tick. U.S. version has dark red case while this French version is pink. Each Version - **$60 $110 $225**

❏ **MKY-1286. "Bradley Mickey Mouse" Clock,**
1960s. 2x4.25x4.5" tall metal case. - **$25 $45 $90**

MKY-1287

❏ **MKY-1287. "Disney Busy Boy" German Alarm Clock,**
1960s. "Hamilton/Made In Germany." 2.5x5x7" tall metal cased wind-up clock topped by 2" tall painted solid vinyl figures of Mickey and Minnie. - **$50 $85 $165**

MKY-1288

❏ **MKY-1288. "Mickey Mouse" Watch,**
1960s. Helbros. 1.25x1.5" metal case with matching metal expansion bands. - **$25 $45 $80**

MKY-1292

❏ **MKY-1292. "I've Been To Disney Village At Donaldson's" Button,**
c. 1960s. 3" diameter. Rim curl has Disney copyright and maker name "Wendell's Mpls." - **$10 $25 $50**

MKY-1289   **MKY-1290**

❏ **MKY-1289. "Acrobatic Clown" Mickey Mouse Trapeze Toy,**
1960s. Kohner, 4.5x7" bag contains 5" tall hard plastic toy. Near Mint Bagged - **$85** Loose - **$12 $25 $45**

❏ **MKY-1290. "Mickey And Donald Magic Slate,"**
1960s. Watkins-Strathmore Co. 8.5x13.75" die-cut cardboard with plastic stylus. - **$8 $18 $35**

MKY-1293

❏ **MKY-1293. "Mickey & Pluto Joggers" Prototype Watch,**
1970. Designed by "Disney Legend" Al Konetzni. 1.25" diameter chromed metal case, leather straps. - Unique, Near Mint - **$375**

MKY-1291

❏ **MKY-1291. Mickey Mouse French Sand Pail,**
c. 1960s. Virojanglor Paris. 5" tall tin litho with vintage 1930s style graphics. - **$55 $135 $265**

MKY-1294

MKY-1294. Floyd Gottfredson Large Framed Specialty Art,
1970. The India ink and watercolor art covers nearly the entire 10.75x14" sheet and was done in 1970 while Gottfredson was still at Disney Studio doing the Mickey Mouse daily strip. Unique, Mint As Made - **$4250**

MKY-1296. Al Konetzni Personally Owned Watches With Handwritten Note,
1970. Both have 1.25" diameter goldtone metal cases, leather straps. First watch is a one-of-a-kind made for his retirement in 1980 and second was given to him by Bradley in 1970, registered edition 0047. Retirement watch - Unique, Near Mint - **$150**
Bradley watch - **$20 $30 $60**

MKY-1295

MKY-1295. "Mickey Mouse Peppy Puppet,"
1970. Kohner Bros. Inc. 4.25x8x2" box contains 4" hard plastic "Miniature Marionette."
Box - **$25 $55 $85**
Toy - **$20 $35 $55**

MKY-1297

MKY-1296

MKY-1297. "Marx Mickey Mouse Little Big Wheel Battery Operated" Toy,
1970. Boxed 5x9.5x7" tall hard plastic toy depicting Mickey in Big Wheel. Includes illustrated 8.5x11" paper sheet advertising Big Wheel and Krazy Kar by Marx.
Box - **$15 $25 $45**
Toy - **$25 $45 $70**

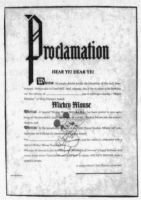

MKY-1298

MKY-1299

MKY-1300

❑ **MKY-1300. "Mickey Mouse" Toy Wristwatch By Marx,**
1971. Blister card is 7x9" and contains hard plastic watch with vinyl straps. Watch produces a "tick-tock" sound as hands move. Carded - **$18 $35 $70**
Loose - **$8 $18 $35**

MKY-1301

❑ **MKY-1301. "Mod Mickey" Miniature Souvenir Frying Pan,**
c. 1971. John Wright who only had a Disney license for one year. 3.25x 4.5x.5" deep cast iron. - **$12 $25 $45**

❑ **MKY-1298. Birthday Proclamation,**
c. 1970. Parchment-like paper is 8.5x11.75" centered by background image of Mickey wearing birthday hat and holding a birthday cake. Text is legal document style and includes mention of a birthday show. Has designated lines for original recipient to fill in information. - **$10 $20 $30**

❑ **MKY-1299. "Mickey Mouse 1932" Daily Strip Reprint Book,**
1971. Italy. 7.75x13.75" with 140 pages. English text. - **$20 $40 $80**

MKY-1302

❑ **MKY-1302. Grateful Dead/Mickey Mouse-Related "Mickey And The Daylites" Concert Poster,**
1972. 14x20" stiff paper poster for December 17, concert featuring Mickey and The Daylites (Mickey Hart, percussionist of The Grateful Dead) and Batucaje Music of Brazil at Pyramid Pins, Garberville, California. Art is by Kelly. First and only printing. - **$40 $75 $140**

MKY-1303

❑ **MKY-1303. "Walt Disney Characters Unscrambler Slide Rule Action,**
1972. Marx. 7.5x12" blister card contains 3.5x11" hard plastic picture puzzle featuring eight Disney characters with bodies divided into three sections. Attached is frame to be placed over one character image and the different sliding sections are then moved to form a complete character image. Near Mint Carded - **$35**

MKY-1304

❑ **MKY-1304. Mickey Mouse And Tinker Bell Figures,**
1972. Marx. Pair of solid soft plastic figures with 6" tall Mickey and 5.25" tall Tinker Bell. Each - **$4 $8 $15**

MKY-1305

❑ **MKY-1305. "Mickey Mouse And The Mouse Factory" Record,**
1972. Sleeve is 7x7" picturing numerous characters and contains 33-1/3 rpm record on Disneyland label. - **$8 $15 $30**

MKY-1306

❑ **MKY-1306. "Mickey Mouse Scooter" By Marx,**
1972. Boxed hard plastic friction toy 2.5x4.25x4" tall. Scooter includes three-dimensional figure of Mickey. Box - **$15 $25 $40**
Toy - **$20 $35 $55**

MKY-1307

❑ **MKY-1307. Mickey And Minnie Mouse Boxed Watch/Pocket Watch,**
c. 1972. Photorific Products, Inc. (Unauthorized.) 4x9.5x1.75" deep box has clear plastic lid, black cardboard bottom. Timepiece is 2" diameter pocket watch which can also be used as wristwatch mounted on 1.5" wide black leather band. Pocket watch snaps into place or can be taken off and comes with metal pocket watch chain. Dial features a 1930s style image of pie-eyed Mickey and Minnie embracing with hearts floating above their heads. Watch is attached to red felt-covered insert. Comes with instruction/guarantee card. Limited production.
Mint Boxed - **$1000**
Loose - **$250 $500 $750**

ing a banjo and Minnie singing. Watch is attached to red felt-covered insert. Comes with instruction/guarantee card. Limited production. Mint Boxed - **$600**
Loose - **$100 $200 $350**

MKY-1309

❑ **MKY-1309. "Mickey Mouse" Unlicensed Pocketwatch,**
c. 1972. Fantasy creation by Al Horne, one of the early dealers in character collectibles, designed as 1930s pocketwatch with silvered metal case and image on dial of pie-eyed Mickey playing piano. Watch is created as actual timepiece rather than toy. - **$100 $200 $300**

MKY-1308

❑ **MKY-1308. Mickey And Minnie Boxed Watch/Pocket Watch,**
c. 1972 Photorific Products, Inc. (Unauthorized.) 4x9.5x1.75" deep box has clear plastic lid, black cardboard bottom. Timepiece is 2" diameter pocket watch which can be also be used as a wristwatch mounted on 1.5" wide black band. Pocket watch snaps into place or can be taken off and comes with metal pocket watch chain. Dial features a 1930s style image of pie-eyed Mickey and Minnie with Mickey play-

MKY-1310

❑ **MKY-1310. Mickey Mouse Toy Watch,**
1973. Marx. Child's toy watch with glow-in-the-dark dial. - **$10 $20 $35**

MKY-1311

❑ **MKY-1311. Konetzni Mock Magazine Cover Original Art,**
1973. Vellum paper sheet is 8.5x11" with art in pencil, watercolor and ink by Joseph Haboush, a member of Disney character merchandise Art Dept. Image is simulated "Time" magazine cover with banner across title "Super Salesman," and featuring a portrait of Al Konetzni wearing Mickey Mouse ears hat. Art was a surprise presentation to "Disney Legend" toy designer Konetzni. Unique, Near Mint - **$275**

MKY-1312

❑ **MKY-1312. Mickey Mouse Pocket Watch,**
1973. In plastic box with advertising card overlay. Train pictured on back of case. Bradley. Complete - **$50 $110 $265**

MKY-1313

❑ **MKY-1313. "Schmid" First Issue Christmas Collector Plate,**
1973. 7.5" diameter decorative china. Reverse text includes "The Disney Family Collector Series/Limited First Edition." - **$100 $200 $350**

MKY-1314

❑ **MKY-1314. "The Best Of Walt Disney Comics 1934 To 1952" Complete Display,**
1974. Western Publishing. 16x25x3" deep cardboard countertop display contains complete amount of 24 reprint books each 8x10.5". Featuring reprints from 1934, 1944, 1947, and 1952 including Mickey Mouse And The Bat Bandit Of Inferno Gulch, comic reprints including the first issue of Uncle Scrooge plus stories from Four Color Comics #62, 159, and 178. Near Mint - **$550**

MKY-1315

MKY-1318

☐ **MKY-1315. Mickey Mouse "School/Utility" Bags,**
1974. Al Nyman & Son Inc. Each is 8x12" nylon with carrying handle and snap closure plus tag and address card. Each Near Mint - **$25**

MKY-1316

☐ **MKY-1316. Mickey Toy Concept Art,**
c. 1974. Paper sheet is 9x10.5" centered by 5x6" original art in ink and wash by "Disney Legend" toy designer Al Konetzni. Depiction is Mickey Mouse three-wheeled riding toy chained to a fire hydrant. Art is signed by Konetzni. Unique, Near Mint - **$125**

☐ **MKY-1317. "Mickey Mouse Cookbook" Hardcover,**
1975. Golden Press. 8.25x11.25" with 94 pages. Filled with great color illustrations on every page of Disney characters preparing food with corresponding recipes including "Peter Pan's Pasta, Bambi's Garden Salad, Wonderland Pancakes," etc. - **$10 $20 $30**

☐ **MKY-1318. Gottfredson Autographed Photo,**
c. 1975. Photo is 5x5" of Floyd Gottfredson, the main Mickey Mouse newspaper daily strip artist in earlier years. Near Mint, Same or Similar. - **$100**

MKY-1319

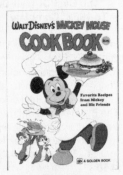

MKY-1317

☐ **MKY-1319. "Spirit Of '76" Puzzle,**
1976. Hallmark Cards. 11x14x1.5" deep box contains puzzle by Springbok Editions. When assembled 17.5x23.5". Near Mint - **$25**

MKY-1320

MKY-1323

MKY-1321

❑ **MKY-1320. Spirit Of '76 Patriotic Figurine,**
1976. Bisque is 4x9.5x6.75" tall painted depiction of Mickey, Goofy and Donald as symbolic patriots, complete with separate bisque flag on metal rod. Issued only for 1976, the year of U.S. Bicentennial celebration. - **$125 $250 $350**

❑ **MKY-1321. "America On Parade" Mug,**
1976. 4" tall milk glass. - **$12 $25 $40**

❑ **MKY-1323. Mickey Mouse Seeds,**
1976. Colorforms. Nine example packets with attached die-cut plastic hanger measures 3.5x9". Each is marked "Packed For 1977." Packets are for Radish, Carrot, Tomato, Cucumber, Pumpkin, Beans, Lettuce, Daisy, Zinnia. These and others hung from store display rack. Each - **$5 $10 $15**

MKY-1322

MKY-1324

❑ **MKY-1322. "Mickey Mouse Seed Shop" Display Board,**
1976. Board is 17x17x3" deep diecut cardboard which sat atop display bin containing variety of garden seed packs. Attached to front is separate diecut piece of Minnie plus two examples of the row markers that were part of each seed package. - **$50 $100 $150**

❑ **MKY-1324. "The Mickey Mouse Phone,"**
1976. American Telecommunications Corp. 15" tall hard plastic. Rotary dial version, also issued with push button numbers. Each - **$45 $75 $125**

MKY-1326

MKY-1327

MKY-1325

□ **MKY-1325. "The Mickey Mouse Phone" Boxed Push-Button Version,** 1976. Large hard plastic phone is 8.5x8.5x15" tall and comes in box with color photo of this phone on four side panels. American Telecommunications Corp. Box design includes word balloon above each phone image reading "Hey Minnie It's For You." Phone is designed with 12" tall Mickey figure in classic 1930s style with pie-cut eyes and attached to the base which has wood grain design on side. This is the push-button variety, also issued as a rotary phone. Box - **$50 $75 $125** Telephone - **$45 $75 $125**

□ **MKY-1326. Walt Disney Bicentennial Sand Pail,** 1976. 5.5" tall by 7" diameter soft plastic pail with handle marked "Made In Italy By Suci For Worcester Toy Corp." - **$15 $25 $45**

□ **MKY-1327. Mickey Mouse Bicentennial Pocket Watch,** 1976. Bradley. 3.5x4.5x1" deep plastic display case with plastic storage tray containing 2" diameter pocket watch with individual serial number. Boxed - **$50 $85 $150** Watch Only - **$25 $50 $100**

MKY-1328

MKY-1328. Disney's America On Parade Magic Slate,"
1976. Whitman. 8.5x13.5" die-cut cardboard slate. Has plastic stylus. Near Mint - **$30**

MKY-1329

MKY-1329. "Walt Disney's America On Parade" Lunch Box With Thermos,
c. 1976. Aladdin Industries. 7x8x4" deep metal box and 6.5" tall plastic thermos.
Box - **$35 $65 $125**
Bottle - **$15 $25 $40**

MKY-1330

MKY-1330. Disney Spirit Of '76 Product Sticker,
c. 1976. Glossy sticker is 9.5x12.5". Sticker backing has ink stamp "Ariston Inc., Hillside, New Jersey." Near Mint - **$30**

MKY-1331

MKY-1331. "Disco Mickey Watch" Boxed Set By Bradley,
1977. Bradley. 8.25x8.75x1" deep box. Set comes with a 45rpm record featuring the songs "Disco Mouse/Walking The Dog." Two-sided record sleeve features 1930s style art of Mickey and Minnie dancing. Watch has animated hands.
Boxed Near Mint - **$125**
Watch only - **$20 $40 $60**

MKY-1332

MKY-1332. "NSDA Convention Anaheim, California 1977" Painted Glass Bottle,
1977. Bottle is 9.5" tall and issued for National Soft Drink Assn. convention. - **$15 $25 $45**

MKY-1333

MKY-1333. "Mickey Mouse Fifty Happy Years" Autographed Book,
1977. Harmony Books. 8.5x10.75" softcover 256-page "Official Birthday Book." Title page of this example is autographed by Floyd Gottfredson and page 22 by Ward Kimball, both early Mickey artists. - **$35 $70 $100**

MKY-1334

❏ **MKY-1334. "Mickey & Minnie Steppin' Out Paperdolls,"**
1977. Whitman. 10x12.75". - **$15 $25 $50**

MKY-1335

❏ **MKY-1335. "Mickey Mouse Nostalgic Radio,"**
1977. Made in China for Canadian Company. Lidco. 12x13x9" deep colorful box contains exceptionally well made electric radio nearly identical in every way to the classic 1930s radio by Emerson. Near Mint Boxed As Issued - **$450**

MKY-1336

❏ **MKY-1336. "Mickey Mouse Die-Cast" Vehicles,**
1977. Azrak-Hamway. Four 4x5" blister cards each containing 2.25" long die cast metal vehicle with three dimensional figure of Mickey. Each Near Mint Carded - **$15**

MKY-1337

❏ **MKY-1337. "Tricky Trike" Toy Carded,**
1977. Gabriel Toys. 5x8" display card holding 5" tall painted hard plastic action toy. Near MintCarded - **$40**
Toy Only - **$10 $15 $20**

MKY-1338

❏ **MKY-1338. Commemorative 50th Birthday Belt,**
1978. Pyramid Belt Co. 2x7.5x2" deep boxed leather belt with brass buckle raised relief image of Mickey holding boxed gift. Near Mint Boxed - **$40**

MKY-1339

MKY-1341

MKY-1340

MKY-1342

❏ **MKY-1339. "Mickey Mouse Magic Glow Fun House,"**
1978. Colorforms. 12.5x16x1" deep box holds set consisting of 5x12x16" pop-up fun house with three different floors with great interior illustrations intended to be used with lamp. All other lights are turned out and lamp is placed behind house which then reveals images hidden in the artwork such as ghosts, skeletons, Mickey and Minnie. Also comes with two large sheets of accessories. - **$30 $60 $125**

❏ **MKY-1340. "Mickey's 50" Birthday Publicity Kit,**
1978. Glossy stiff paper folder 9x11.75" contains three different press releases on "Walt Disney Productions" stationery, a promo 45 rpm record and Volume 13, #4 Sept-Nov 1978 issue of Disney News magazine. - **$25 $45 $90**

❏ **MKY-1341. "Mickey Mouse" Comic Strip Reprint Book Signed,**
1978. Abbeyville Press Inc. 9.75x13.25" hardcover with 204 pages, featuring full color reprints of Mickey Mouse 1930s comic strips by Floyd Gottfresdson. His inked autographed greeting and signature is on blank fly leaf page to collector friend Charlie Roberts. Signed - **$30 $60 $100** Unsigned - **$8 $15 $30**

❏ **MKY-1342. "Mickey's Birthday Party Show" Movie Poster,**
1978. Poster is 27x41" glossy one-sheet for feature length film celebrating Mickey's 50th birthday. - **$20 $35 $60**

MKY-1343

❑ **MKY-1343. Mickey 50th Anniversary German Movie Poster,**
1978. Poster is 23.5x33" paper with text in both German and English including "Fox-MGM Technicolor" and "Walt Disney Cartoon Jubilee." - **$25 $50 $85**

MKY-1344

MKY-1345

❑ **MKY-1344. Mickey 50th Anniversary German Movie Poster,**
1978. Poster is 23.5x33" paper with text in both English and German, apparently issued for an anniversary compilation cartoon. - **$25 $50 $85**

❑ **MKY-1345. "Mickey's Birthday Party Show" Publicity Book,**
1978. Book is 9x12" with 16 pages. Issued for NBC-TV special. - **$15 $30 $60**

MKY-1346

❑ **MKY-1346. "Mickey's Birthday Songfest" Folio,**
1978. Folio is 9x12" stiff paper covered issue for Mickey's 50th birthday, 36 pages. - **$15 $25 $50**

MKY-1347

❑ **MKY-1347. Birthday Card Mobile,**
1978. Montgomery Ward. 6x10" closed stiff paper card opening to 18" of die-cut character punch-outs of Mickey, Donald, Pluto and Goofy to be assembled into a "Fun-Time Mobile." Card refers to Mickey's 50th birthday and also mentions that a special gift was available if card was brought to a Mongomery Ward store. - **$15 $25 $40**

MKY-1348

MKY-1349

☐ **MKY-1350. "Mickey Mouse Commemorative Watch,"**
1978. Bradley. Box is 2.5x5.5x.75" deep and contains goldtone watch issued for 50th birthday. Comes with small registration form and is numbered with incised "37235" on reverse.
Box - **$15 $25 $40**
Watch - **$20 $40 $60**

MKY-1351

☐ **MKY-1348. "Mickey Mouse: The First Fifty Years" Exhibition Booklet,**
1978. 8x8" with 16 pages. - **$12 $25 $50**

☐ **MKY-1349. "LIFE" Magazine,**
1978. Issue for Mickey's 50th birthday. Inside has 3-page article emphasizing then current projects such as Black Cauldron and The Fox And The Hound. - **$12 $25 $50**

☐ **MKY-1351. Mickey Mouse Visible Mechanism Wind-Up,**
1978. Gabriel. 3x4x9.25" tall hard plastic that walks forward when wound and also has manually movable arms. - **$35 $65 $115**

MKY-1350

MKY-1352

☐ **MKY-1352. Mickey's 50th Birthday First Day Covers,**
1978. Each is 3.5x6.5" with individual hand-inked edition number on reverse. - **$8 $15 $30**

MKY-1353

❑ **MKY-1353. "Mickey Mouse" Girl's Wristwatch,**
c. 1978. Bradley. 3x6x2.5" tall hard plastic display case with hinged lid over 1" diameter goldtone metal case watch with vinyl straps. Case - **$15 $25 $50**
Watch - **$25 $50 $75**

MKY-1354

❑ **MKY-1354. "Disney's World On Ice" Original Design Art,**
1979. Vellum paper sheet is 10.25x12.25" with inked original art by "Disney Legend" toy designer Al Konetzni. Depicted is Mickey in disco outfit wearing roller skates under title. Unique, Near Mint - **$100**

MKY-1355

❑ **MKY-1355. "Mickey Mouse Glow-In-Dark Calendar,"**
1979. 10.5x13" spiral-bound on stiff glossy paper. Each month features a large full color action scene with Disney characters. Front and each picture page has areas designed to glow in the dark. - **$8 $15 $30**

MKY-1356

❑ **MKY-1356. Stockbroker's Necktie,**
1970s. Cervantes. Silk/polyester blend tie with 4.5x5" stitched image of Mickey painting a rising line on a monthly report graph. - **$10 $20 $40**

MKY-1357

❑ **MKY-1357. "Mickey Mouse Krazy Ikes" Kit Carded,**
1970s. Whitman. 9x9.5" blister card holding figure building parts set for 4.5" tall Mickey figure. Carded - **$10 $15 $25**

MKY-1358

☐ **MKY-1358. "Mickey Mouse Pop-Up Playset,"**
1970s. Colorforms. 12.5x16x1" deep box with pop-up scene that opens to 11" height depicts Mickey, Minnie, nephews, Pluto, Horace and Clarabelle. Includes accessory pieces including instruments and party items. - **$30 $60 $125**

MKY-1361 **MKY-1362**

MKY-1360

MKY-1359

☐ **MKY-1359. "Mickey Math Educational Ruler,"**
1970s. Walt Disney Distributing Co. 3.25x15x.5" deep box contains large hard plastic ruler. Can be used for addition, sub-traction, division and other mathematical problems. Near Mint Boxed - **$25**

☐ **MKY-1360. "Tricky Mickey Magic Colorforms,"**
1970s. Colorforms. 10x16x1" deep box. Insert board has cardboard disk with wooden knob to turn. Complete with accessories and booklet. - **$15 $30 $60**

☐ **MKY-1361. Mickey Mouse Cel From Eastern Airlines Commercial,**
1970s. Image is 2x3.75". - **$50 $85 $135**

☐ **MKY-1362. Baby Mickey Mouse Cel,**
1970s. Acetate sheet is 10.5x12.5" with 4x6" painted side view of him crawling and reaching forward. No. 29 from a numbered series for a Disney TV show. Near Mint - **$125**

MKY-1363

☐ **MKY-1363. Mickey Mouse Jack In The Box Toy,**
1970s. Carnival Toys Inc. 5.75x5.75x5.75" tall tin lithographed toy. When crank is turned, "Pop Goes The Weasel" plays and a figure of Mickey pops out. He has hard plastic head and fabric body. - **$50 $75 $150**

MKY-1364

❏ **MKY-1364. Newspaper Comic Strip Signed By Gottfredson,**
1970s. Strip is 3x12.5" vintage complete four-panel comic for August 26, 1933 neatly removed from a newspaper. Title is "The Big Chance" and depicts Mickey receiving a letter and rushing to tell Minnie that "They're Gonna Let Tanglefoot Run In Th' Big Race." Third and fourth panels have signature "To Charles Roberts Best Wishes Floyd Gottfredson." Gottfredson was the artist on the Mickey Mouse comic strip from 1930 until his retirement in 1975. Same Or Similar - **$35 $65 $110**

MKY-1365

MKY-1366

❏ **MKY-1365. Mickey And Minnie Porcelain Figurines,**
1970s. Mickey is 2.25" tall and Minnie is 2.75". Over-the-glaze paint. Unmarked. Each - **$10 $15 $25**

❏ **MKY-1366. Mickey And Minnie Ceramic Figurines,**
1970s. 4" tall pair with additional over-the-glaze paint. Pair - **$15 $30 $50**

MKY-1367

❏ **MKY-1367. Walt Disney Character Bendables,**
1970s. Durham Industries Inc. Three 5x8.5" blister cards each containing 4.5" tall rubber figure. Included are Donald, Mickey and Pinocchio. Each Carded -**$10 $20 $30**

MKY-1368

❏ **MKY-1368. "Mickey Mouse" Toothbrush Holder,**
1970s. Painted and glazed ceramic 2.25x5x4.75" tall. - **$20 $40 $75**

MKY-1369

MKY-1370

MKY-1372

❑ **MKY-1369. "Mickey Mouse Hallmark Candle,"**
1970s. 4x4.5x7.25" tall painted figural. - **$8 $15 $25**

❑ **MKY-1370. Mickey Mouse 3-D Puzzle,**
1970s. 9.5x11.5" deep plastic frame holds 3-D style puzzle picture with figural plastic pieces of Mickey. Has small magnets on reverse to hold them to the tin sheet underneath. - **$10 $20 $30**

❑ **MKY-1372. "Mickey Mouse" Dakin With Bag,**
1970s. 7.75" tall poseable vinyl complete with cardboard tag. With Bag & Tag - **$25 $50 $75**
Figure Only - **$15 $30 $45**

MKY-1373

MKY-1371

MKY-1374

❑ **MKY-1371. Giant Santa Mickey Pepsi-Cola Premium Doll,**
1970s. Animal Fair. 34" tall stuffed plush with hard plastic eyes and felt belt with vinyl buckle. Marked "Made For The Pepsi-Cola Company" with Disney copyright. We believe these were issued one per store to be used for promotional display. - **$50 $100 $150**

❑ **MKY-1373. "Happy Birthday" Mickey Mouse Party Plates,**
1970s. Beach Products. 9" diameter sealed set of eight paper plates. Near Mint Sealed - **$18**

❑ **MKY-1374. "Mickey Mouse Sew-Ons,"**
1970s. Colorforms. 8x12.5x1" deep boxed set designated on lid as Canadian version. - **$15 $30 $50**

MKY-1375

❏ **MKY-1375. "Mickey And Minnie Mouse" Trash Can,**
1970s. Cheinco. 7.5x10x13" tall tin lithograph waste container. - **$20 $35 $75**

MKY-1376

❏ **MKY-1376. Mickey Mouse Faux Watch Bracelet,**
1970s. Strap is 1" wide by 9" long with attached 1.25" diameter die-cast metal simulated watch dial. - **$15 $30 $60**

MKY-1377

❏ **MKY-1377. "Mickey Mouse" Retro Cuff Links,**
1970s. Hickok. Pair of 1.25x2" figural cast metal cuff links attached to original cardboard holder with string tag, "Authorized Limited Edition From The Original 1934 Dies Out Of The Hickok Archives." Carded - **$15 $25 $40**

MKY-1378

❏ **MKY-1378. Child's Feeding Dish,**
1970s. "Japan" 5.25x9.25x.75" deep china dish compartmentalized into food area and cup holder space. - **$12 $25 $35**

MKY-1379

❏ **MKY-1379. Mickey Mouse Telephone Mug,**
1970s. Heavy clear glass 5.5" tall has small Bell Telephone Co. logo. - **$25 $45 $80**

MKY-1380

❏ **MKY-1380. "Mickey's Spaceship,"**
1970s. Eagle Affiliates. 8.5" tall hard plastic mug held by cardboard wrapper strap within unopened original shrinkwrap. Near Mint Packaged - **$35**

MKY-1381

MKY-1384

❑ **MKY-1381. "Walt Disney Ceramic Greenware Figure Maker,"**
1970s. Jaymar. 11.5x16x3" deep box contains casting molds and accessories for Mickey, Minnie, Donald and Pluto. Near Mint Boxed - **$30**

❑ **MKY-1384. Mickey Mouse Coin-Sorting Bank,**
1970s. 1.5x5x7" tall hard plastic. Back of bank is clear plastic so coin sorting mechanism can be viewed. - **$15 $25 $50**

MKY-1385

MKY-1382   MKY-1383

❑ **MKY-1382. "Mickey Mouse" Bank,**
1970s. Animal Toys Plus Inc. 8.5" tall by 4" diameter hard vinyl bank. One hand is designed to hold a coin and the arm is movable for placing coin in bank. - **$15 $30 $60**

❑ **MKY-1383. Mickey Mouse Bank,**
1970s. Hard vinyl with one movable arm and head. 6.5" tall. - **$12 $25 $45**

MKY-1386

❑ **MKY-1385. Mickey Mouse Large Plaster Bust Bank,**
1970s. Unmarked. 7x9x11.5" tall painted plaster depicting Mickey's head atop a block of swiss cheese. Coin slot is on top of head, back of base has plastic trap. - **$20 $35 $70**

❑ **MKY-1386. "Mickey Mouse Play Money Set,"**
1970s. Kingsway. 8.5x11.5" blister card includes play money with character portraits, credit and I.D. cards featuring Mickey portrait and castle illustration, vinyl wallet and plastic money clip, both depicting Uncle Scrooge plus five plastic coins with raised Mickey portrait/castle. Carded - **$8 $18 $35**

MKY-1389

❑ **MKY-1389. Mickey/Minnie Mouse Purse,**
1970s. Disney Fashion Parade by Lanco. 5x6x1.5" deep vinyl with shoulder strap. - **$10 $20 $40**

MKY-1390

❑ **MKY-1390. English Bicycle Bell Attachment,**
1970s. "C.J. Adie & Nephew Ltd." 2" diameter by 1.75" tall chromed metal. - **$15 $25 $45**

MKY-1388

MKY-1387

MKY-1391

❑ **MKY-1387. "Mickey Mouse Guitar,"**
1970s. Carnival Toy. 6x17" display card holds 15" tall hard plastic guitar. Carded - **$15 $30 $60**

❑ **MKY-1388. "Walt Disney Character Appliques By Streamline" Store Display,**
1970s. Large 8x16x34" tall display with metal frame and pair of revolving columns with top die-cut attachment being thick mason board with thin cardboard covering. - **$60 $110 $225**

❑ **MKY-1391. "Le Journal De Mickey" Huge Outdoor Advertising Banner,**
1970s. French. 36x79" vinyl-coated fabric for outdoor use to promote publication. - **$40 $70 $150**

MKY-1392

❑ **MKY-1392. "Le Journal De Mickey" Huge Outdoor Advertising Banner,**
1970s. French. 27.5x112" vinyl-coated fabric for outdoor use to promote publication. - **$40 $70 $150**

MKY-1393

❑ **MKY-1393. Disney Characters "Musical Collectibles" Promotion Figurine,**
1970s. Schmid. 2x5.5x3.75" tall painted and glazed ceramic store display. - **$15 $25 $50**

MKY-1394

❑ **MKY-1394. Mickey Mouse "Wind-Up 'Walking' Toy,"**
1970s. Durham Industries Inc. 6x9" die-cut blister card contains 4" tall hard plastic figure with built-in key. Near Mint Carded - **$25**

MKY-1395

❑ **MKY-1395. "Mickey Mouse/Donald Duck Disney Dancer,"**
1970s. Gabriel. Each is 2.5x3.5x1" deep hard plastic. Each has a die-cut plastic jointed figure attached to backdrop by a wheel which is spun causing figure to move about as if dancing. Each - **$8 $15 $25**

MKY-1396

❑ **MKY-1396. Walt Disney Characters Kaleidoscope,**
1970s. Hallmark. 9" long. - **$25 $45 $70**

MKY-1397

❑ **MKY-1397. "Mickey Mouse Sing-A-Long Radio,"**
1970s. "Concept 2000." Boxed 5x7.5x9" tall hard plastic three-dimensional replica of band wagon topped by vinyl figures of Mickey as bandleader with accordian, Donald with guitar, Pluto as singer, plus small removable microphone for "Sing-A-Long" use. Box - **$10 $20 $30**
Radio - **$20 $35 $60**

MKY-1398

MKY-1401

❏ **MKY-1398. "Mickey Mouse Sing-A-Long Radio,"**
1970s. Simpsons-Sears Ltd. Toronto. 3x8.5x6.5" tall hard plastic battery operated. Box - **$10 $20 $30**
Radio - **$15 $30 $50**

❏ **MKY-1401. "Mickey Mouse Watch,"**
1970s. Bradley. 2x3x3" deep plastic display case contains watch with 1" diameter metal case. Mickey's head nods as seconds tick. Near Mint Boxed - **$75**

MKY-1399

MKY-1400

MKY-1402

❏ **MKY-1402. Minnie Wristwatch,**
1970s. Bradley. 1.25" diameter chromed metal case with dial illustration of Minnie whose hands point at the numerals. Leather strap has images of Mickey. - **$50 $80 $140**

❏ **MKY-1399. "Mickey Mouse Talking Alarm Clock,"**
1970s. Bradley Time. 4.5x5.25x8.75" tall hard plastic clock in box. Attached to top is hard vinyl figure of Mickey from waist up depicted as engineer. Box - **$10 $20 $30**
Clock - **$15 $25 $40**

❏ **MKY-1400. "Teach 'N' Play Clock,"**
1970s. Illco. 8x11.5x3.5" deep display box containing 8" tall Mickey figural hard plastic with inset wind-up toy clock. Near Mint Boxed - **$40**

MKY-1403

MKY-1404

□ MKY-1403. "Windup Climbing Mickey Mouse" Boxed Fireman Toy,
1970s. Durham. 4x5x11" tall box contains hard plastic toy with built-in key. Toy consists of 9" tall Mickey as fireman figure plus base with two-piece ladder that extends to height of 17". Mickey climbs to the top of the ladder and then slides down.
Box - **$25 $50 $75**
Toy - **$40 $65 $100**

□ MKY-1404. "Mickey Mouse's Car" By Polistil,
1970s. Box is 2.5x4.5x6.5" tall and contains 3.75" long cast metal and plastic car. Car has three-dimensional rubber figure of Mickey. Box - **$10 $20 $30**
Toy - **$25 $45 $65**

MKY-1405

□ MKY-1405. "Mickey Mouse Radio Control Camper Van,"
1970s. Boxed 4x10.5x5.25" tall hard plastic battery toy with separate hand-held remote control unit. Box - **$12 $25 $40**
Toy - **$25 $45 $80**

MKY-1406

□ MKY-1406. "The Wonderful World Of Disney" Snow Dome,
1970s. Hard plastic 3.25x4x2.5" tall with clear front view three-dimensional figures of Mickey and Minnie with Sleeping Beauty's castle. - **$25 $45 $65**

MKY-1407   MKY-1408

□ MKY-1407. "Walt Disney Character Weather Watch,"
1970s. Skil-Craft. 10x12.5" blister card contains hard plastic "Child Window Thermometer." Near Mint Carded - **$35**

□ MKY-1408. Mickey Mouse Figural Pencil Sharpener,
1970s. Hard plastic 4.75" tall. - **$12 $25 $35**

MKY-1409

MKY-1410

MKY-1412

❑ **MKY-1412. "Mickey Mouse" Wristwatch,**
c. 1970s. Bradley. 1-1/8" square silvered metal case. Has unusual one-piece sil-vered metal bracelet-style wrist strap. - **$25 $45 $75**

MKY-1413

❑ **MKY-1409. "Mickey Mouse Good Grooming Club" Set,**
c. 1970s. The Dep Corp. 8x8.5x2" deep box holds two 7.5" soft plastic figural con-tainers, one bottle is "Mickey Mouse Shampoo" and the other is "Donald Duck Lotion." Near Mint Boxed - **$50**

❑ **MKY-1410. Mickey Mouse Lamp,**
c. 1970s. Wis-Ton, Canada. Large 9" tall soft vinyl Mickey figure attached to 5.25" diameter vinyl base with total height of 14". - **$20 $30 $50**

MKY-1414

MKY-1411

❑ **MKY-1411. "Mickey Mouse Pocketwatch,"**
c. 1970s. Bradley Time. 2" diameter hard plastic watch in box. Box - **$10 $20 $30** Watch - **$20 $35 $60**

❑ **MKY-1413. Mickey Mouse As Sorcerer's Apprentice Carved Wood Figure,**
c. 1980. Limited edition by Anri of Italy. 3.5" tall. - **$60 $120 $175**

❑ **MKY-1414. "Mickey & Minnie Mouse Doctor And Nurse Playset" By Colorforms,**
1981. Includes colorful background board depicting doctor's office and two oversized sheets of die-cut vinyl characters and accessories. - **$15 $30 $50**

MKY-1415

MKY-1418

☐ **MKY-1415. Mickey Mouse Lever-Action Car,**
1981. Modern Toys. 3x4x3.25" tall tin lithographed and plastic car with three-dimensional vinyl figure of Mickey with movable head. Right side of car has small lever that when pulled back and released causes the car to speed forward. - **$15 $25 $40**

MKY-1416

☐ **MKY-1416. World On Ice Banner With Mickey,**
c. 1981. Large 30.5x61" rubberized vinyl banner, believed for first year of World On Ice performances and used as show promotion, not as souvenir item. - **$30 $60 $125**

☐ **MKY-1418. "Mickey Mouse Talking Phone,"**
1983. Hasbro. 8x12.5x6" deep box contains battery operated hard plastic phone. Phone has rubber tube cord. Top of unit has viewing screen and knob is used to change character image. Each image has matching character voice activated when certain button combination is pressed. Near Mint Boxed - **$60**

MKY-1419

MKY-1417

☐ **MKY-1417. "The Disney Channel" Salesman's Promotional Folder,**
1982. 10x14" on stiff glossy paper issued to promote upcoming The Disney Channel which began broadcasting in April 1983. - **$8 $15 $25**

☐ **MKY-1419. "The Rescuers/Mickey's Christmas Carol" Lobby Card Set With Envelope,**
1983. Set of eight 11x14" stiff glossy paper for double-feature release. Set - **$15 $25 $45**

MKY-1420

MKY-1422

❑ **MKY-1422. "Cooking With Mickey Around Our World,"**
1986. Has 292 pages of "Walt Disney World's Most Requested Recipes" divided into twelve sections, each with tabbed divider page featuring Mickey as chef illustrations. - **$12 $25 $45**

❑ **MKY-1420. Mickey Mouse Wrist Watch Original Concept Art,**
1983. 14x17" paper sheet with large art done in pencil and colored marker featuring Mickey on watch dial. Art was produced for Bradley. Unique, Excellent. - **$225**

MKY-1423

❑ **MKY-1423. "Mickey Mouse 60th Anniversary Limited Edition Commemorative Serigraph,"**
1988. Image is 8x10" from the short "Nifty Nineties." Comes with laser background. Mint As Issued - **$240**

MKY-1421

❑ **MKY-1421. Disney Christmas Collector Plates,**
1985. Schmid. First china plate is 7.5" limited to 20,000, second 1986 plate is 8.5" limited to 25,000. Each - **$10 $15 $20**

MKY-1424

❏ **MKY-1424. "Mickey's 60th Birthday" Boxed Bisque,**
1988. Disneyland/Disney World. 4.5" tall. Plain generic box. Cost **$45**. Mint As Issued - **$65**

MKY-1425

❏ **MKY-1425. "Mickey Mouse 60th Anniversary" Metal Figurine Boxed Set,**
1988. Pixi. 3.5x4.25x1.75" deep box contains three painted lead figures by French company. From a series and this is "Disney Memory/60th Anniversary." Comes with illustrated certificate card stamped with collection name and stock #4604 as well as inked edition "121." Figures are Walt, a chair and Mickey. Mint As Issued - **$250**

MKY-1426

❏ **MKY-1426. "Steamboat Willie" 60-Year Commemorative Medal,**
1988. Rarities Mint Inc. 1.5" diameter .999 silver troy ounce commemoration for Mickey's first appearance in 1928 in "Steamboat Willie" short. Reverse has "Mickey's Sixty" official logo. Medal is displayed in 4.5x6.5x1" deep velveteen covered box with logo lid. Mint As Issued - **$50**

MKY-1427

❏ **MKY-1427. "Mickey Is Sixty!" Commemorative Magazine With Cel Insert,**
1988. Time Inc. 8x10.75" specialty publication comprised of 64 pages in full color supplemented by "Exclusive Disney Animation Art" cel of Mickey as Sorcerer's Apprentice. Cover art is by Andy Warhol and content includes contributions by Ray Bradbury, George Lucas, Steven Spielberg, Jimmy Carter, many others. - **$8 $15 $30**

MKY-1428

❏ **MKY-1428. "Mickey's Sixtieth Birthday" Sculpture,**
1988. From the Disney Capodimonte Collection by retired sculptor Enzo Arzenton. Edition size of 192. - **$2650**

MKY-1429

❏ **MKY-1429. Disney M-G-M Grand Opening Cel,**
1989. Hand-painted animation cel is 5.5x5.5" produced in limited edition only for opening day of Disney M-G-M Studios theme park.
Mint As Issued - **$250**

MKY-1430

❏ **MKY-1430. German Figure Set,**
c. 1989. "Ferrero Kinder." Set of eleven different hand-painted hard plastic figures, each about 1.5" tall. All are similar to Disneykins of the 1960s but are much more detailed. Set includes two different Mickeys, Minnie, the nephews, Goofy, Pluto, Beagle Boys, Black Pete and police officer. Set is accompanied by 1.5x4.5" paper with illustration of the figures plus their names in German. Set - **$35 $65 $125**

MKY-1431

MKY-1432

❏ **MKY-1431. "Mickey Lunch Kit" Figural Lunch Box,**
c. 1989. Aladdin. 9x10.5x9.5" tall hard plastic with 6" tall plastic thermos. Box - **$10 $15 $45**
Bottle - **$10 $15 $45**

❏ **MKY-1432. Mickey Mouse Cel,**
1980s. Image is 5.25x7". From a 1980s TV appearance. - **$100 $200 $300**

MKY-1433

❏ **MKY-1433. Mickey Mouse Cel,**
1980s. 10.5x12.5" acetate sheet has 5x7" image. #6/52 from a numbered sequence. - **$55 $110 $160**

MKY-1434

❑ **MKY-1434. Mickey Mouse Cel,**
1980s. 10.5x12.5" acetate sheet with 3.25x4.25" hand-inked cel image. - **$60 $110 $160**

MKY-1435

❑ **MKY-1435. Mickey And Pluto Serigraph Cel,**
1980s. Matted and framed individual images combined into 5x9.5" dual image from 1939 cartoon short, "The Pointer." Reverse of frame has label notation of limited edition of 9500 pieces by "Walt Disney Productions." Mint As Issued - **$200**

MKY-1436

❑ **MKY-1436. Wizard Of Id/Mickey Mouse Sketch,**
1980s. Paper is 3.5x8.5" with 3x3" inked art by Brant Parker, creator of Wizard of Id comic strip and a former Disney artist. Unique, Near Mint - **$175**

MKY-1437

MKY-1438

❑ **MKY-1437. Carl Barks Signed Mickey Mouse Print,**
1980s. 9x11" image size. Limited edition of 174. Mint As Issued - **$325**

❑ **MKY-1438. "Mouskamania Puzzle,"**
1980s. Hallmark Cards Inc. Springbok 11.5x11.5x2" deep boxed 1000-piece jigsaw puzzle assembling to 24x30" color photo scene of exceptional vintage 1930s Mickey collection of Disney collector Bernard Shine. - **$12 $25 $35**

MKY-1439

MKY-1440

MKY-1442

❏ **MKY-1439. "Walt Disney Schmid" Store Display Figurine,**
1980s. Schmid. 2.5x5.25x6" painted and glazed ceramic. - **$12 $25 $50**

❏ **MKY-1440. Mickey Mouse Band Leader Miniature Metal Figure,**
1980s. Detailed but only 1" tall. Sold briefly at Disneyland. - **$75 $140 $250**

❏ **MKY-1442. Mickey Mouse Riding Butterfly Enamel On Brass Jewelry By Wendy Gell,**
1980s. Beautifully crafted 1.25x2.25" piece of jewelry with hinged circular clip on reverse rather than a pin. - **$15 $30 $60**

MKY-1441

MKY-1443

❏ **MKY-1441. Mickey "Adventureland" Poseable Figure,**
1980s. Arco Toys Ltd./Mattel. 8.5x11" blister card packaged set of 4.5" tall flexible bendy Mickey as jungle explorer plus accessory pieces of pith helmet, rifle, boat and oar, binoculars, monkey, smaller bendy of a witch doctor. Carded Near Mint - **$30**

❏ **MKY-1443. Mickey Mouse Conductor Limited Edition Wooden Figure,**
1980s. Anri of Italy. Number 12 in club series limited to 5000. 4.75" tall. - **$60 $150 $225**

MKY-1444

MKY-1444. Figure Bank,
1980s. Leonard Of Japan. 3.5x3.5x5.25" tall cast metal figural finished in silver luster depicting Mickey in tuxedo holding his hat and sitting atop a suitcase. Foil sticker on underside, complete with trap. - **$12** **$25** **$35**

MKY-1445

MKY-1445. Mickey As Chef Salt & Pepper Set,
1980s. Large pair of 4.5" tall glazed ceramic matched shakers. - **$10** **$20** **$30**

MKY-1446

MKY-1446. "Disney Video Cassettes" Promotional Clock,
1980s. 10.25" diameter by 1.5" deep battery operated hard plastic. Issued on a promotional basis to video store owners. - **$25** **$50** **$90**

MKY-1447

MKY-1447. "Mickey's Corn Popper" Battery Operated Toy,
c. 1980s. Illco. 3.5x8x6.5" tall hard plastic. Mickey pushes the cart around with bump-and-go action as his head moves. Inside lights and balls pop around as the song "It's A Small World" is played. - **$15** **$30** **$60**

MKY-1448

MKY-1448. "Pelham Puppets" Mickey Mouse Store Display Marionette,
c. 1980s. Exceptionally large Mickey marionette with attached wood hand control unit. Mickey is 10x10x25.5" tall with composition body, felt ears and shirt, cloth pants and black flexible rubber legs. Control unit has metal plate marked "Pelham Puppets/Made In England." Production of these displays was quite limited. - **$275** **$550** **$800**

MKY-1449

MKY-1450

☐ **MKY-1449. The Sorcerer's Apprentice Pencil Drawing,**
1990. Image of Mickey is 4.5x4.5" and broom is 2.5x5.5". Has penciled signature and date "Ken Anderson '90." Anderson began his career in 1934 as art director to many films including Snow White and The Pastoral Symphony section of Fantasia. - **$250 $500 $750**

☐ **MKY-1450. "Mickey's Holiday Treasures" Troy Ounce Of Silver,**
1990. Rarities Mint. 1.5" diameter. Limited edition of 10,000 with individual proof number. Mint - **$40**

MKY-1451

☐ **MKY-1451. "Disney Collectible Classic Charlotte Clark Dolls" Boxed Reproductions,**
1990. Limited editions of 10,000 by Applause. Each 16" tall. Includes numbered certificate. Each Near Mint Boxed - **$85**

MKY-1452

☐ **MKY-1452. German Museum Disney Exhibition Catalogue,**
1991. Catalogue is 7.75x8.5" with 208 pages, about 1,000 copies published for a Disney Expo at the Film Museum of Potsdam, Germany. All in German, plus many photos covering German-issued Disney items and a history of Disney in Germany from 1927-1945. Sixteen full color pages show merchandise of rare toys and porcelain figurines including Rosenthals. - **$45 $85 $165**

MKY-1453

☐ **MKY-1453. "Minnie on the Beach" Figure,**
1993. Very unusual Capodiamonte figure; a sold out edition of only 197. - **$750**

MKY-1454   MKY-1455

❑ **MKY-1454. "The Disney Channel" Promotional Champagne Bottle,**
1993. 12" tall clear glass filled with jellybeans. Near Mint - **$40**

❑ **MKY-1455. "Through The Mirror" Bronze Sculpture,**
1996. Limited edition of 200. Sculpted by Paul Vought. Signed by Carl Barks. Mint As Issued - **$550**

MKY-1456

❑ **MKY-1456. Mickey Mouse Cel From The Disney Channel's Mouse Works,**
1999. Acetate sheet is 10.5x12.5" with 3.5x3.75" image. Mint As Issued - **$125**

MKY-1457

❑ **MKY-1457. "Mr. Mouse Takes A Trip" Serigraph,**
1990s. Image is 4.25x8" with Walt Disney Co. seal. From a limited edition of 9,500 pieces. Mint As Issued - **$175**

MKY-1458

❑ **MKY-1458. Mickey And Minnie Serigraph,**
1990s. Acetate sheet is 10.75x14" with 6x6.5" image of Minnie covering Mickey's face with lipstick kisses, based on the 1939 "Mickey's Surprise Party" short. Background is color laser scene. Limited edition with "Walt Disney Company" seal at bottom right. Near Mint As Issued - **$150**

MKY-1459

❑ **MKY-1459. Mickey And Minnie Serigraph,**
1990s. Acetate sheet is 10.75x14" with 5.5x7" cel image of Mickey and Minnie skating based on the 1935 "On Ice" short. Background is color laser depiction of frozen lake waters. Limited edition with "Walt Disney Company" seal at bottom right. Near Mint As Issued - **$150**

MKY-1460

❏ MKY-1460. Mickey With Donald's Nephews Cel,
1990s. Mouse Works TV. Cel consisting of four 10x12" acetate sheets, each with different character image for combined image of 4x5.5" on color laser background. Near Mint - **$200**

MKY-1461

❏ MKY-1461. Mickey Animation Cel,
1990s. Acetate sheet is 10.5x12" with 3x4.75" full figure painted image. Laser background sheet. Near Mint - **$300**

MKY-1462

❏ MKY-1462. Mickey Wristwatch Retro Re-Issue Boxed,
1990s. "Pedre." Reproduction of the first Ingersoll watch from 1933 in 2.5x4.5x1.75" deep box with hinged lid. Mint As Issued - **$225**

MKY-1463

❏ MKY-1463. "Mickey/Minnie Japanese Candy Tin,"
1990s. Lithographed tin container 6x10.75x1.5" deep. Contains two layers of taffy with each piece wrapped in identical wrapper depicting Mickey with guitar and Minnie holding umbrella. Lid is marked "Milaoshu/Tang." Near Mint As Issued - **$55**

MKY-1464

❏ MKY-1464. Mickey And Minnie As Roman Citizens Ceramic Figures,
1990s. China. Sold at Caesar's Palace Casino, Las Vegas. Each 5" tall. Each - **$8** **$12** **$20**

MKY-1465

MKY-1467. Fantasia Limited Edition Sericel,
1990s. Image is 5x6.75". Limited edition of 5000 with "The Walt Disney Company/Sericel Certified" seal. Mint As Issued - **$265**

❏ **MKY-1465. "Mickey Mouse Waddle Book Collector's Edition" Set,**
1990s. Applewood Books. 8.25x11x1" deep boxed limited edition and authorized exact reproduction of the 1934 "Mickey Mouse Waddle Book" published originally by Blue Ribbon Books. The Applewood edition includes an extra set of punch-out waddle characters Mickey, Minnie, Pluto and Tanglefoot plus folder for other "Disney Collectibles Books." Reproduction publication was limited to 1,000 copies at original $70 purchase price each. Mint As Issued - **$95**

MKY-1468

MKY-1466

❏ **MKY-1468. "Mickey's Busy Book,"**
1990s. Book is 6.5x7.25" with eight pages. Near Mint - **$15**

❏ **MKY-1466. "Mickey & Minnie" Creamer/Sugar Set,**
1990s. Painted and glazed ceramic set 4.25" tall. - **$15 $30 $60**

MKY-1469

MKY-1467

❏ **MKY-1469. "Lenox Bandleader Mickey" Ornament Inspired By Macy's Parade Balloon,**
2000. Box is 4x4x6.25" and contains quality clear glass ornament issued for the 2000 Macy's Thanksgiving Day Parade. This is the first in a series. Displays NYC landmarks including World Trade Center. Mint As Issued - **$90**

MKY-1470

MKY-1473

❑ **MKY-1473. Mickey Mouse Monopoly Game,**
2004. Mint As Issued - **$40**

❑ **MKY-1470. Rice Krispies Cereal Box,**
2000. Promotes Mini Bobble Head inside. -
$15

MKY-1474

❑ **MKY-1474. Mickey Plush Keyring,**
2004. - **$6**

MKY-1471

MKY-1472

MKY-1475   **MKY-1476**

❑ **MKY-1471. Mickey Mini Bobble,**
2004. Premium from Rice Krispies box. -
$10

❑ **MKY-1475. Mickey Keyring,**
2004. - **$6**

❑ **MKY-1472. Mickey Mini Bobble,**
2004. - **$22**

❑ **MKY-1476. Mickey Keyring,**
2004. - **$6**

WANTED!

EARLY DISNEY (1930-1950) COMIC CHARACTER TIMEPIECES WITH BOXES

EXAMPLES:

1934 Big Bad Wolf/III Pigs Wristwatch
1934 Mickey Mouse Alarm Clock
1935 Donald Duck Wristwatch
1937 Mickey Mouse Wristwatch w/Charms
1938 Mickey Mouse Lapel Watch
1939 Donald Duck Pocket Watch
1939 Snow White Wristwatch
1947 Donald Duck Wristwatch
1947 Little Fiddler Pig Wristwatch
1949 Louie Duck Wristwatch

OTHER EARLY NON-DISNEY CHARACTER TIMEPIECES ALSO WANTED

SEND DESCRIPTION AND/OR PHOTOS TO:
JERRY HOWELL
635 WHITAKER STREET
MOREHEAD, KY 40351
JERHOWELL@GMAIL.COM